MASS NEWS

MASS NEWS practices, controversies, and alternatives

DAVID J. LEROY
Florida State University

CHRISTOPHER H. STERLING
Temple University

Prentice-Hall, Inc., Englewood Cliffs, New Jersey

Library of Congress Cataloging in Publication Data
LeRoy, David J.   comp.
    Mass news.

    (The Prentice-Hall series in speech communication)
    Bibliography: p.
    1. Journalism—Addresses, essays, lectures.
I. Sterling, Christopher H., joint
comp. II. Title.
PN4733.L46   070   72-5849
ISBN 0-13-559898-2
ISBN 0-13-559880-X (pbk.)

The Prentice-Hall Series in Speech Communication
Larry L. Barker and Robert J. Kibler, Consulting Editors

Printed in the United States of America

10 9 8 7 6 5 4 3 2 1

Prentice-Hall International, Inc., London
Prentice-Hall of Australia, Pty. Ltd., Sydney
Prentice-Hall of Canada, Ltd., Toronto
Prentice-Hall of India Private Limited, New Delhi
Prentice-Hall of Japan, Inc., Tokyo

To the women in our lives

Judy, Lisa, and Simone

and

Ellen, Jennifer, and Robin

Contents

Preface

Why mass news? The institution of the press in America is a vague concept and this lack of precision has no doubt been responsible for some of our persistent controversies about "the press" and its rights and responsibilities. We cannot claim credit for originating the notion that there are many separate media under the umbrella term "the press." By introducing a reader devoted almost exclusively to the three major sources of the public's news—the wire services, newspapers, and television—we hope to focus concern upon the assessment of their strengths and weaknesses. It is from this limited number of news sources that most Americans acquire awareness and knowledge of the world beyond immediate experience. Further, it is the mass news media that faces political attack and around which legal maneuvering revolves. This view discounts to an extent the impact but not the value of journals, quarterlies, weekly news magazines, and other media which cater to an informed but small group of people. In fact, it is often only when their concerns are picked up and touted by the mass news media that we realize the power of the mass news system in America.

Further, we think that this volume can be valuable to the concerned citizen, the sociologist, the social psychologist, and the teacher in both mass communication and the humanities. This is because we focus first on the "news bureaucracy" and how it shapes the news. Any number of worthwhile and meaningful suggestions for media improvement have failed because the authors did not comprehend that the crux of the issue lay in the way the task was performed—*not* in the intelligence or good will of the reporter, editor, or owner. Next, we cast many of the current as well as recurring charges against the press as controversies. In a sociological sense we cast the issue as a type of social problem. We ask the reader to consider who makes the charges, who answers, and how the controversies are resolved. This knowledge, along with that of bureaucracies, should allow the reader to grasp the enormous complexity of some issues such as biased reporting, the bad news syndrome and the grinding paternalism of the mass news industry toward its critics.

Although this may lead some to a pessimistic view of improvement in mass news performance, we are in general, optimistic. Our closing section deals with alternatives already underway, including a new interpretation of the First Amendment, press councils, underground media, professionalism, and the upheaval in broadcasting through licensee challenges.

Focusing on the mass news media then can be a valuable aid in bringing coherence to the debate about the role and responsibility of the most important segment of the press. Depending on which poll you wish to cite, from two-thirds to three-fourths of the public rely only on newspapers and television for their news.

The quality of a democracy depends upon its citizens and their ability to make informed and enlightened decisions. The most persuasive source of this intelligence is the mass news media. Thus, the question is: Which is more amenable to immediate improvement, the press or the electorate? It is possible to have a literate and catholic mass news system. We hope that this introductory reader can function as a modest contribution to that development.

D. J. LeRoy

C. H. Sterling

Note
to the
Instructor

Much has been cut from the first to the final draft of this volume. Most journalists would instinctively understand the economic necessity of such editorial decisions—others may not. The purpose here is to note what has been excluded and to suggest some rationale for using this book.

We have left out the classic sociological papers which are readily available from reprint houses. In the humanities, we left out those essays that assess critically, often abrasively, the intellectual paucity of the journalistic enterprise. Since the empirical studies of news, journalists, and role sets are limited and tentative, we felt no need to burden the undergraduate with studies which required extensive commentary and interpretation. In the area of politics we have excluded a number of speeches, hearings, and polemics which are readily available, free of charge, from your Congressmen or (for a modest fee) from the Government Printing Office.

Finally, we have excluded theorists without portfolios. Certainly McLuhan's work and others' are valuable and provocative teaching tools. However, we felt it indiscreet to force insights in this reader best dealt with in the framework of student-teacher interaction. Thus, we also excluded from the other end of the continuum the almost obligatory reprinting of codes of ethics and regulatory codes of the various mass news organizations.

From the outset, we knew that this volume could best serve as a supplemental text. We still faced the issue of whether to give full bent to all of the various theories, models and functions of the mass media (e.g., the Charles Wright functional analysis approach). After considerable thought, we have excluded any detailed presentation of functions and effects of mass news. The effect of mass news, while of great social importance, is an underdeveloped research area. There is a large number of scholars who have generated all types of functions and purposes for the media. Still, an instructor's choice of a model for the functions of the mass news media is more a question of aesthetics than empirical evidence. Also, one's discipline influences the choice. A sociologist of the functional school will be quite clear in his demands of the news media, whereas a journalism scholar could have a historical bent, which predicates a more eclectic approach. Hopefully, we have been flexible enough to allow many schools of thought to absorb the reader.

Given the limited space available for selections, we still feel that it is important for students to know how the news is collected and processed by a news organization, which reveals some bias on our part. To demand journalistic reforms without a comprehension of the organizational constraints in the craft is to court frustration. All manner of social reforms have failed, not because they lacked nobility in purpose, but because they lacked a grasp of what must be changed in the social structure.

Of necessity, the controversies section had to limit itself to a few issues. Although the introduction to the section may create an impression of order and progression in controversy, order is really imposed by a scholar's or student's attempt to phrase the problem and find a solution. It is fallacious to cast these persistent problems as crisp and neat issues. Further, they are, in reality, biased issues with (for example) real people being subpoenaed amidst the shifting sentiments of a Congress and court system seeking a new baseline for future action to resolve persistent social problems. Just as the shoreline beaches and dunes shift with current, winds, and seasons, issues in mass news will continue to acquire different configuration. If this paradigm is correct and incorporated in one's analysis, there should occur a more tolerant attitude toward the contradictions and anomalies persisting in this area. Principally, this is the reason for printing case studies, which hopefully cast a broader net over the issues in a given confrontation.

The final section, dealing with alternatives in mass news is offered with some trepidation. Folk wisdom has it that a little knowledge can be a dangerous thing. Students should be aware that reforms and change cannot be accomplished in a semester or quarter. Press councils, license challenges, or negotiations with a cable operator require a substantial commitment of time and labor.

In the future, we may offer a teacher's guide with some interesting projects for a wide variety of fields such as psychology, sociology, and, of course, journalism and broadcasting courses. In the meantime, if you have any suggestions or criticisms, we would like to hear from you.

MASS NEWS

part one **CONTEXT
OF
MASS NEWS**

Introduction

Mass news is a distinction drawn to focus attention upon a limited spectrum of the news and information available to the American public. It is common for news industry spokesmen to cite the thousands of newspapers, magazines, newsletters, and radio and television stations available to the American public. The fact that a majority of these thousands of outlets are carrying identical stories, pictures, and even prefab editorials is overlooked. The newspapers, television, and radio stations are fed daily their international, national, regional, and state news from perhaps less than ten national operations that supply news, as a business venture, to local media outlets. These organizations are the national news wire services (Associated Press and United Press International), the three television networks, and the large metropolitan newspapers syndication services (*New York Times, Washington Post,* and the *Los Angeles Times*).

But what about the thousands of *specialized* trade and business magazines, newspapers, and journals? They must generate millions of valuable or interesting news items each year. Indeed they do, but they are read by a select few, and unless someone puts this information into the national news system, the public will not know of its existence.

Mass news can be defined from three different standpoints: how the news is distributed; its audience; and, ironically, by what is attacked, investigated, or vilified by governmental agencies and politicians. Consider the latter. Does the president of the United States see fit to attack for biased reporting the *Turkey Growers Gazette,* or others with larger circulation, such as the show business paper, *Variety,* or even such journals as the *New Republic, National Review,* or *Commentary?* Politicians attack news media that reach the largest and most influential audience—for example, television and a few national newspapers such as the *New York Times* or the *Washington Post.*

Public opinion polls bear out the veracity of the politicians concern. About 65 percent of the American public receives most of its news from the electronic media and newspapers. In a recent Roper poll only 13 percent of those surveyed said that they received most of their news from sources other than the mass news outlets (magazines, journals, and books). Further, 31 percent of those interviewed depended on television *alone* for their news, while 21 percent said they depended only on newspapers, with the remainder citing both as news sources.[1]

The fact is that most American people depend entirely on television and newspapers for the substance of their news. Like it or not, the public does *not* seek out competing news sources, much less different interpretations of important events. If any competition of ideas is to reach the public, it is going to have to occur on a favorite network news program or in the *Daily Bugle.*

Thus, from the thousands of voices, we are constrained to two major transmitters of news—television and newspapers. They constitute what we call the mass news system and are interlocked into a web by the two wire news services. Consider, also, the numbing realization (as noted in the Roper poll above) that the trend is toward increased dependency on *one* news source—television; and this trend appears to be on the upswing (from 19 percent in December 1959 to 31 percent in January of 1971), while newspapers remained the same (approximately 20 percent for the same period).

The labeling of the phenomenon of mass news stems from its distribution by an organized and massive system; from its huge audience (perhaps 40 to 50 million in a given day); and from the fact that the public gets its news from these sources. Most of this book is concerned with the content and practices of mass news media. It should be noted that the very requirement that media collect, edit, and disseminate this daily intelligence requires profound compromise in terms of human organization, level of thought, and mode of reception.

Mass news is then merely one instance of an institution in mass society. This suggests that mass news is part and parcel—like railways, sanitation trucks, police, manufacturing, and servicing agencies—of a complex, bu-

---

[1] The data discussed in the text are from the pamphlet, "An Extended View of Public Attitudes toward Television and Other Mass Media: 1959–1971," available from Television Information Office, 745 Fifth Avenue, New York, N.Y. 10022.

reaucratized society wherein each institution is so pervasive and so interdependent that the failure of one link, due to a strike or equipment failure, threatens the overall functioning of the total society.

For example, the economic "health" of a city without newspapers is threatened—advertisers cannot reach their potential consumers; public attendance at cultural and sports events diminishes. In recent years, America has never had any substantial period without television and radio programming. In 1967 there was a strike by network broadcast employees which involved some of the network news personnel. The overall effect was not crippling, however, since network executives continued to broadcast the news.

Perhaps we cannot appreciate the importance and impact of any institution until it is withdrawn. The mass news media are linked to our market- and consumer-oriented economy and are supported by advertising. Although the cost of mass news and entertainment media are eventually absorbed by the citizen in the price of his automobile or bar of soap, the individual continues to think of his mass news and mass media entertainment as "free."

MASS SOCIETY, MASS COMMUNICATION, AND MASS NEWS

Colin Cherry pointed out that one does not communicate with masses but with individuals in massive numbers. In fact, the individual is lost in much discussion about news and society as we are presented with statistics that denote staggering numbers of people reading the newspaper or viewing television newscasts. The individual, in many instances, is reduced to a cipher—one of millions assembled into something called an "audience."

Throughout much of the discussion to follow, it will become apparent that individuals have little substantive power to influence the mass news system. This is because news is locked into what sociologists call a mass society. However, a knowledge of mass society and its institutional strengths and weaknesses can be used to advantage by individuals organized into certain powerful groups that influence public opinion. Before we begin such a discussion, however, we must sketch in some background for the economic and psychological parameters of society, the news media, and their interaction.

Although most Americans pride themselves upon being pragmatic, they nevertheless adhere to certain myths or philosophies to explain or rationalize their existence. Frequently the present is contrasted with a romanticized past and is often found wanting. Assumptions about mankind and ideal society are forever offered by sociologists and politicians as guides for understanding the past, present, and future. Let us begin by examining what is commonly labeled *mass society*.

Melvin De Fleur in *Theories of Mass Communication* and Dennis McQuail in *Toward A Sociology of Mass Communication* note that mass society is often contrasted with a romanticized notion of nineteenth-century village culture. Compared to the good old days, today is terrible, given our urban, industrialized, sprawling cities and equally undistinguished suburbs. For example, consider the two following definitions taken from an introductory sociology textbook:

1. Society is . . . a relatively self-sufficient unit that consists at any one time of a number of persons carrying on a common interdependent life which has continuity through successive generations.
2. Mass society is . . . a large number of persons widely dispersed spatially, having diverse interests, and anonymous to each other.[2]

Add to this Kornhauser's idea of mass society

In which many or most of the major institutions are organized to deal with people in the aggregate and in which similarities between the attitudes and behavior of individuals tend to be viewed as more important than differences.[3]

In this scheme of things, individuals are seen as alienated, fragmented into small and weak social groups, with the power of the family and traditional authority weakened by a mass society. The mass media of communication are seen as one of the few cohesive forces in society, reaching into almost every home with television programs and daily newspapers. Some early theorists saw the individual in a mass society as a helpless amoeba, liable to sinister manipulations by advertisers and propagandists. The mass media were seen as perfect instruments for reaching and shaping the masses according to whims of the power elite.

Subsequent research has shown that the individual in mass society is not a mindless animal. True, the man in the street is not a paragon of erudition and reason, but neither is he a robot. The effects of mass communication continue to be a controversial issue for many concerned scholars and citizens. The research to date has primarily been devoted to the effects of entertainment programs and advertising, with news-related research being a distant third in terms of number of studies. It would be interesting to deliver a definite treatise upon the effects of news, but the best one can do is to point to public opinion polls.

What seems to be the case is that people are creatures of habit. They will vote for the same political party year after year, and watch or read the same news media year after year. This suggests that human behavior is relatively stable.

Although usage or news attendance may be a habit, another issue involves learning from the news. There is little inherent in the news media

2 George A. Lundberg et al., *Sociology*, 4th ed. (New York: Harper & Row, Publishers, 1968), pp. 756 and 754 respectively.
3 Quoted in Dennis McQuail, *Toward A Sociology of Mass Communications* (London: Collier-Macmillan Limited, 1969), p. 19.

that fosters learning. Consider taking an examination after viewing a newscast or reading your evening newspaper—how well would you do? News in America tends to be entertaining or relaxing and is not considered an opportunity for a learning experience. Most people pay attention to the news in their leisure time. Society may require a number of individuals (such as politicians, press agents, and mass communication scholars) to pay close attention to news, but most people attend to the news because they want to. Most mass news tends to go in one ear and out the other. Much of the information seems to make little lasting impression. Unless one is interested in a particular topic such as the balance of payments or the fate of the yellow-barked birch tree, little attention is directed to it and little is remembered.

One of the most popular ways to make people pay attention has been sensationalism: the screaming headline, the tone of imminent doom in the newscasters voice. In a sense, the news is like a wall of noise; like music, it can be pleasant, but it does not necessarily lead to intellectual development.

Let us ask the broader question: What is an adequate news system for Americans? The answer requires some knowledge of both our history and democratic theory.

The soil of the American dream lies in the seventeenth century. Within European monarchies, men conceived new forms of government which would allow the individual to reach the limits of his innate skills and to enjoy the fruits of his labor. This notion, called libertarianism by many historians, saw man as a rational creature operating in a free market place of goods and ideas. Given that man was rational and important in his own right, he would naturally seek to fullfill his own enlightened self-interest. As each man sought what was right and desirable for himself, society would benefit since what was good for the citizen was good for the society. Libertarianism celebrated *individual fullfillment.*

The American founding fathers were steeped in this philosophy, but also bore the scars of some of its failures in England. Some men were greedy, and some groups less than philanthropic in their activities. Thus the American constitution provided for checks and balances against the accumulation of power in one group or governmental body. Further, a list of amendments was added to the constitution to insure individuals and institutions their unalienable rights. One of these, of course, was "the press."[4]

Assumptions about the freedom of the press revolved around a notion called the "marketplace of ideas." An unfettered press insured that all ideas would be made public and, more important, once published and debated, the truth would triumph because rational men would discover what was truthful.

---

4 This is an idealized and pluralistic description. For an elitist interpretation, see Thomas R. Dye and L. Harmon Zeigler, *The Irony of Democracy* (Belmont, Calif.: Wadsworth Publishing Co., Inc., 1970), pp. 3–87.

The press was only one feature of a society that strove for the minimal amount of government and that advocated individual freedom. A curious facet of American constitutional liberty is that it often, especially in the case of the press, grants "negative" freedom. Congress can "pass no law" to abridge the freedom of the press; this is essentially freedom without definition. The press is not required to be truthful or intelligent. There are a few laws to protect individuals from libelous coverage—a case can be tried only after the publication of the article.

It was left to the publishers of papers and their readers to define what constituted the press. In an eighteenth-century society where few could read and vote, the press was merely an adjunct to one's circle of friends. America was then still a village culture, with a majority of the people involved in agriculture.

The changes in the press in the nineteenth and early twentieth century have been profound. Principal among these was a shift from the subscriber or patron support to the advertiser support of most newspapers today. This shift occurred as mass education led to increased literacy, as technical advances allowed large numbers of newspapers to be printed, and as mass production took hold. With an increased number of marketable goods, advertising was necessary to induce the public into purchasing the manufacturer's daily and seasonal goods. Industrialization created urban centers where skilled and semi-skilled workers no longer grew their own food or made their own clothes. There were circulation wars between competing newspapers, yellow journalism, and sensationalism, but *objective* journalism emerged as a reporting norm for sound business reasons.

Objective reporting was fostered by a number of factors. Newspapers sought to *increase* their circulation—not drive away subscribers with slanted or insulting stories. The drift was toward news for everyone—the "lowest common denominator." The newspaper became entertaining with comic strips, advice columns, and sports reports. The telegraph had allowed the rise of the news (or wire) service. Newspapers in the hinterlands often had to rely on the mail for news about New York, Chicago, or Washington. With the telegraph, news syndicates undertook to provide newspapers with more recent news. Reporting became objective since newspapers subscribing to the wire service represented all political, religious, and ethnic viewpoints; objectivity stressed unslanted description. Above all, wire service reporting stressed facts, not interpretation or comment. The news per se had become a salable commodity and was subject to the same constraints inherent in any type of mass production.

The last major change was the rise of the electronic mass media. Radio allowed people to hear the news before it was printed. Thus, radio killed the newspaper extra but never really challenged the "news" supremacy of newspapers. Television did challenge this supremacy, but the process was gradual and didn't reach fruition until the sixties. It did not reduce the number of American newspapers substantially, but the number of people dependent on television for news is still growing.

Thus, the changes in American newspapers can be attributed to urbanization, education, and the development of the newer media. Newspapers and television rely on advertiser support. One now talks in terms of markets rather than community—publishers and accountants talk of ratings, cost per thousand impressions, and all the jargon of a merchandizing economy. Whatever happened to libertarianism in this evolution?

Libertarianism collapsed as a viable theory of government soon after its inception. At best, it is a myth, a charming and emotional explanation of our ideals. Human rationality fell to new psychologies embodied in Freud and in early behaviorists. One of the crucial assumptions of libertarianism was that groups were transient—free individuals were the key to libertarianism. Competition assured the best for one and all. But what happens when large industries combine and stifle individual competition? What do you do when political parties become machines controlling the candidates offered to the people?

Theoretically, people still could control their destinies, but most of the crucial decisions were made by a small group of industrialists, political bosses, and pressure groups. Some political scientists found it desirable to have elites or groups since the apathetic public did not concern itself with important issues in government and business. When Robert Dahl asked *Who Governs?* (the title of his now famous book), his answer was that groups did, but *not* without deference to the public who could act against disreputable leaders. The crucial assumption in the pluralist theory of democracy advocated by Dahl was there was a time when the citizen could act against the group through the vote or boycott. But subsequent research has shown that individuals must exert substantial pressure— either through numbers or economic power—to challenge the entrenched power structures. The growing awareness that the single individual is practically powerless had its effect in scholars' and critics' perceptions of the responsibilities of the press.

It was soon apparent to even the casual observer of American life that the press constituted a separate and powerful institution. As the number of Americans increased, the relative number of newspapers did not keep pace. Put another way, the number and variability of the American newspaper did not reflect the diversity of American life. Newspapers became entertainment packages, with political intelligence and reporting of important events of the day reduced to a modest percentage of their pages. Recall also that the marketplace of ideas depends on ideas gaining access to the channels of communication. In large industrialized and urban centers of population, one's friends alone could not begin to reflect the needed information required for simple survival in an urban environment. There was no way to require newspapers to more accurately reflect society, given the negative freedom granted them in the First Amendment. While broadcasting does have some requirements for balance and fairness in journalism (contained in a Communications Act passed by Congress), electronic journalism was not a serious contributor to the American intelligence until the sixties.

Improving the performance of the press meant only suggesting improvements to editors and owners. Historically, a number of government and private commissions have dealt with press performance in reporting events such as minority news, comprehensiveness, and so on. Their reports have been ironically redundant—critics and scholars of American journalism have been suggesting the same reforms since the forties. The principal document in this case was the Hutchins Commission Report entitled *A Free and Responsible Press.*[5]

Subsequent investigations such as the Kerner and Eisenhower reports on press performance have essentially restated the Hutchins commission suggestions. Simply, the Hutchins Commission felt that the press, given its freedoms, should accept the responsibility for journalistic performance. A shift in thinking has evolved, as evidenced at times in the Supreme Court, by certain activist groups and scholars. Previously, the press tended to wrap itself in its First Amendment privileges when challenged or criticized. The new interpretation suggests that freedom of the press resides in the people, not in whom Nicholas Johnson calls the media barons. Certainly, as you will see later, this is the case for broadcasting. The newspaper remains somewhat "freer" (assuming there is a viable concept of relative freedom).

What constitutes this newer interpretation of freedom of the press? Essentially the argument is that the people should have the right to demand fair and balanced journalistic performance from their news media. The owner or manager of the media does not have free vein to exclude unpopular opinion, or overly slant coverage. In a sense, the individual has a right to expect a marketplace of ideas from his local television station and newspaper. This notion contradicts sentiments of American journalism. The American journalist defends his craft by noting that *no one* telecast or newspaper can meet imposed requirements. It is incumbent upon the individual to attend to a variety of news sources. According to this view, no media can be a complete smorgasbord of ideas and events. Rather, each news media is but one part of the larger mosaic; the shape and structure of the complete picture rests with the citizen, not the journalist.

However, as we have already noted, the average American depends on only two sources of news—television and his daily newspaper. Americans will probably not learn about any new idea, concept, event, or governmental program unless it appears in the mass news media. The mass news media have absorbed a role that they do not want: They are the providers of the nation's intelligence.

What the Hutchins commission required of the press can be summarized into the following five points:

1. The press must provide a truthful, comprehensive, and intelligent account of the day's events in a context which gives them meaning.
2. It must be a forum for the exchange of comment and criticism.
3. It must project a representative picture of the constituent groups in a society.
4. It must present and clarify the goals and values of society.
5. It must offer full access to the day's intelligence.

[5] Report of the Commission on Freedom of the Press, *A Free and Responsible Press* (Chicago: University of Chicago Press, 1947).

This is a prescription that can be met by few newspapers today, but it is a guideline for judging the effectiveness of one's local newspaper or television station. These ideas, of course, cannot be passed into law, since the constitution explicitly prohibits it. Perhaps they can best function to inform the citizen and the media owners of the goal toward which they strive.

In this introduction we have sought to give the reader some background in a few of the crucial ideas that shape thinking about news and society. Our libertarian heritage continues to influence conceptions of the press. The key phrase is, of course, the marketplace of ideas. Some scholars have sought to explicate various "theories" of the press.[6] In fact they have referred to the Hutchins commission as the forerunner of a concept known as the social responsibility theory. Here one asks that the publisher and journalist accept the social responsibility for their actions, rather than just printing the news and letting the public be damned. While the laws governing broadcasting reflect this thinking, the newspaper remains unfettered by coherent and explicit philosophy of its role and function in society. Some practice what Stuart Hyde has called the show biz theory of the press. Here the telecast or newspaper is more oriented toward its entertainment function rather than its informational duties. When an editor talks about his newspaper as a "product" or television journalist labels his newscast a "show," we have crossed over to the world of commerce and razzle dazzle. The press is designed to be one institution among many interdependent systems constituting mass society. The press was conceived in seventeenth-century terms, but its evolution to the twentieth century has resulted in a number of changes that unfortunately make it less responsive to its public. Our aim throughout this reader is to remind ourselves that even if the single individual is powerless in American life, there are avenues open to him to reach desired ends. A real need is for some background for an understanding of mass news.

For example, it is important to know how news bureaucracies function since some reforms will require changes in organization. Failure to recognize this will merely increase frustration. We then discuss persistent practices for the outrageous anti-intellectual bias of most mass news. To this we have added a discussion of the typical patterns associated with mass news controversies. Knowledge of these patterns should allow the reader to sense what is viable in a public controversy and what is mere political rhetoric. Finally we conclude with a discussion of some alternative media and structures promising to broaden both individual participation in the news media as well as the content of mass news. Through all of this we assume that the news is vital to the republic's continued existence and that concerned individuals can and do influence the news establishment. If knowledge is power, then knowledge in America possesses the *potential* of power if it is utilized by individuals who persist in arguing that the mass news system *can* be improved.

[6] Frederick S. Siebert et al., *Four Theories of the Press* (Urbana: University of Illinois Press, 1956).

part two   **PRACTICE**
OF
MASS NEWS

section A News Media Bureaucracy

The selections in part 2 explore the current operating practices of mass news media, concentrating on news economics and technology. Let us begin by repeating some crucial distinctions. While it is easy to talk about "the institution of the press," it is not a monolithic or coherent entity; rather, it includes a fragmented cluster of men and organizations sprinkled throughout the nation. It is a curious mixture of local enterprises, regional and national services. Consider, for example, what happens when congress decides to study automobile pollution. The legislators are able to call the corporate heads of two or three corporations and begin the investigation. Who speaks with similar authority for American journalism? Like quicksilver, the "press" seems to be a cluster of concerns. Mass news is the product of jerry-rigged conglomerates of local outlets, wire services, and television networks, often owned and managed by entrepreneurs concerned only with profits and show biz.

We propose to approach the news in a different fashion. Consider the following articles as examples of news bureaucracies. Throughout the readings try to keep in mind that news is an abstract, intellectual enterprise. What impact is bureaucracy going to have on how that task is accomplished? By way of introduction, we discuss briefly such issues as bureaucracy, deadlines, and some notions about gatekeepers. In the opening selection, Ben H. Bagdikian, assistant managing editor of the *Washington Post* and long-time student of news media, discusses some of the special factors of the news business in this country which he explores at length in the Rand Corporation study cited in the bibliography. Bagdikian's major finding—that news is a privately-controlled commercial commodity, subject to many of the marketing limitations and practices of private enterprise—is the key to all that follows in this book.

From Bagdikian's essay we turn to three articles detailing the functions and operations of television, newspapers, and the wire services. This may puzzle you, since with few exceptions, none discusses "news" in any depth. Rather, the emphasis is on how the news is collected, edited, and produced. Without an appreciation of the strengths and weaknesses of the news bureaucracy, many criticisms and suggestions for reform of the American institution of the press are bound to fail. Reform must not only change attitudes of those concerned but also their group mores and their working conditions. Irving Fang, former ABC television newsman, tells of the people, jobs, and procedures at the TV station, stressing the early evening local telecast common in most markets. Julian Harriss and Stanley Johnson then analyze the equally complicated role of getting out the morning paper—a combination of specific job slots and print technology. The basic job in each case is the same—to beat the clock deadline with the most complete and best news presentation possible. The major difference between the two media is, of course, in their widely varied technical requirements which call for the newspapers' longer "lead time" (from initial report to news in the hands of the public), and usually much higher television expenses (for cameras and other electronic equipment). A comparison of the two articles helps illustrate the strengths and weaknesses of the two major means of reporting news.

The most important single element in mass news is detailed in the selection on the press (or wire) associations by Edwin Emery, Phillip H. Ault, and Warren K. Agee. There is surprisingly little written about Associated Press and United Press International, and yet these two giants of news reporting provide the large proportion of daily international and national news content seen on television, heard on radio, and read in print. The wire services are, in reality, a pool of reporters shared by many different news media all over the country.

To sum up part 2, Christopher H. Sterling, one of the editors of this volume, briefly explores the major limitations of mass news, concentrating on actually getting the story (newsgathering), presenting the story (news reporting), the story itself (content), and news reception and effects at home. These limits are primarily inherent, that is, they grow out of the nature of the media as opposed to the news process itself. To understand these limitations and their reasons, and to understand how the various elements of mass news function, is to clarify many controversies surrounding mass news (which will be discussed in part 3).

chapter 1 # Some Peculiarities of American News

BEN H. BAGDIKIAN

Among world news systems, America's is peculiar.

In other countries there are national newspapers issued in one or two important urban centers and distributed as the primary serious journals throughout the country. Local papers are marginal and parochial, classified geographically and culturally as "the provincial press."

In most countries radio and television also are centralized, with few local originating facilities. Programs typically emanate from a central studio owned and controlled by a government monopoly.

In the United States, the typical American consumer receives all his daily printed and broadcast news from a local private enterprise. There are historical reasons for this unique pattern in the United States and social reasons why it should continue. Though there are contemporary trends diminishing local independence, compared to world systems the American news continues to be rooted in the local community.

Ben H. Bagdikian, "Some Peculiarities of American News," from *The Information Machine: Their Impact on Men and the Media*, pp. 68–85. Copyright © 1971 by the RAND Corporation. Reprinted by permission of Harper & Row, Publishers, Inc.

The American news is even at odds with its own technological and corporate environment. It transmits most of its information through national monopolies, the telephone and telegraph systems. Its major suppliers of national and world news are two highly centralized national services, the Associated Press and United Press International. The newspaper industry as a whole is one of the country's largest and as such operates in an economic environment of corporate giantism and oligopoly. Yet the news itself continues to be dispensed through a highly fragmented collection of local firms.

In the United States no national newspaper is readily available in all parts of the country at its time of publication. The *New York Times* comes closest to being a national newspaper, but it is printed only in New York City and despite its considerable influence does not displace a significant portion of national newspaper reading.

The *Wall Street Journal* is published simultaneously in six different locations and is readily available in more cities than any other daily, but specializes in business and finance. The *Christian Science Monitor* of Boston is distributed nationally but its countrywide circulation is small.

Broadcasting in the United States also operates through local firms; national networks dominate prime-time television and are important in national broadcast news. But even the networks and their affiliates operate exclusively through local outlets.

No other country approaches this degree of localism in news institutions. In Russia, for example, metropolitan Moscow has less than 3 percent of total U.S.S.R. population, but Moscow-based dailies have 87 percent of all Russian daily circulation. In Japan, metropolitan Tokyo has 11 percent of national population, but Tokyo-based dailies have 70 percent of national circulation. In Britain, metropolitan London has 14 percent of population, but its dailies have 70 percent of national circulation.

In contrast, metropolitan New York and Washington, D.C., together have 6.6 percent of national population and together their daily papers supply only 9.6 percent of daily papers throughout the country.

Technical innovations in the coming years could change the fundamental pattern of public information distribution in the United States, and it is logical to ask whether the unique localism in the United States can or should be preserved. This question is worth asking because prevailing explanations for the absence of national news media in the United States seldom touch on its profound social basis.

The usual explanation for the lack of national newspapers is that the United States is so large geographically that it has been impossible to transport a paper speedily from its city of origin to all other cities. This has been one influence. But if it were the controlling factor, it would be predictable that new technology would quickly eliminate the pattern of local newspapers, since remote reproduction of large quantities of documents will become increasingly fast and inexpensive. One need not even wait for future developments. Present technology permits effective centralized control of newspaper production over great distances. Russia is two and a half times larger than the United States but manages to control most of its papers from Moscow.

Still another explanation usually offered is national affluence that can support many papers. This, like geographical size, is a factor but not a controlling one. A number of countries have a higher rate of per-capita newspaper buying but support fewer individual papers.

Country	Daily papers sold per 1000 population	Number of individual daily papers
Sweden	501	117
Britain	488	106
Japan	465	174
New Zealand	380	41
Australia	370	60
Denmark	347	67
Switzerland	344	126
West Germany	332	416
United States	312	1754

Data from *Statistical Abstract of the United States, 1968,* Table 1272, p. 862.

Note, for example, that Japan, with about half the population of the United States, sells about 50 percent more papers per capita, but has only one-tenth as many individual dailies.

The American broadcasting news system follows somewhat the same pattern, with a large number of individual radio and television stations spread throughout the country. This is primarily the result of governmental regulatory policy rather than market mechanisms that govern placement of newspapers. But it is significant that government policy places a high value on localized radio and television stations. Governments of other industrialized countries favor centralized systems.

Centralizing radio broadcasting would be technically simple. Commercial radio signals ricochet between the surface of the earth and layers of the atmosphere during the evening, propelling themselves over very long distances in every direction. Thus, it would not be difficult to produce nighttime coverage of the entire continental United States from a single transmitter. As a matter of fact, this was done from 1934 to 1938 when WLW in Cincinnati was permitted to operate at 500,000 watts.

Daytime radio signals fade more quickly, but with easily achieved power and selected frequencies a single station can still be heard within ranges of several hundreds of miles, so that a few stations could easily cover the entire United States.

Despite this technical feasibility of a few stations covering the entire country, there are 6,200 commercial AM and FM radio stations operating in 2,672 separate American communities. The largest number of radio stations in a single area is 34.

If the only desired end in the distribution of radio stations were diversity on a national scale, this could be achieved more easily, economically, and with greater variety than the present scattered locations. It would be possible, for example, to have 100 powerful radio transmitters that could reach every radio in the United States, rather than 6200 weaker ones reaching only their own locales. And the 100 centralized ones would provide more choice for the average listener, whose present maximum local stations are 34, with most communities able to receive far fewer. But the 100 centralized stations would not conform to the special force of localism in the United States.

Television cannot be so easily propagated from a few national transmitters because its carrier wave has a range less than a hundred miles and is even more disturbed than radio by intervening masses. But if national coverage with several channels were desired, it could be produced by several centralized studios whose programs would be relayed to each locality by relatively simple translator stations that are automatic. Instead, there are 639 commercial television transmitters in operation in 285 metropolitan areas, each with facilities for originating its own programs, rather than merely relaying national ones.

The fundamental reason for this persistent localism in American news institutions is a peculiarity in American political organization and the prevailing pattern of family money spending.

More governmental functions are left to the local level in the United States than in other developed countries. Schools, property taxes, land use, public health, large areas of business regulation, and many other political and social activities are controlled by locally elected and locally controlled bodies in the United States, while in other countries many of these are controlled by national governments or administered by national bureaucracies.

These locally controlled policies have maximum immediate impact on family life, such as schooling for children, design and location of homes, routes of local highways, and rates of personal property taxes. Such decisions are made by a complicated but highly localized set of political bodies. There are 18,000 municipalities and 17,000 townships. Within these are 500,000 local government units of one kind or another directly elected by local residents, 100,000 of these being directly elected local school boards, and 70,000 of the local jurisdictions possessing the power to impose taxes on their constituents.

No national newspaper or national broadcast news program can tell the local citizen what he needs or wants to know about these local activities that affect his family life. Furthermore, what is relevant to one local jurisdiction is only minimally significant for the next, since school systems, property taxes, and similar matters follow strictly local lines and cease to apply across the local boundary. Continuing information from relatively small districts is a unique imperative of the American social system.

Another powerful force for localism in the mass media is the large amount of local money spending by the average family. Mass purchasing power requires enough spending decisions to support advertising as a major economic activity.

American family income has been rising rapidly. From 1929 to 1962 average family personal income, measured in constant 1954 dollars, rose 70 percent. This, and the demands of modern urban and occupational life, have made necessities of some consumer goods that previously had been luxuries or nonexistent—refrigerators, cleaning compounds, formal city clothes. And, as national styles of work and social life evolved, other consumer goods became essential for coping efficiently with the environment—telephones, a family car, and electrical appliances like vacuum cleaners, radio and television sets. So, even at the lowest levels of income, the pressure for large-scale consumer purchasing became significant.

The great majority of this family money spending is done locally among competing enterprises. There are 1,700,000 retail stores in the United States. The average American family spends $5,000 a year in them. Many of these stores advertise in competition for this disposable family income, and most of their advertising is in the general locality of their stores, in the mass media of the region.

Thus, there is both a political and an economic base for the localized pattern of American news media.

But there are conflicting forces at work, some in the direction of the traditional fragmentation of news firms, and some in the direction of a more homogenized, national pattern of a few organizations dominating the country. At present, there seems to be a tenuous equilibrium between the forces, with a surprising degree of stability among small journalism units despite the national trend toward large national corporations. The nature of new technology and the way it is organized could be crucial to the fate of this equilibrium.

The stability and profit of small, local journalism firms are remarkable, considering their rarity in other countries. In the daily-newspaper business, for example, there is a common pattern of a few large firms controlling a disproportionate share of the total market. In the United States, 8 percent of the largest papers have over half of all circulation. The smaller papers, those under twenty-five thousand circulation, con-

Circulation of Papers	Number of Papers of this Size	Percentage of all Papers	Percentage of Total Market
500,001 and over	11	0.6	14.0
250,001 to 500,000	28	1.6	15.6
100,001 to 250,000	93	5.3	24.4
50,001 to 100,000	112	6.4	12.3
25,001 to 50,000	255	14.5	14.6
10,001 to 25,000	462	26.3	11.8
5,001 to 10,000	467	26.7	5.3
Less than 5,000	324	18.5	1.9
Total Papers	1,752	100.0	100.0

Editor and Publisher Yearbook, 1969, p. 17. Percentages of papers and of total market added.

stitute 70 percent of all daily newspaper firms but they have less than 20 percent of national circulation.

In the usual corporate trend, where in a field of 1,752 firms the top 2 percent have 30 percent of all the business, consolidation would proceed until most smaller operations would be absorbed by the giants. There is, in fact, a strong trend in the newspaper business toward consolidations, mergers, and chains, though these do not take the conventional form of centralized production, planning, and sales and do not seem to enjoy the usual economies of scale. But, while consolidation grows, the distribution of the market among smaller papers remains fairly stable, thanks to the emphasis on local self-government and local merchandising.

Location of broadcasting stations is decided by the Federal Communications Commission, and though these decisions are influenced by market demand, they are more influenced by limitations of positions on the dial. And, since there is no simple measure of "customers" for broadcasting because the consumer does not pay directly for his broadcast, determining how stations share their market is somewhat blurred. The distribution of profitable stations, by size of their community, of the 2,624 AM and AM-FM stations reporting profits to the Federal Communications Commission in 1967 is shown on the following page.

Here, as with newspapers, one sees advantages with domination of larger markets, but relative stability in the smaller ones.

The pattern of economic activity of television stations by size is more difficult to discern in official data, since the Federal Communications Commission does not issue comparable information for television. There are fewer television stations nationally, and fewer per market. There are over two hundred television markets; the top ten markets have more than a third of all TV households in the country and the top forty markets have two-thirds. Since there is a narrow limit to the number of television

Population Category of Community where Station Is Located	Number of Stations in Communities of this Size	Average Percent Profit on Gross per Station Before Federal Tax
2,000,000 or more	146	28%
1,000,000 to 2,000,000	106	27
500,000 to 1,000,000	217	19
250,000 to 500,000	241	15
200,000 to 250,000	58	15
150,000 to 200,000	89	13
100,000 to 150,000	116	13
50,000 to 100,000	71	11
25,000 to 50,000	239	13
10,000 to 25,000	465	11
5,000 to 10,000	457	13
2,500 to 5,000	294	12
Less than 2,500	125	12

From *AM-FM Broadcast Data, 1967*, F.C.C. Document 27306, February 7, 1969-B, Table 8. Percentages of profit added.

stations in any market because of the frequency shortage in the air—seven is the VHF maximum—there is a poor fit between available audience and available stations. Pittsburgh, for example, has $23 million a year in advertising revenues for its three television stations. The New York market has $130 million in television advertising revenues, or 5.6 times as much, which presumably would support 5.6 times as many stations, which would be sixteen or seventeen stations. But in New York there are only seven stations. Thus, the physical limitations of electromagnetic space in broadcasting through the air distorts any tendency to let television broadcasting adjust itself to potential audience or demand for advertising.

The news media from the start were carriers of local merchandising information. The newspaper in the United States began as a printed extension of bulletin boards of taverns and coffeehouses, its content mainly of ship arrivals and their offerings of cargo. These papers sold for six cents each, a very high price in the eighteenth century, designed for the affluent in the local population. The nonadvertising content consisted largely of reprinted stories from the English papers which arrived on the same ship as the merchandise. Until the Revolution, the most common name for American newspapers was *Advertiser*.

This pattern was enhanced by the absence of very large cities in the eighteenth-century North American continent. When the first dailies were established, the two largest cities, New York and Philadelphia, each had twenty-five thousand population.

Most of these early papers were published either by the local postmaster or by a local printer. Colonial postal service was crude and unreliable, a private monopoly granted by the Crown, and operating in only three cities. The population was a dispersed agricultural one, kept deliberately unindustrialized by the mother country, lacking the urbanization that might have encouraged a different press pattern.

As the country grew it developed a different demographic pattern from Europe, which already had its population clustered around large cities. The American frontier expanded and its population kept proliferating outward to virgin territory. A lively apprentice system produced many printers who had a reputation for itchy feet and parched throats, drifting drinkers who fell out of one job to another just beyond their reputation, but leaving behind the idea of a locally printed sheet.

Other factors helped create many small papers instead of a few large ones. One was the absence of a tax on papers. The European attempt to control the press through stamp taxes was so burdensome in many countries that it inhibited new papers. This concentrated circulation in the few papers that were rich and stable enough to pay the heavy duty on individual editions, and that tended to be very establishmentarian.

In the United States there was both constitutional and statutory encouragement for a free and growing press. Congress was forbidden to make any law abridging the freedom of the press. And the new postal system set up by Benjamin Franklin, an ex-printer, and William Hunter favored local printers. Each subscriber to a newspaper was charged nine pence sterling a year for every fifty miles the paper had to be carried by the postal system. On the other hand, papers sent from one printer to another went free. Thus, the individual subscriber was penalized by distance while his local printer was not; this encouraged printers to clip and paste other papers from distant cities and reprint locally.

In 1833, the largest American daily, the New York *Courier and Enquirer,* had a circulation of forty-five hundred, and that probably exaggerated, and most other American papers had less than a thousand circulation. The same year, the London *Times* and at least two Paris papers had circulations of more than fifteen thousand each.

The most spectacular burgeoning of the press came in mid-nineteenth century, largely because of new communications technology, like paper production from wood, high-speed presses, railroads, and the telegraph. The prices of many papers dropped. It became possible to buy a daily paper for a penny. In 1800, there had been 235 individual newspapers in the country, by 1850, 2,300. By 1860, there were more than three times as many papers in the United States as in England and France. Always local merchandising and local government stimulated indigenous papers, and the number of dailies rose to a peak of 2,461 in 1916.

But with World War I the number of newspapers in the country began to decline and has continued to decline until today there are 1,750 papers, a drop of 30 percent. And since that time there has been a rise in strictly national news media, separate or nearly separate from the local papers and broadcast stations. The rise was slow until the last twenty years, during which it has become marked.

Since 1940, total daily newspaper circulation in the United States has risen about 50 percent, roughly the same as population. But the carriers of daily national news have outpaced this. The *Wall Street Journal*'s circulation in its home state increased 2,100 percent, but outside New York it went up 4,700 percent. The *New York Times*'s circulation in greater New York rose 30 percent, outside its own city, 165 percent. The *Christian Science Monitor*'s circulation in its home city, Boston, actually dropped slightly, but elsewhere in the country it rose 26 percent.

National news magazines, an invention of the period, have gained even more rapidly. In the 1940–1968 period, *Time, Newsweek,* and *U.S. News and World Report* increased their circulation 585 percent.

Responding to the same growing appetite for national news, new special supplementary news services for daily papers concentrated on serious Washington and world reportage and analysis. The New York Times Service was going to 16 North American papers in 1956 and to 211 in 1969. The Los Angeles Times/Washington Post News Service started in 1962 with 21 papers and in 1969 had 189. *Congressional Quarterly,* a relatively sophisticated summary and statistical analysis of legislative activity in Washington was subscribed to by 1 paper in 12 in 1955, but in 1968 by 1 paper in 6, even though it had a rival in a new service, Center for Political Research.

But, during the same period of marked growth of national news media, there was growth in strictly local ones. Hundreds of specialized papers, many classed as "underground," sprang up, with a circulation estimated at 4 million. "Establishmentarian" weeklies, mostly serving small areas, also grew. During the decade 1958–1967, daily newspaper circulation rose 5 percent, but circulation of standard commercial weeklies rose 51 percent. Some operators forecast even more spectacular growth. John E. Tilton, of Suburban Papers, Inc., of Minneapolis, said, "In the next 20 years, someone will start another 2000 suburban newspapers."

Nevertheless, commercial pressures for ever wider jurisdictions, made all the more tempting by easier and cheaper long-distance transmission of information, raise the possibility of increasing separation between local media and national.

Two factors push in this direction. One is the growth in popular consciousness of national and world affairs, the result both of increased cosmopolitanism and education and the enlargement of the role of the national government and world events in the life of the average family.

The other factor is the trend in contemporary advertising and merchandising reversing the historic role of rooting the local media to their immediate communities.

In the late nineteenth century, newspapers for the first time took seriously the possibility that at least one newspaper could be sold to each household each day. By then it was technically possible to manufacture enough papers for this kind of saturation. Advertising was becoming an important national economic activity and assuming an ever larger share of the newspaper's revenues. In 1867 $50 million a year was spent on ads; in 1900 this had gone up ten times, by 1950 a hundred times.

Merchants generally buy space or broadcasting time on the basis of the cost of exposing their advertising to a thousand persons, or cost-per-thousand. As individual newspaper production plants developed the capacity to print one complete newspaper for every house in the community, and advertisers clearly became indirect subsidizers of these plants, the working of the marketplace made it inevitable that it would be less expensive for the advertisers to support one plant in a community instead of two or three or a dozen. Even with the increased advertising rates that a local monopoly could charge, the cost-per-thousand was cheaper than advertising in two or more competing papers.

Since World War I the number of individual newspapers has declined, though the surviving papers have become fatter and devote a larger percentage of their space to advertisements. Since World War II advertising content in daily papers has gone from 52 percent to 61 percent, the size of papers from twenty-two pages a day, of which eleven were ads, to fifty pages in 1965 for the average daily, of which thirty were ads.

Fatter papers meant larger plants, more presses, more typesetting machines, and larger work forces. Processing of advertising is more demanding and expensive than that of news matter. Costs rose. But, once plates were on the presses, labor costs remained relatively level and the cost of added circulation was largely the cost of paper and ink. And, since advertising was placed more on the basis of cost-per-thousand than any other single factor, it was advantageous for a paper to increase its production, even if it meant extending its sales beyond the limits of its immediate city.

Conversion of newspapers into substantial manufacturing plants inhibited growth of new papers in new communities. Surviving papers gained monopolies in their own communities and pushed beyond the city limits to nearby communities. Consequently, the cost of starting new papers in the new communities at the edges of the metropolises was unattractive, since the established nearby papers were always prepared to produce papers for the new communities at small incremental cost. The country created more and more communities, and served them with fewer and fewer newspapers.

The consequences of this reversal of the traditional American tendency for each community to serve its self-governing functions with its own news medium are difficult to measure. But the change from 90 percent of

Year	Daily Papers	Cities with Dailies	% of Daily Cities with Competing Papers	% of Urban Places with Own Dailies
1880	850	389	61	90
1910	2202	1207	57	53
1920	2042	1295	43	48
1930	1942	1402	21	44
1940	1878	1426	13	41
1945	1744	1396	8	—
1961	1763	1461	4	29
1968	1749	1500	3	—

From *Subcommittee on Antitrust and Monopoly,* "The Failing Newspaper Act," Part 6, p. 2842, Table 1, "Trends in Ownership of English-Language Dailies of General Circulation and Content in the United States, 1880–1968," percentage of daily cities with competing papers added. Number of urban places from *Historical Statistics of the United States,* p. 14, and *Statistical Abstract of the United States,* p. 16.

urban places with their own daily paper to less than 30 percent is a radical one, and it may have radical consequences. It could be a contributing factor to the growing inability of municipalities to control their social and political affairs, to the psychological loss of community identity characteristic of newer towns and cities, and to the sluggishness with which urban governments responded to postwar social pathologies and the slowness with which this pathology, once felt, came to national attention.

The need for systematic community communication in the United States is self-evident from the number of important functions left to local decision. Jack Lyle, in his book *The News in Megalopolis,* notes that the local press is usually thought of as a watchdog over local government, and while this is true, there is a positive function as well: ". . . officials want to get information to the public . . . because of the proliferation of public agencies, such bodies are actually competing for the attention of the individual citizen and for coverage within the news media."

Lyle's research showed that community communications depend more than anything else on the presence of a locally based printed news medium. When he asked local officials how frequently their activities were covered by news media, both city-government and school-district activities showed coverage in this way:

Local weeklies	53%
Local dailies	53
Metropolitan dailies	17
Radio and TV	0

Banfield and Wilson in *City Politics* note that a city like Chicago has

341 different officials with identifiable authority in city and county matters and "in most cases there is no formal mechanism by which all these governments can be brought together."

The growing number of radio and television stations has not relieved this trend because broadcasting pays little attention to systematic local reportage. Robert Paul Boynton and Deil S. Wright, in a study of council managers in cities of over 100,000 population, found that "Local news is the base of a newspaper's operation. A high percentage of its total space is allotted to community concerns. Radio and television have other primary interests."

Boynton and Wright polled city managers on their judgment of mass-media influence on municipal affairs, with these results:

Degree of Influence	Newspapers	Television	Radio
Highly influential	51%	8%	2%
Moderately influential	42	50	33
Limited influence	7	23	49
No apparent influence	0	20	16

"Communication Gap: Is Anybody Up There Listening?" by Robert Paul Boynton and Deil S. Wright, *Public Management*, March, 1968, p. 2.

This parallels a survey by the Bureau of Advertising of the ANPA which, in 1966, polled a cross-section of readers on the "best way" to find out about local affairs, to which 48 percent cited newspapers, 13 percent television, and 15 percent radio. Both the newsmakers and the news consumers depend on the local printed newspaper for important community information.

The basic causes for present community malaise in the United States can hardly be laid at the door of absent or delinquent news media. Even with ideal local attention to civic affairs, it would be difficult to cope with the bewildering maze of governmental and quasi-governmental units, often uncoordinated and frequently at cross-purposes. But apathy or frustration produced by this random agglomeration of civic functions is deepened by the lack of locally based news-media that even try to follow and publicize systematically the more important developments. In a country of 100,000 autonomous school districts and 400,000 other local governmental units, it is significant that fewer than 30 percent of the communities in whose boundaries they lie has any locally based news medium.

This poor fit between community units and news media comes largely because newspapers and radio and television stations, even though they carry a place name in their identification, do not arrange their output by civic boundaries but instead by merchandising territories. As the automobile determines the range for shopping, merchandising territories increasingly ignore civic boundaries. And, as these shopping territories enlarge, the growing production power of the mass media follows them through communities whose civic affairs they largely ignore.

The effective boundary line of most newspapers is a territory called "retail trade zone," which varies in definition from place to place but commonly ends in neighborhoods where the paper's daily sales fall to between 5 and 20 percent of the total households.

Broadcasting stations occupy territories called "markets," which are usually the area of the effective range of their broadcast signal.

About 400 markets are calculated for daily newspapers and about 230 markets for broadcasting stations. Within these are most of the 500,000 units of local government. Given the total space for serious local news in newspapers, and the total time devoted in typical broadcasting stations, it would be impossible to give systematic reportage of all the important public-affairs developments in each of the significant public bodies within the market areas of individual news media.

In 1969 a majority of the FCC raised questions about the transfer in ownership of the only television station in Hutchinson, Kansas, KTVH, Channel 12. The Commission was concerned with concentration of ownerships, but KTVH is typical of other television stations in its jurisdiction, which represents problems regardless of ownership.

KTVH covers about 18,000 square miles with its strongest signal, with average penetration of 90 percent of the 344,000 homes. If the 23 counties for which KTVH is the primary station have their share of all local governmental units in Kansas, they contain over 800 different governmental bodies, including 210 municipalities and 110 school boards. About 350 of them levy taxes.

If the station devotes typical TV time to local news (not including sports), and if each of the governmental bodies in its area made only one newsworthy decision a month, and if the station happened to cover this decision, and if the station devoted all of its local newscasts exclusively to the deliberations of these public bodies, each would have reportage of thirty seconds a month.

KTVH is part of the Kansas Broadcasting System for the purpose of selling commercials. This network of television stations advertises itself as "a 93 county major television market of 403,400 television homes, 1.3 million people in a five state area with a consumer spendable income of over $3.5 billion. . . ."

For merchandisers, such a network is effective. As reporters of events within their boundaries, it reduces each civic function to a fraction of a minute per month.

Yet the merchandising function continues to favor ever larger geographical territories, so that the cost of reaching each consumer will drop. This is impelled not only by the larger shopping ranges made possible by the automobile, but also by the growth of unified national brands, commonly available "at your local" (anonymous) drug, department, or grocery store. Standard-brand cosmetics, food, and cigarettes do not need to specify particular stores or addresses in order to stimulate sales by wide-area broadcasting or newspaper advertising.

Among newspapers, two categories of standardized retail goods make up 42 percent of all newspaper advertising: automobiles with 28 percent, and foods with 14 percent. In television, in 1970, four categories of nationally standard brands made up almost 60 percent of all television advertising: foods with 19 percent; toiletries, 17 percent; tobacco, 12 percent; and drugs, 11 percent.

The retail outlets for these standardized items are also becoming regionally and nationally standardized by a relatively small number of recognizable and dominant firms. The combination of near-universal recognition of both store names and brand names means that broad, homogenized advertising becomes more effective, and the small medium with a special audience less competitive.

Especially with broadcasting, whose entertainment and news also are increasingly produced in a national source, the financial rewards lie with enlargement of area and of gross population, even to the deliberate exclusion of a station's immediate home base.

The Federal Communications Commission recently took note of this tendency. "We have . . . noted that there is a tendency on the part of stations in suburban communities in metropolitan areas, to identify themselves with the entire metropolitan area rather than with the particular needs of their communities." The FCC intervened when the only full-time radio station in Camden, New Jersey, was about to be sold to a Texas corporation which intended to eliminate all local programming serving the 117,000 population of Camden in order to attract advertising for programming designed for the metropolitan Philadelphia area across the Delaware River, although Philadelphia already had twenty-eight of its own radio stations.

Technology helped eliminate the idea of every community with a news medium of its own. But even broadcasting once started as a local service. When the British Broadcasting Corporation started in 1922, there was no practical network system in existence. Consequently it established twenty strictly local stations with only $\frac{1}{4}$ kw power (American communities now have stations with many times that power). When communications technology improved, the BBC became a centralized operation out of London. Frank Gillard, managing director of radio for the BBC, says that the result has been that the former development of local talent in discussion, entertainment, and culture atrophied as only the highly professionalized work of London reached the air, and that "democracy in the country breaks down at the local level."

If England, which depends far less on local decision making for the health of its basic institutions than the United States, is apprehensive about a breakdown at the local level for lack of local media, the United States has cause for concern. Although the United States has far more local media than any other country, it is far more dependent on such media than any other country. And these local media are expanding their territories, largely at the expense of neighborhood, community, and city information and programming. The commercial imperative is not news but to reach the largest possible undifferentiated gross numbers of audience for purposes of national and regional advertising. And this advertising is less and less tied to particular communities.

●　●　●

chapter 2 Mass News: Business and Bureaucracy

DAVID J. LeROY

BUREAUCRACY

The news media evolved their present bureaucracies more from necessity than from a rational analysis of the tasks to be performed. As newspapers became daily in their production and larger in size and circulation, owners had to hire assistants to help him produce the daily product.

Bureaucracies display certain predictable attributes which may have detrimental effects for both journalism and the public. First, all bureaucracies have a hierarchy of authority, because production of a product requires a division of labor—assembly line workers, foremen, supervisors, and managers. The requirements for each job are determined by management, not by the worker. There is a system of rules and procedures covering one's job and one's interaction with the employer or the union. An individual is hired, fired, or promoted by the rules which include criteria for assessing technical competency for each position. Although these requirements for employment may reduce nepotism and favoritism in hiring and promotion, they also reduce to a cold impersonal level most interpersonal transactions with one's supervisor and employer. This impersonal coldness is what most of us dislike about large bureaucracies. In a bureaucracy, one is dealt with according to the established procedures and few exceptions are permitted.

We are concerned here mostly with those individuals who collect, write, and edit the news. We omit consideration of the printers, mailers, cameramen, film editors, and other laborers. In most instances, especially if they are unionized, these individuals are already thoroughly bureaucratized. Initially, the union contracts were undoubtedly necessary to protect the worker from the capricious and demeaning treatment of the media owners. However, each job is now enshrined in minutely specific detail in the union contract. The result is a rigidity in task behaviors which can seriously usurp the creative efforts of those in journalism. Yet, since everyone knows his job and what is expected of him, the regular appearance of our daily newspaper or telecast is insured. Regardless of how one feels about the bureaucratization of the back shop employees, it does exist and it has ramifications for both the media owner and the journalist. Thus, while it is dramatic to tear down the front page shortly before press time or to send camera crews to the scene of a midnight disaster, each decision has a dollars and cents repercussion, especially with union personnel. Too many deficit-creating decisions by an editor can have only one result—unemployment.

DEADLINES

Each news medium has a deadline that has to be met. Viewers expect to see the news program at its announced time, while newspaper readers expect their papers at its usual time. For the print media, deadlines are necessitated by transportation difficulties. Excessive delay in printing the daily paper may result in the trucks becoming tied up in rush hour traffic causing the out-of-town deliveries to be hopelessly delayed. Only weekly and monthly magazines have what can be termed reasonable flexibility concerning deadlines. Yet, even weeklies must come close to their deadlines to insure mail delivery. Also, since advertisers may have national or regional sales campaigns underway, it is important that weekly magazines meet their deadlines.

Thus the news media are symbiotic with the other necessary institutions in a mass society. They mesh with government, business, and leisure industries and fulfill various important functions to insure operation of the whole society.

Deadlines also have social consequences for the journalist in that they introduce psychological stress. Not only must one do his job, but often it must be done in a hurry to insure the story's inclusion in the forth-coming edition.

Why the rush? In the early days of competing daily newspapers, espe-cially those in larger cities where the paper depended heavily on street sales, the paper with the "latest" or "freshest" news stood to increase its circulation. In some instances there were extra or bulletin editions for important news such as presidential deaths, invasion, or civil disorder. With the rise of the electronic media, the bulletin and extra newspaper editions have disappeared, their function having been taken over by radio and television. Further, in all but a few cities today there are no competing afternoon or morning papers. Rather, one paper appears in the morning and another in the afternoon. Yet, the puzzle remains—why all the stress on freshest or latest news?

Journalism is as sentimental as any other occupation. The notion here revolves around the idea of "fresh" news—to get the latest story of major importance into the forthcoming edition. Today's deadlines exist to insure efficient distribution, but newsmen insist on complicating the issue by requiring that the freshest news be included in the *next* edition or newscast. Ironically, the fast-breaking story is often reported only in a sparse general outline or bulletin form. Further, it is interesting to note that the editors are already under deadline stress when the decision is made to insert the latest information about a senate debate, flood disaster, or airplane crash. Perhaps this element of stress explains why much of the bulletin news which is slipped in shortly before air or press time turns out, in retrospect, to be trivial or unnewsworthy. Some critics have argued that the fresh news emphasis is misplaced, and that one should strive to achieve thorough coverage, not to be the first with a head-line and one paragraph of general or inaccurate information about a de-veloping event.

GATEKEEPERS

In the complex process of collecting and assembling the news for dis-tribution, a number of people must make crucial decisions about which news items will be printed or broadcast and which will be discarded or saved for another day. The label, "gatekeeper," is most commonly em-ployed to identify these key decision makers.

The most important gatekeepers can be classified by their job type. For example, the telegraph or wire editor is responsible for selecting stories from the Associated Press or United Press International teletype service. Generally these are stories dealing with regional, national, and interna-tional news.

The organization and size of the particular paper or station influence the other types of editors employed. Some editors deal with incoming calls, assign reporters, and, in general, monitor the local news input of a newspaper or station. The managing or city editor decides what is included and what is excluded in the paper or telecast. He may also decide the placement or play of a story. Since the number of individuals who make gatekeeping decisions is rather small, they have been a continuing focus of study by academic researchers for many decades. Because these men determine our daily diet of news, their attitudes and work habits have been studied more, perhaps, than those of any other news media worker. Unfortunately, at this time no adequate survey of gatekeeping research is available. What follows is an impressionistic review of a number of field studies.

Findings dealing with telegraph or wire editors can be summed up briefly. These gatekeepers have a quota of news to pull from the wire. They have more stories available than they can use. At best, their decisions are secondary, since the crucial behavior already occurred when someone up the line at the wire service decided that event X was important enough to cover and event Y was not. If the paper or station subscribes to two wire services, then the editor sometimes must choose between AP's version of the story and UPI's.

Ironically, even given the abundance of available material, the wire editor's choices are quite predictable. There will usually be a story about the president, what happened in Congress today, the current flood or riot in a nearby state, and a human interest story. Human interest stories tend to bring out an editor's particular idiosyncrasies—some editors love horse stories, others like dogs, some like stories about children.

In summary, wire editors have a quota of stories to select each day, and the variety of these stories tends to be somewhat stable. They have some latitude in selecting material when two wire services are available. But in general, they have little real impact on the makeup of the newspaper or newscast. The front page of one local newspaper usually resembles another since there are only two wire services available.

In decisions regarding local news coverage, the managing or assignment editor plays a crucial role. Here again, the range of variation is not great, since some reporters regularly cover special areas or beats like city hall, the police precincts, school boards, and council meetings. Some editors may have a strong commitment to local issues such as pollution or the PTA, but usually the same things are covered day after day.

The inevitable conclusion is that the early research into gatekeeping and decision behavior for journalists was rather primitive, if not naive in conception and design. A number of researchers in this area are now arguing for an expanded conceptual model to better explain the behavioral components of journalistic behavior. In general, they argue that decisions are not best represented by the older linear models—that news items flow from point one to gatekeeper A who makes a decision about an item, and that the surviving news stories flow to point two and gate-keeper B. As was suggested in discussing the wire editors, the conclusion from the early studies was that an individual gatekeeper made what was in essence a number of trivial choices. The previously held assumption was not supported—that conscious, premeditated decisions by one person bestowed coverage on certain events or people. Rather (as you will see later in Bailey and Lichty's article), gatekeeping decisions are embedded in the organization. It is difficult to find one person who makes "monumental" decisions. (The exception would be in times of dire emergency, such as a presidential assassination, when a decision has to be made quickly. Here the decision requires the commitment of large sums of money, personnel, and perhaps the disruption of traditional production schedules. But these instances are rare, and the day to day flow of events is taken care of by the current bureaucratic organization.)

Empirical researchers have generated a jargon to label their new models for investigating journalistic behavior. Terms such as cybernetic and systems analysis, servo-mechanism, and feedback loops appear in today's research papers. Essentially what is usually being discussed is nothing more than bureaucracy and interpersonal interaction on the job. The bureaucracy of journalism is rather primitive in comparison with an industrial corporation such as General Motors. For the news media, many methods and procedures for performance are still immersed in tradition and ritual.

chapter 3 The Television News Day

IRVING FANG

At seven o'clock each weekday morning, the dayside assignment editor at one of our large city television stations arrives at work. Let us consider him and his co-workers, for they are fairly typical of local television news staffs of comparable size everywhere. Even where news staffs are much smaller, most of the same tasks are performed, although on a reduced scale, by employees with combined job functions.

The dayside assignment editor of our typical news staff walks into the newsroom and goes straight to the bank of teletypes, even before he hangs up his coat. In a few seconds, he scans the last 30 minutes of copy transmitted by the AP, UPI and the local news wire (if his city has one). Seeing nothing that will require the immediate alerting of camera crews, he hangs up his coat, plugs in the coffee pot, and begins his day. For the rest of the day either he or the nightside assignment editor will either rip or

Irving E. Fang, "The Television News Day," from *Television News: Writing–Filming–Editing–Broadcasting*, pp. 13–36. Copyright © 1968 by Irving E. Fang. Reprinted by permission of Hastings House, Publishers.

glance at the "wires" (all the teletype wires) roughly every 15 minutes. As air time nears, the trips to the teletypes will be increased to every five minutes; this frequency will be maintained until the newscast is done. Throughout the day other staff members will look at the wires, out of both personal interest and the knowledge that when a major news story breaks, they will probably learn of it first by teletype.

DAILY ASSIGNMENTS

If the dayside assignment editor has found nothing on the wire requiring his immediate attention, he begins to plan the day's camera schedule for three crews. From a box containing 31 consecutively numbered "future" folders, one for each day of the month (after a date has passed, that folder is used to accumulate assignments for the same date of the following month) he takes the folder for the present day.

The assignment editor rips all the wires. His practiced eye runs down each item, searching for several kinds of stories:

a. A story which should be covered today.
b. A feature story, which can be filmed any time.
c. A future news assignment.
d. An out-of-town, national or international story with a local angle.
e. A story which should be presented with still photos, maps or drawings.
f. A backgrounder or some other story which should be called to some staff member's attention.
g. Out-of-town stories for which film might have been shot—or yet might be shot—by another television station or a free lancer.
h. Hard news: major news stories which can be reported as is. As the day wears on, almost every major story will have been updated several times.
i. A cute "bright."
j. Specialized items of interest to the sports editor and the weather reporter.

As the assignment editor scans the wires, the first news team arrives to start their day. A reporter, a cameraman and a soundman report to work. The editor tells the cameraman that he is tentatively scheduled to cover interviews with an author, a senator and air pollution officials. This informs the cameraman that he will probably mount his camera on a tripod all day, rather than on a shoulder pod, and that he will be lighting static indoor scenes. He and the soundman go off to assemble their gear and, if they haven't already done so, load film into magazines. They also know they have an hour to get to and set up for their first assignment. This time, the camera is not hooked to its shoulder pod, but the pod goes along in the car, just in case.

Although a cameraman and a soundman usually work together week after week, the assigning of reporters is more flexible. Some stories may not need reporters; for example, the filming of an art exhibit, a parade, or a circus performance. Camera crews are sometimes assigned to non-news tasks such as filming segments of a documentary. On the other hand, reporters may be sent where camera crews are not needed (e.g., to search records) or not allowed (e.g., at a trial). Also, camera crews necessarily move from story to story more slowly than reporters do. A reporter may be assigned to work with different camera crews during the day, either to cover more stories or because he has particular knowledge in a certain subject area. And if a reporter edits his own film (i.e., determines the cuts—a film editor does the physical editing) he may have to leave his crew in mid-afternoon. Sometimes the reporter travels in his own car; sometimes he travels with the crew, and takes taxis if he has to break away.

Stories of neighborhood problems, such as a demand for a traffic light or objection to a zoning decision, usually require no advance study by a reporter. Sympathetic questioning by a skilled reporter plus intelligent camera work at the scene of the problem usually produce a good story. If both sides to the dispute can be brought in front of the camera, the story is even better, especially when a writer can later intercut the arguments to produce short and punchy statements by each party in turn. Very rarely, a camera is witness to a heated discussion by both sides present at the same time, perhaps brought together by the reporter. One or both parties may grow quite angry at the television newsmen off camera. On the other hand, the camera may record an absolutely fascinating argument, either with the reporter or, more properly, between the antagonists.

At 10:30 a.m., the lab man arrives at the station. He begins to heat the chemicals in the tanks of his color film processor (his tasks became more complex when the station "went to color" in news). The smaller black-and-white film processor remains on the premises, but it is rarely used now. All news film is shot in color at his station, including the film shot by "stringers," the free-lance cameramen who earn extra cash each week by filming spot news stories, often at night when the station's regular camera crews are off duty.

Two other men begin their day at 10:30 a.m., a writer and a film editor. The film editor is ready to begin work almost immediately. Before the night newsroom film editor (who arrives at 3 p.m.) leaves each night, he clears the editing benches of the day's debris. The morning film editor's first task is to take apart the reels which comprise the previous night's late news. The station presents two news shows, at 6 p.m. and 11 p.m. The 6 p.m. reels are broken into individual story segments after the program ends. Some of the stories are re-edited for the 11 p.m. newscast.

The 11 p.m. reels are broken the following morning. The film editor spends about 30 minutes breaking the two 400-foot reels into a dozen or so smaller reels. He labels each little plastic reel and types a file card. The cards are catalogued alphabetically by topic and/or person, and are cross-filed if necessary. All the reels are placed in a film can, which the editor dates and stores on a shelf.

Meanwhile, the first writer to arrive spends his first 30 minutes scanning the day's shooting schedule, the morning wire copy and the newspapers to which the newsroom subscribes. He keeps up with news events from local to international levels for several reasons:

1. He may be called upon to look at film or tape concerned with this news event or a subsequent event related to it.
2. The news event may be mentioned by someone whose words he must edit.
3. He may find in the news event something worth following up. Here, his purpose duplicates that of the assignment editor. It is a useful redundancy. The more staff members who read news extensively, the more depth of coverage the newscasts are likely to have.
4. He may write a non-film story, an editorial or a humorous essay based on a news event.
5. He may refer, in passing, to a news event in his copy or another story.

At 11 a.m., the newsroom messenger arrives. Until the news department hired its own messenger, it had to make do with commercial messenger service or use whatever staff member had some free time. The messenger makes frequent trips to the airport to get or ship film. He intercepts camera crews, picking up their film in order to save them a trip to the lab. He brings them spare parts if any of them report equipment failure. When available, he carries film between the lab and the film editing room. He carries reels from the film editing room to the projection room, and brings them back after the newscast. All the while, he learns the workings of the television news operation and, when he has time, apprentices for the job which interests him most.

The news director makes his own schedule and keeps it flexible. At 10 a.m. he arrived at the station for a management conference on the news budget. Unlike some television news departments run on a shoestring and producing lackluster newscasts which do little but keep the Federal Communications Commission at a safe distance, his news department actually makes money for his station. The twice daily newscasts are interesting and informative. Their audiences represent a large slice of all viewers in the city, and the viewers tend to be faithful. Watching one or both newscasts is as much a part of their day as eating supper. Local advertisers request time within or adjacent to the newscasts, and some segments are sponsored. Station management, aware that it takes money to make money, plows much of the profit back into the news department in salaries, equipment and a budget to cover purchases of film, artwork, rental of helicopters and other costs to improve the newscasts.

At 3 p.m., two more writers, a film editor and the nightside assignment editor report to work. Crews and reporters have been given lunch breaks. Crew 1 is given time to check equipment before going home for the day. Newsreel cameras and sound gear get rough handling, yet they are precision built. All the equipment needs attention and frequent maintenance. Otherwise, the cameraman and soundman risk equipment failure at crucial moments.

The other writer goes to a television monitor for both the incoming "feed" from New York of the network news, and a special network videotape service of international, national and sports film stories for use on local newscasts. From some 15 available clips in the videotape special service, the writer may choose four. He will edit them if necessary, but keeps his editing to a minimum, for videotape editing remains a cumbersome process. Instead, he directs the videotape engineer to dub the clips he wants onto a separate reel in the order he requests, with cue marks in between. He will prepare a script for each videotape clip, so that the director will have timings and end cues. The writer will also strip the wirephoto machine, looking for stills to use in connection with the videotape, usually at the beginning or end of the tape. He will also look for stills which will stand by themselves as the only visual elements in a story. All stills will be sent to the art department for touch-up and for mounting on cards. The newscast may use 30 cards of various kinds in 30 minutes.

The nightside assignment editor will take over duties from the dayside editor in the space of half an hour. The transfer of responsibility and information must be smooth and complete. If not, the nightside editor may not do what the dayside editor promised would be done: important phone calls will not be made; phone calls that are received will not be understood (e.g., "Say, anybody know why Detective Joe Green was supposed to call us?"); and news stories will not be assigned as they should be.

BUILDING THE NEWSCAST

As the afternoon hours pass, a pile of individual story scripts grows on the news director's desk. A 4 p.m. he begins to build the newscast from wire copy, film scripts, videotape scripts and local material such as a weather report. The writer who looked at the videotape and monitored the network news also rewrites news stories from the wire copy. He chooses the major stories of the day, selects the latest information available and summarizes them briefly, writing in broadcast style. He will continue to watch the wires closely until both the local and network newscasts have been completed. The network newscast is received from New York one to three hours before it is played back (depending on national time zones). If late news contradicts what has been taped already, or if a bulletin of overriding importance appears on the teletype, the writer will write a script to cover a portion of the taped network newscast with a slide, or with a local newscaster, live, to report it. Besides rewriting wire stories for the local newscast, the writer also chooses a half dozen wire copy stories which he doesn't bother to rewrite. He simply staples the copy to sheets of paper and writes the word "PAD" at the top of each sheet. If the newscaster runs out of copy before the end of the program, he will have these additional items to read.

The total time, as tentatively outlined, is 25 minutes 15 seconds. The 30-minute newscast, of course, does not permit airing 30 minutes of news. Its format includes an opening one-minute commercial, four one-minute commercials within the program, a 20-second opening, a 20-second closing and 20 seconds at the end for a "promo" (a promotional commercial for a later television program) and a station break, leaving 24 minutes for news.

However, five minutes each day is allotted to sports and weather news. A sports reporter and a sports writer have been working independently of the main news operation, assembling the items for their segment. They add two films to the reels being built by the film editors.

Subtracting five minutes from 24 leaves the news director with 19 minutes of time available for 25:15 of film, tape and copy. The news director now has a chore he must cope with each day: what to cut—he always has more news available to him than he can use. If he did not have more, he would worry, for he would sense a weakness in the overall quality of the newscast material. He would also worry if too much had to be trimmed away, because that would mean a lot of effort and expense was going to waste. Ideally, he wants to trim the script to 18:45, with 15 seconds for leads into commercials. But first he assembles his individual scripts for each story into a newscast script within the framework of the format.

The news director now has his script. It is, however, 6:30 too long. Many of the times are approximate. Taking out a stopwatch and reading at the pace he knows the newscaster uses, the news director reads the rewritten wire stories, all of which are marked, as an approximation, as segments of 30 seconds. As he reads, he edits out a phrase here and a sentence there, finishing with a saving of 45 seconds. He knows the seven minutes allotted to fire story is also approximate. He may be able to trim this story, but he does not want to cut anything out that would hurt a major local story, his lead story of the day, one which the news staff covered in depth. He goes to the screening room, where the writer and film editor are now piecing together on paper what they have just seen. The news director asks about the quality of the story and its length. The writer praises the film and asks the news director how "tight" the newscast is. When he is told, the writer asks for at least five minutes. The director asks him if he wants more. They settle on six minutes.

It is now 4:30 p.m. The newscaster, the director and the assistant director, or A.D., arrive. Each page of the script has been typed in quintuplicate. The assistant director sorts the pages into five separate scripts, slipping in "slug" sheets where pages are still missing. The top copy goes to the newscaster. The second copy to the director, who circles a word five seconds ahead of each film and videotape. When the newscaster reads that word, the director will order "Roll film" or "Roll tape," knowing that each film clip and each tape story will be physically halted in their machines precisely five seconds of rolling time ahead of the first frame of film or the first videotape picture that is wanted. The director also calculates which of three television studio cameras he will focus on the newscaster each time he appears, which camera on the sports reporter and which camera on each card on the two racks in the studio; additionally, he decides which cards go on which racks.

The newsroom set in the studio is fixed. It does not change from day to day. It is never "struck" unless it is redesigned. The set is pre-lit; that is, once a lighting director has arranged the lights, no changes are made in lighting so long as there are no complaints and no changes are made in the set; the single exception is the occasional need to light a prop used to illustrate a story.

The third copy of the script goes to the assistant director. During rehearsal he will time each story and keep a running time as well, marking these times on the pages of his copy. The fourth copy will go to the audio engineer. Although the audio engineer gets instructions from the director, his copy of the script enables him to cut away from film and tape exactly at the final word of the end cue, so that the studio sound is crisp and clear, with neither unwanted words going over the air or "upcuts" (the loss of words because the sound was brought in a second or two late). The final copy goes to a TelePrompTer typist, who reproduces the script in large letters on a roll which will fit into a device above a television camera lens. As the newscaster reads, a TelePrompTer man will roll this script to keep pace. To the viewer at home, the newscaster seems to be looking right at him, *telling* him the news. Actually, he is reading. Sometimes, he uses the script in his hand just as a prop. Other times, he reads each in turn.

As a rule, except on some smaller stations, neither the director nor the assistant director are newsmen. They consider a newscast a "show" which is handled much like any locally produced show, except that they get the script very late, feed it live and occasionally accommodate changes while the program is on the air. Otherwise, to them it is another show using two or three cameras, one or two film chains, videotape, slides, etc. It uses a set which must be lit, and it begins and ends at specified times, with breaks for commercials. Their concern is not with content, but with format.

At some television stations, a member of the news staff, perhaps a writer or assignment editor, doubles as director, assistant director or as producer. The latter is responsible for the content and production of a newscast. In many cases, the news director serves as the producer. In some news operations, there is no producer as such; several staff members share the work and the responsibility for the content of the newscast.

The newscaster has the most desirable job in the television news department. He is paid more than others, sometimes disproportionately more. To station management, he is the "talent," and to everyone, in and out of the station operation, the newscaster alone is identified with the news program. The newscaster is the representative of the station and the news department in addressing Kiwanis luncheons, and the like. However, accompanying the occasional glamour and star system treatment is a measure of insecurity. If audience ratings fall, the newscaster is likely to be blamed and may be replaced. Chances are he will seek employment in another city unless he chooses some other occupation. He also feels the competition not only of newscasters elsewhere, but of reporters and other news staffers who aspire to his position.

On some stations the newscaster is an announcer who was appointed newscaster by virtue of his stage presence, his authoritative voice, his delivery skill or his looks. If he does not immerse himself in the day-to-day news operation, but merely contents himself with picking up a finished script, other news staffers scornfully label him a "reader."

Today, many newscasters go considerably beyond such detachment from news and the building of the newscast. The newscaster is often also a reporter; on small stations he is likely to be *the* reporter. Even further, the combination newscaster-news director is common. The newscaster then has responsibility for the content of the newscast. Or, to put it another way, the news director not only produces the newscast, but delivers it.

While the director and the assistant director mark their copies of the script for cue words and camera cuts, the newscaster reads his copy for content. He is particularly concerned with factors which may be detrimental to delivery. If he comes across a name or a word which he is not sure he will pronounce properly, he checks it with a writer or looks the word up in a dictionary or a gazetteer. The newscaster also watches for words he feels a writer chose in error.

The newscaster takes his script to a quiet corner and reads it aloud to himself, getting a feel of words, phrases, meaning and a rhythm pattern. He pencils slash marks at places he will pause for breath and he underlines words he will emphasize. Here and there he edits words and phrases, eliminating those he considers unnecessary to the meaning and changing others to permit a smoother reading.

After he has read the script and is satisfied with it, the newscaster either goes to the make-up department or puts some on himself. Make-up for a newscaster is usually limited to "pancake," to avoid appearing washed out under the hot studio lights, although sometimes features are highlighted or subdued, depending upon the skill with which the make-up is applied. As a rule, newscasters grin and bear this "show biz" aspect of presenting the news.

At 5 p.m., one hour before the 30-minute newscast begins, everyone connected with the air production of the program (as distinct from news assembly) gathers in the studio and the adjoining control room. More distant rooms, such as master control, quality control, projection and videotape are already staffed. The reels which the film editor has built of the individual stories, based on an order list from the news director, are taken to the projection room and mounted on sound projectors.

In the control room are the director, the assistant director and the technical director, who is seated before a panel of buttons and levers called a switcher. On the wall in front of the three men are a bank of television monitors showing what each studio camera sees, what each projector sends, what the videotape room sends, what the control room is sending out and what the television station is beaming.

In a room adjoining the control room (or "control booth") is the audio control booth, with a plate glass wall, enabling the audio engineer to see the director and the monitors while shutting out all unwanted sound. His room is equipped with turntables, tape recorders, audio switching controls and volume "pots."

In another room is a booth announcer. He introduces the newscast and the newscaster, gives station breaks, reads "promos" for the later programs, reads some commercial copy and introduces the next program. The only equipment in his soundproof room is a microphone and a television monitor, except for his headset, consisting of earphones and a tiny microphone, which can be shoved aside. Everyone in the control room has a similar headset, and so do the stage manager and each cameraman in the studio. The projectionist and the videotape engineer have either headsets or a two-way speaker system to complete the informational hookup under the control of the director.

In the studio proper are the television cameramen (not to be confused with the film cameramen who go into the field to record news stories), a "boom mike" man responsible for all the studio microphones, a prop man responsible for cards and furniture, the man who operates the Tele-Prompter, an electrician responsible for lighting, a stage manager who is both a sub-director and the man who cues the newscaster, and, of course, the newscaster plus others who will appear in the newscast, such as the sports reporter, a news reporter, a feature reporter, the weather-man or a guest.

REHEARSAL

The rehearsal brings together for the first time all the elements of the newscast. The headlines or the "tease" film or statement which may pre-cede the newscast give the audio engineer a chance to adjust his "pots" to get the sound levels he wants. He also balances the announcer's mike level during the "open." More importantly, for the first time, the written copy for each story is read against the edited film and videotape. The newscaster paces himself and may edit some more words so that copy matches film. If something on film escaped the watchful eyes of the film editor and the writer, a dozen other pairs of eyes will catch it at rehearsal. If the film editor has transposed two film stories in a hurried assembling of the projection reel, it will be caught here. Like theatrical rehearsals, a rehearsal of a newscast starts and stops, as the director orders changes. The TelePrompter man runs through his script roll.

While each segment is practiced, the assistant director times it with his stopwatch, and notes that time on his copy of the script. When the rehearsal is finished, he adds up the segment times, and informs the di-rector, producer and newscaster of the total. It may be necessary to cut some copy, or even to excise a film or tape story, which usually means rolling quickly through the film or tape during the program when the reel has reached the point where the particular story begins. Only if the script allows no time for a roll-through, will the film be physically cut. On the other hand, if the newscast runs short of its allotted time, the newscaster will "fill" with "pad" copy, either until the program ends, or a pre-set "backtime" segment is reached, enabling the newscaster to con-clude strongly, rather than sloppily with pad copy.

While the rehearsal continues, the technical director glances fre-quently at the clock. Everything stops when he reports, "Two minutes

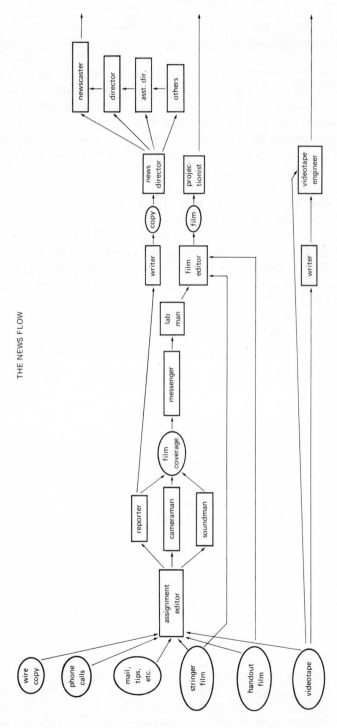

THE NEWS FLOW

HOME VIEWER

newscaster
director
asst. dir.
others

news director
projectionist

copy
film

writer
film editor

lab man

messenger

film coverage

reporter
cameraman
soundman

assignment editor

wire copy
phone calls
mail, tips, etc.
stringer film
handout film
videotape

videotape engineer

writer

to air." Now the projectionist and the videotape engineer rewind the reels back to the first cue positions. The television cameramen swing their heavy cameras into opening position, "get on" the suitable lenses and focus. The TelePrompter is rolled back to the newscaster's opening words. The director, the assistant director and the audio engineer stack the pages of their scripts, and leaf through them to make sure all pages are in numerical order. The newscaster does the same with his copy. He straightens himself in his chair, picks up a pencil or whatever other prop he uses, and assumes an expression of intelligent seriousness.

"One minute to air."

"Thirty seconds."

The stage manager gives a final flip to the trailing cord of his headset and calls out, "Fifteen seconds. Quiet on the set . . . . Ten . . . . Five . . . ."

With his eyes fixed on the sweep-second hand of the clock mounted on the wall in front of him, the director addresses, in turn, the technical director, or T.D., beside him and the stage manager listening by headset: "Four . . . three . . . two . . . one . . . Up on one (telling the T.D. to fade in from black to camera number one) . . . Cue him."

The stage manager, standing beside the camera designated as number one, jabs a forefinger toward the newscaster.

And the newscast begins.

chapter 4　# The Reporter in the Newspaper Organization

JULIAN HARRISS
and
STANLEY JOHNSON

Reporters are the most essential members of the newspaper organization. They are the ones who gather and refine the commodity which is the *raison d'être* of the newspaper—the news. All others who serve the publication are there for the purpose of making it possible for the reporter's stories to get into print, accurately and attractively presented, for distribution to waiting readers. All this is true, but reporters cannot afford to be arrogant about it because they would have no newspaper to carry their stories without the contributions of other members of the organization.

The editors and other staff members who supervise or collaborate with reporters do have an important function, for without them the newspaper would lack organized coverage of all events and would lose much of its reader appeal. Too, the price that a reader pays for his newspaper does not begin to cover the publication's cost, and the newspaper must have employees who can sell part of its space as advertising to make up the difference and to assure the reporters their periodic salary checks. Other employees are needed to sell thousands of copies of the newspaper and see that delivery is made to waiting readers. Moreover, those readers would have to wait a very long time to receive their newspapers if efficient mechanical workers were not available to convert typewritten material into printed pages. Thus, reporters fit into one of the three different functions involved in the process of publishing a newspaper—writing, printing, and selling. These are the duties of the editorial, mechanical, and business departments, respectively.

Editorial Department. News must be gathered from various sources as it occurs and must be written into readable, interesting form, then edited and displayed in the newspaper. This is the function of the newspaper's editorial department. Secondary functions of the newspaper are to instruct or influence the public through editorials and special articles, and to entertain by means of comics, fiction, and other features. All these materials are processed by the editorial department.

Mechanical Department. News must also be transferred from the typewritten sheet of the reporter into metal type (or slugs and, for large dailies, into stereotyped plates) in the composing room and thereafter be printed upon thousands of pages of newsprint in the pressroom. This is a complicated, technical, mechanical process. Hence, every newspaper has a mechanical department.

Business Department. To finance these two operations, advertising space must be sold, subscriptions must be obtained, and the news commodity must be delivered—hence the advertising and circulation divisions. A third division comprises problems of management and business administration. In the smaller newspaper, advertising, circulation, and management may be combined as one business department. In the larger newspapers they may be greatly expanded and sharply differentiated.

DETAILS OF ORGANIZATION

A typical organization of a newspaper in a city of 100,000 to 200,000 population is shown in the accompanying diagram. The numbers in parentheses following titles of staff members refer to numbers in the diagram.

The publisher (1) is usually the owner, or chief owner, of the newspaper. He may be more or less closely associated with its actual operation. If closely associated, he may be also general manager (2) or editor (19).

He has the power (if he chooses to exercise it) to dictate all policies, editorial or otherwise. Under the publisher, the general manager is supervisor and coordinator of all departments.

The business manager (3) is shown with authority over the advertising (4), circulation (6), and office manager (8). In many instances, however, he assumes merely the rank and position of office manager. In this event the advertising, circulation, and business managers report directly to the general manager or publisher.

In the mechanical process of printing a newspaper the metal type is set on typesetting machines (large headlines sometimes set by hand) in the composing room (11) and assembled in page *forms*. From these forms a *matrix* is made by impressing the forms against newspaper mats of special cardboard. From these matrices semicylindrical plates are cast in metal to be bolted upon the rotary presses. The process of making these plates is known as *stereotyping* (15) and is usually carried on in a special room shown between the composing room and pressroom (17) organizations in the chart.

The foregoing description of the mechanical process (11 through 16) applies to *letterpress printing*, which is commonly used by newspapers. In recent years another printing process, known as *offset printing*, has been developed and improved, and it is being used by an increasing number of newspapers. It replaces stereotyping by a negative and platemaking process, and it requires a different kind of press. Type for offset may be set by letterpress procedure or by machines which set words on film or tape.

From the editorial department the copy for the day's newspaper is sent [by all of the editors (21–29) indicated in the chart] to the composing room, to be set in type. A makeup editor (20) must plan where the various stories are to be placed in the newspaper. In other words, he makes up the newspaper. He determines where each story and picture will be placed on each page as the *galleys* of type are *locked up* in the page forms. On many newspapers the makeup editor is also the managing or news editor (20).

Most of the news that appears in the newspaper is provided by staff reporters (28) through the city editor (24), by national news agencies through the telegraph editor (23), and by correspondents (out-of-city reporters) through the state news editor (25). The women's editor (22) and sports editor (21) and their various assistants or reporters are allied with, and sometimes subordinate to, the city editor.

The editorials which appear in newspapers are written by the editor and editorial writers (26). Editors having administrative duties may write few editorials.

The *copy* (news manuscript) written by the staff reporters is carefully

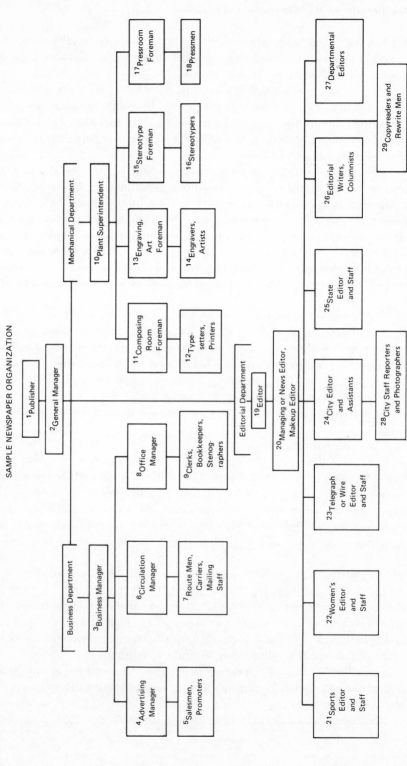

SAMPLE NEWSPAPER ORGANIZATION

¹Publisher

²General Manager

Business Department

³Business Manager

⁴Advertising Manager

⁵Salesmen, Promoters

⁶Circulation Manager

⁷Route Men, Carriers, Mailing Staff

⁸Office Manager

⁹Clerks, Bookkeepers, Stenographers

Mechanical Department

¹⁰Plant Superintendent

¹¹Composing Room Foreman

¹²Typesetters, Printers

¹³Engraving, Art Foreman

¹⁴Engravers, Artists

¹⁵Stereotype Foreman

¹⁶Stereotypers

¹⁷Pressroom Foreman

¹⁸Pressmen

Editorial Department

¹⁹Editor

²⁰Managing or News Editor, Makeup Editor

²¹Sports Editor and Staff

²²Women's Editor and Staff

²³Telegraph or Wire Editor and Staff

²⁴City Editor and Assistants

²⁵State Editor and Staff

²⁶Editorial Writers, Columnists

²⁷Departmental Editors

²⁸City Staff Reporters and Photographers

²⁹Copyreaders and Rewrite Men

corrected and improved by *copyreaders* (29). Stories received by telephone from reporters or others, and stories not already in proper form for publication, are prepared by *rewrite* men (usually staff reporters on office duty). On metropolitan newspapers most headlines are written by copyreaders. (On the average-sized daily most of the copyreading and headline writing is done by the city, telegraph, and state editors.)

Photographers (28) serve under the city editor and usually are allied with reporters on assignments. Pictures must be converted into engravings (or metal *cuts*) in order to be reproduced in print. Larger newspapers have their own photoengraving plants (13). Smaller newspapers send their pictures to commercial photoengravers. Both cuts and *mats* (the matrix reproduction of a cut) are received from various other sources—press bureaus, publicity organizations, and the like. For newspapers using the offset process of printing, metal engravings and mats are not needed.

Departmental editors (27) are in charge of special features and columns or full-page departments, such as radio and television, motion pictures, the special Sunday sections (Sunday editor) and business and finance. On the smaller newspapers these special departments are allotted to various staff reporters. The departmental editors are usually under the managing editor.

The staff organization described above (and the diagram) is by no means uniform for all newspapers. The method of operation and the titles of staff members will vary among newspapers, but the essential functions as revealed above must nevertheless be performed, and this is a typical organization which can do the job.

THE MORGUE

Not shown in the chart but accessible to all reporters and editors is the newspaper's "morgue"—its reference files. The purpose of the morgue is to supplement current news stories (and editorials) with previously gathered information and story aids. Pictures, cuts, and mats are of primary importance. "See if we have a picture" is the first suggestion of the city editor concerning many stories. The morgue should also contain the biographies of prominent persons, ready for instant use in obituaries and stories of achievements. Clippings of stories used in the past, economic and social data, historical sketches, and "background" in general for a great variety of stories will be found in the morgue. The city directory, *Who's Who*, unabridged dictionaries, encyclopedias, and various reference books will supplement these materials. Depending on the size of the newspaper, the morgue may vary from a few files to a large reference library.

NEWS CHANNELS

News enters the editorial department of the newspaper through several channels and from many sources:

1. From local sources through the newspaper's own staff of reporters, who gather the news from regular beats, background it with information from the morgue, and do most of their writing in the newspaper office under the city editor.

2. From national and foreign sources through the news agencies (services, bureaus, syndicates)—Associated Press (AP), United Press International (UPI), and others. In addition many commercial syndicates furnish much feature material. Most of this material is received by telegraph or teletype and is, except for copyreading and headlining, already properly written for publication. The telegraph or wire editor is in charge, but he gives credit (by use of name or initials) to the press service for every such story used. Usually initials of a press service are in the *dateline,* which is the line at the beginning of an out-of-city story giving both date and place of origin. A local story needs no dateline.

3. From state and regional sources through correspondents. Much of this material is properly written and ready for publication. If not, it must be rewritten or heavily edited. Such stories often have "Special to the (name of newspaper)" preceding or in the datelines. The state news editor is in charge.

4. From various individuals and organizations, such as chambers of commerce, lecturers, and promotion agencies, through the mail, telephone, and personal calls. Most of this material is rewritten by the city staff under the city editor.

Through whatever channel it may subsequently pass, all news must be gathered and written at its source by reporters, and most news is, at its source, local news. An exception is news at state capitals and at the national capital affecting distant communities. In gathering and writing news a reporter faces substantially similar problems whether he is a staff reporter, a press-service reporter, or a correspondent.

BEATS

A city editor would expect the following sources to yield perhaps 90 per cent of the local news and would instruct reporters to gather news from the various daily assignments, or *beats,* as indicated:

1. The city police station, county jail, fire department, and hospitals.
2. The city hall (headquarters for city legislative and executive officials).
3. The county courthouse (headquarters for county officials and state courts).
4. The state capitol or state offices (headquarters for state officials).
5. The federal building or offices (headquarters for the post office, federal law-enforcement and other offices and federal courts), and the Weather Bureau.
6. Schools, colleges, and associated organizations.
7. The chamber of commerce, business houses, industries, labor organizations.
8. Civic, fraternal, and professional organizations.
9. Churches and associated organizations.
10. Youth organizations and welfare agencies associated with the local Community Chest or United Fund, and also "health associations" (such as heart, tuberculosis, cancer) which are financed independently.
11. Motion-picture houses, radio and television stations, and organizations offering theatrical productions, athletic events, and other forms of entertainment.
12. Funeral homes.
13. Convention centers, hotels, airlines, railroads, and other firms engaged in accommodating meetings and visitors.
14. Varying local news sources, such as ships and shipping, mines and mining, oil, lumber.

It is apparent from this list of beats that the reporter has a regular and routine job. He does not stroll about the streets looking for stray news. Every day he is responsible for covering definite offices and organizations where most news emanates. Even news of murders, fires, and accidents is to be encountered at regular sources—the police and fire departments, and hospitals.

The fourteen beats listed will be altered and determined by physical locations and other conditions. If a chamber of commerce is situated near the police station, the police reporter perhaps will be required to cover the chamber of commerce also. If the city jail (police station) and the county jail are widely separated, a single reporter may not be able to cover both. Just how the beats are set up, and the number of reporters assigned to each, will be determined on a time-saving and step-saving basis adjusted to the number and ability of reporters on the payroll. In a city of 100,000 to 200,000 population, six to a dozen reporters may constitute the staff.

THE STORY PROCESS

To clarify and relate the various factors of the newspaper organization, the steps in the story process from news event to reader may be listed as follows:

1. Upon the occurrence of a newsworthy event the reporter compiles the facts by interview and investigation and makes rough notes for his story.

2. He writes the story, usually returning to the office for this purpose. In critical circumstances he may write the story on the spot and send it to the city editor by messenger. Or he may telephone the facts, in which case the story is written by a reporter on rewrite duty in the newspaper office.

3. The typewritten story is delivered to the city editor (and copyreaders) for copyreading and headlining. The copyreader corrects any mistakes and attempts to polish or improve the story if necessary.

4. The city editor or news editor (or both) makes a record of the story, sometimes indicating its preferred position (for example, "page 1 must" to specify placement on the first page), and sends it to the composing room.

5. The foreman of the composing room gives the copy to a typesetting machine operator to be converted into metal type. If it is a long story or a rush order, he cuts the copy into numbered *takes* and distributes them to several operators. Large headlines are set on a special machine or perhaps by hand. The takes of type are reassembled in galleys, and a galley proof (printed impression) is made. *Proofreaders* indicate typographical errors in the galley proof, and the necessary corrections are then made in type by resetting the lines and replacing them in the galley trays.

6. The galleys of type are assembled on a *stone* (table) under direction of the makeup editor and are locked up in page forms.

7. From these forms a matrix of each page is made, and from it the semicylindrical metal page is cast (in the stereotyping room). The metal type of original flat page forms is now melted down and returned to the typesetting machines.

8. The semicylindrical page forms are locked upon the rotary presses in the pressroom, and the newspaper is printed, cut, and folded in one mechanical operation.

9. The printed newspapers are delivered to the circulation department for mailing, for delivery by routes, and for street sales.

chapter 5 # Press Associations

EDWIN EMERY,
PHILLIP H. AULT,
and
WARREN K. AGEE

THE ROLE OF PRESS ASSOCIATIONS

The clatter of press association teleprinters, delivering stories hour after hour with almost relentless precision, stirs a sense of subdued excitement in the newsrooms of the country. This is the world in action. Even veteran newsmen who work with the teleprinters at hand year after year always wonder subconsciously what dateline will emerge next on the continuous rolls of paper. The automatic keys spell out dispatches from Washington, London, Saigon, the state capitals, and a thousand other cities.

Supplying the news dispatches that come from the teleprinters in such abundance are the Associated Press and United Press International, the two largest, most intricate and fiercely competitive news-gathering agencies in the world. Without the service of a press association, a daily newspaper or broadcasting station would find distribution of a well-balanced news report to its audience virtually impossible.

The press associations take over where the local and area news coverage of the city desk ends. Even the largest dailies and the broadcasting networks with extensive staffs of their own correspondents in Washington and abroad are heavily dependent upon the press associations for domestic and foreign dispatches.

Intense hour-to-hour rivalry between AP and UPI exists in their effort to deliver dispatches that are comprehensive, accurate, objective, and perceptive—and to get them there first. Both services emphasize a writing style sufficiently simple and interesting to be understood by a mass audience.

This competitive urge is one of the attractions of press association work, especially for younger reporters and editors; it adds a zest to newsgathering which has disappeared to some degree from the local news staffs in many cities where only one newspaper now exists. Commercially, this competition to be faster and better than your rival has great importance, because the AP and UPI are in constant battle to take away customers from each other. (The AP calls them members; the UPI refers to them as clients.)

Although the services they deliver to newspapers, television, and radio stations here and abroad are similar, the two press associations are organized quite differently. The Associated Press, which is much older, is a cooperative newsgathering association. Each American newspaper which purchases its service becomes a member of the cooperative and has a voice in setting the association's newsgathering and financial policies; also, it is obligated to turn over its local news coverage to the cooperative. Television and radio stations taking AP service become associate members without voting rights; the total now exceeds that of newspaper members. The Associated Press was founded in 1848 by six New York publishers, primarily to cooperate in the gathering of news from ships arriving in eastern harbors from Europe. It has been in continuous existence ever since, having gone through several major reorganizations including one in 1900 which established it in its present form.

United Press International is a privately owned company, dealing on a contract basis with newspapers, television and radio stations, and other organizations which have need for a news report. Its individual clients influence the shape of the UPI news report only through their suggestions and criticisms, solicited by the UPI management, or through their ultimate power to cancel the service. An Associated Press member can withdraw on two years' notice; the usual United Press International contract with a client runs five years. The United Press was founded in 1907 by E. W. Scripps, the owner of a large group of newspapers, with the purpose of supplying news to papers which could not obtain Associated Press membership under the then-existing rules. In 1958 the United Press absorbed the International News Service, which had operated as a relatively weak third American competitor in the field since William Randolph Hearst founded it in 1909. The combined service became known as United Press International.

The Associated Press and United Press International are now comparable in strength, the UPI having improved its position by the merger with INS.

The Associated Press reported that at the start of the 1970's it was serving approximately 8500 newspapers and television and radio stations around the world; the United Press International reported it had approximately 6000 clients for its news and picture services. The UPI was operating in 114 countries and territories, the AP in 104. Both press associations leased more than 400,000 miles of telephone wires in the United States for transmission of news and pictures, and both used globe-girdling radio teletype circuits and underwater cables to carry their news reports to and from Europe and Asia. For the United States alone, the two associations reported these figures: AP, service to 1750 publications and 3100 television and radio stations; UPI, 1600 publications and 2300 television and radio stations. Each had an annual budget above $50,000,000.

Regardless of whether it is called a member or a client, the net result for each daily newspaper is much the same. It receives the UPI or AP news report by teleprinter for a specified number of hours each day, for which it pays a fee based upon its circulation and the amount of news received. Prices range from roughly $100 to $400 a week for a paper of 25,000 circulation up to $6000 a week for the metropolitan dailies, depending on the special services purchased. Both news agencies offer supplemental sports and financial services.

Most small dailies, and even some very large ones, operate successfully with only one of the two major wire services. Of the 1750 American daily newspapers, approximately 45 percent subscribe only to AP, 30 percent only to UPI, and 25 percent to both services. More than 500 dailies purchase news from both to have a wider choice of news stories to publish. When both services provide stories on the same news events, as they do scores of times daily, the telegraph editor of the two-service newspaper selects the dispatch which arrives first, if an urgent news break is involved, or the one which seems to him more complete, concise, and interesting. Sometimes the two dispatches are combined to provide a more well-rounded and complete story.

The rival agencies keep close watch on selected lists of these two-service papers to determine the "play" their respective stories receive.

Bad "play" on a big story—or worse, being badly beaten by the rival agency on a news break—brings sharp backstage criticism from the New York home office down upon the head of the offending bureau involved.

HOW PRESS ASSOCIATIONS FUNCTION

The news reports of each press association are carried to newspapers by leased telegraph circuits from offices scattered across the United States. The stories arrive in the newspaper office on a continuous roll of paper in a teleprinter, a machine resembling an automatic typewriter whose keys are activated by impulses transmitted over the telegraphic circuit from a press association office. This paper is cut into segments by the telegraph editor, who selects from it the stories he will publish in his newspaper that day. Originally transmission was on Morse dot-and-dash circuits, but these were replaced long ago by automatic teleprinters. When a major news break develops, the first portion of it is marked "urgent" or "bulletin" and transmitted along the circuit on a priority basis.

Each press association divides its flow of news into P.M. and A.M. reports, or cycles, the former for afternoon newspapers and the latter for morning papers. These reports always begin with a "budget," or checklist, of the most important stories that are to be transmitted. The budget represents a summary of the basic stories then available, or known to be forthcoming during the next few hours, plus sports and feature highlights. Usually it contains 10 to 12 items. The news editor is thus enabled to plan his makeup to ensure space for stories that he most likely will want to run. Since the large majority of American newspapers are published in the afternoon, and most news occurs during daytime hours, the P.M. reports are generally handled with a greater sense of urgency.

Basic stories on major news situations are transmitted early in each cycle. If later developments occur on a story, a new "lead" is moved on the wire. This reports the latest news on the situation and ends with a transitional paragraph which blends into the earlier dispatch at a specified place. On big, fast-breaking stories a press association may carry half a dozen leads in a cycle; these are edited so compactly that the dispatch which ultimately appears in a client newspaper reads with smooth continuity, even though it may contain segments of several leads.

Such methods are necessary because press association clients are constantly going to press and must print what is available on a given situation at press time. To use a phrase popular with United Press International, somewhere there is a deadline every minute. This is a major difference between press association and ordinary newspaper writing: the press association correspondent must keep feeding latest developments in a "spot" story onto the news wires immediately, even when their meaning and ramifications are not fully disclosed; the newspaper staff correspondent (called a "special" by wire service men) usually has more time before his deadline to digest and consolidate his information. Press association men always work under time pressure. When we consider this, the amount of background and interpretation an experienced press association man can weave into a fast-breaking story is remarkable.

The press associations have main trunk teletype circuits running across the country, serving the major metropolitan newspapers. From these main trunks, regional and state circuits strike off at relay bureaus to serve the smaller papers in different areas of the country. The editors who control the flow of news onto these secondary wires, known as "wire filers," must see that the newspapers on each receive a balanced menu of regional news along with the most important national and foreign dispatches. Thus an Associated Press member in Arizona will receive some stories of interest only to readers in the Southwest which will not be delivered to another member in Florida. These members will receive identical dispatches on the day's major news from Washington and London, however. Proper channeling of the daily news report, so that each newspaper gets the largest possible number of stories pertinent to its needs, is a basic problem for press association editors. Many stories are shortened when relayed on secondary circuits, because smaller newspapers do not have the space to publish them in full. Dispatches from the press associations bureaus abroad are sent to the New York home offices for processing and filing on the domestic circuits.

As an example of the press association wire operation, a story originating in a small bureau may be distributed around the world, if various wire service editors along the way consider it sufficiently interesting; or it may never go farther than the circuit serving the newspapers in a nearby region. The bureau of origin transmits it on the state or regional wire. The editors at the control point for this circuit may consider the item to have national appeal and offer it to the editors in New York for nationwide transmission. When it reaches the New York general office, an editor may put it on circuits serving newspapers overseas. Every wire service story undergoes this selective screening process, by which the editors tailor the news report on each circuit to fit the needs and interests of its client newspapers.

Creation of teletypesetter circuits has been a major recent development in press association news transmission. On these circuits the news is delivered to client newspapers on a teleprinter roll, typed in capital and lower case letters with the lines justified to fit a newspaper column width for quick typesetting. Simultaneously, each newspaper receives the stories in perforated tape ready for use in automatic typesetting machines. Use of computers to justify the lines and insert hyphenation speeds up transmission. Under the original Morse code dot-and-dash system, about 35 words a minute could be transmitted. This was increased to 60 words on the all-capital letter teleprinters. Today computers and fast transmission circuits enable movement of special material such as stock market lists and baseball box scores at more than 1000 words a minute. The Associated Press and the Los Angeles *Times* in experiments have transmitted market reports at ultrahigh speeds of 50,000 words a minute, from one computer to another. After being stored in the receiving computer, the words come out on tape, to be run through ordinary typesetting machines. Further developments in uses of fast transmission will be forthcoming during the 1970's.

SPECIAL WRITING TECHNIQUES

It is evident that a news story which goes through all these vicissitudes of editing en route from reporter to client editor's desk requires special writing techniques. It may be published 500 words long in one newspaper and only 100 words in another. Thus the writer must keep his fundamental information near the top of the story so the dispatch can be trimmed easily without having any key facts omitted. A remarkable new computer system has been developed by the American Newspaper Publishers Association to do some of this story trimming automatically. If a wire service dispatch is 300 newspaper lines long, for example, the computer can shorten the story to almost any length the editor desires.

A press association reporter must write concisely, in simple sentences. Because his dispatches will be printed in newspapers of differing political persuasions and social viewpoints, he must be carefully objective in handling stories, even the complicated, controversial ones which require background and interpretation. The primary goal of press association writing is clear and swift communication of ideas and events, and the staff man's stock in trade is straight news, well written. More distinctive forms of self-expression find their way onto the wires, but those who wish to specialize in this type of writing usually choose other outlets.

Television and radio's instant news coverage of events in progress has had heavy impact on the press associations. Like newspapers, broadcast news staffs have changed their traditional operating methods, putting more stress on interpretative and analytical material.

Roger Tatarian, editor of United Press International, has described the trend that took place in his organization during the 1960's. Much of what he states also applies to the Associated Press:

> The UPI 10 or 15 years ago was basically happening-oriented. Its product was overwhelmingly based on action—action just over, action under way, or action imminent. This, in a word, is spot news. Spot news remains fundamental, of course, but the organization today is far more situation-oriented than it used to be. The restructuring of the report has been done in recognition that while newspapers can't usually be the first to disclose a major event to the public, it is in newspapers that these subjects can best be explored and reprised in a more meaningful way.
> We are keenly aware that newspapers cannot compete with television or radio in giving readers an up-to-date account of a continuing thing like a space flight; or that a morning newspaper today can hardly report that Army beat Navy 20–7 yesterday when half the nation watched it on TV yesterday and the others who cared undoubtedly knew who won from radio. Our objective now is to write stories that are equally useful to those who know the central fact, and those who do not.

While the press associations permit their established writers more freedom in interpreting news situations now than in the past, they are on guard against political or social slanting of dispatches. The more complicated the world becomes, the more difficult it is for press associations to find a proper balance between quick-breaking facts and interpretation that gives them perspective without distortion. This calls for highly skilled reporting and editing.

OTHER PRESS ASSOCIATION ACTIVITIES

Both the United Press International and Associated Press were founded to provide news for American newspapers. That remains their primary function, but they have branched out into several additional services. Each now delivers its news to newspapers and broadcasting stations in many foreign countries. A constant flow of overseas news comes to this country while news originating here is being dispatched throughout the world. Much of this global two-way news flow is accomplished by radio transmission, but because it is sometimes subject to interruption, both agencies also operate leased cable circuits under the Atlantic to London.

From New York radio teletype circuits operating around the clock transmit news both east and west for both the AP and UPI. In either operation, a transmitter on Long Island beams the signal by radio to Tangiers, where a relay station boosts the signal and beams it to Europe, the Middle East, South Asia, and South Africa. In London, the incoming beam is fed into teletype circuits covering more than 20,000 miles in Europe. In each country, the news is translated into that country's language and then put onto a separate national teletype network (translation into Spanish for Latin-American countries is largely done in the New York offices). The file to Asia is beamed by radio from San Francisco to booster relay stations at Manila and other points. Thus an important bulletin news story can flash by teletype within a minute or two on a Rome-London-New York-San Francisco-Tokyo transmission network. Pictures likewise are transmitted throughout the world by radio facilities.

The foreign bureaus of the American press associations usually are headed by an American, but they also employ local nationals in substantial numbers as reporters, editors, and translators. The number of foreign correspondent jobs available to Americans on the press associations is thus smaller than many people may believe.

In normal times approximately 500 U.S. citizens serve overseas as correspondents of U.S. media, the majority of them for the press associations. It is apparent that the commonly held desire of young newsmen to become foreign correspondents is not easily fulfilled. The overseas contingent was much enlarged during the war in Vietnam; however, many persons who received press credentials to Saigon were accused by the permanent press corps of being more curiosity seekers than hard-core reporters.

At many points around the world the American organizations are in sharp competition, in both newsgathering and sales, with such foreign news agencies as Reuters of Great Britain and Agence France-Presse. The impact of these foreign agencies upon the American press is negligible, however, since only a very few metropolitan papers purchase any of their material.

The American press associations have become important transmission belts for presenting a picture of life in America to foreigners. The hunger in many countries for news about the United States has been growing in proportion to this country's increasingly dominant role in world affairs. The Associated Press and United Press International carry a heavy responsibility in their selection and writing of news for the overseas audience, so that a well-balanced picture is presented. This does not imply censorship, the hiding of unpleasant news, or peddling of propaganda, but a judicious budget of stories to provide a multifaceted view of American life. For a great many citizens of foreign countries, press association dispatches provide the chief source of information about life, political policies, and attitudes in the United States.

The only foreign press association with important news outlets in the United States is Reuters, the British agency. The Reuters news report, which is edited principally in London, is purchased by some metropolitan

American newspapers and TV-radio network news departments as a supplementary service.

Special news service for television and radio stations is a major part of the agencies' operations. This is transmitted on different teletype circuits from the newspaper service and is rewritten from the stories in the basic report to please the ear rather than the eye. The style is more conversational, with simpler sentence structure and less detail. Distribution of this specially processed radio report was inaugurated by the United Press in 1935. The Associated Press followed reluctantly five years later.

Another important service provided to newspapers by the press associations is news picture coverage. Both AP and UPI operate coast-to-coast circuits for transmission of news photographs, a growing number of them in color. The larger newspapers are connected with these circuits and receive photographs, about 80 or 90 a day, instantaneously as they are transmitted. Smaller newspapers receive selected airmailed pictures of glossy prints or mats processed from the wire photo circuit by regional control points. The news agencies supply pictures to foreign clients by radio-photo, leased circuits, and mail.

Some newspapers purchasing the nationwide direct service receive the news photos in their offices over facsimile machines, which translate the electrical impulses of the transmission circuit into black-and-white photographs by means of a scanning device; these pictures are ready for immediate engraving and printing. Other newspapers obtain glossy black-and-white photographs from negatives activated by the transmission circuit on equipment in their own plants. Both UPI and AP have staffs of photographers, who are assigned to stories much as are reporters. In addition, the Associated Press distributes many pictures taken by photographers on the staffs of member papers. UPI also supplements its staff picture coverage with photos from newspaper sources.

United Press International operates a daily motion picture newsfilm service for use on television news programs, an audio news service for radio station voice pickups on news events, and an Ocean Press radio news report to passenger liners at sea. Among its supplementary offerings the AP includes a color slide service for television stations, a mailed tape service, and a book division which produces a news annual and other special volumes.

On still another front, the Associated Press and United Press International, the latter through its subsidiary United Feature Syndicate, provide comic strips, women's features, political columns, and a host of other syndicated material for newspaper publication.

Thus the two organizations have journeyed far afield from their original purpose of providing dispatches for newspapers. However, the daily newspaper report continues to be the core of each agency's operations.

The UPI and AP now serve not one but three of our mass communications media—newspapers, television, and radio, plus special services to magazines.

CRITICAL VIEWS OF AGENCIES

Students of the American press sometimes are critical of the heavy dependence of newspapers and broadcasting stations upon the press associations; this criticism is aimed more at the role of the wire services than at their daily performance. There is an undercurrent of uneasiness among these critics because more than 1700 daily newspapers look to these two organizations for the great bulk of their nonlocal news. Anyone who listens to a succession of radio newscasts and hears the identical words from the radio news wires spoken to him repeatedly on different wave lengths realizes the dependence of radio stations in particular upon the press associations. In fact, an overwhelming percentage of the American people are largely dependent upon the two organizations, through their various newspaper and TV-radio ramifications, as well as their use by the weekly news magazines, for knowledge of what is happening in the world. In the eyes of the critics this constitutes a danger involving conformity of reporting and thought, and some question the qualifications of wire service newsmen to select the news which is transmitted.

The argument is more philosophic than practical. The economics of newspaper publishing makes it impossible for even the largest, richest newspapers to have staff reporters stationed around the world in sufficient numbers to give them exclusive reports, for the costs would be prohibitive. Therefore some form of cooperative newsgathering is necessary. And the men and women who select the news to be transmitted are as competent in performing this task as may be found; their judgment is constantly under question by veteran wire service officials and by the thousands of editors they are serving.

National concern with conduct of the Vietnam war during the late 1960's caused close scrutiny of press association coverage from Saigon. Considering the difficulties involved, most informed critics gave the press associations good marks for their reporting from the war zone, particularly their efforts to reach beyond the official version of events.

So long as the United Press International and Associated Press remain free of governmental control or subsidy, operate in a highly competitive manner, and hold to their principles of objective news coverage, the perils of undue conformity are relatively small. The efficiency and far-reaching news lines of the press associations contribute greatly to the mammoth amount of information about the world available to readers and listeners throughout the United States.

The editors of client and member newspapers, and wire service executives themselves, subject the press association news report to a constant scrutiny for accuracy and completeness. When instances of insufficient or inaccurate coverage come to light, steps are taken quickly to remedy the wordiness. The competitive factor is a very wholesome one. The Associated Press Managing Editors Association has committees of newsmen making year-round studies of AP operations.

The press associations are scolded at times by critics because they must depend upon the reporting services of part-time local "string" correspondents in some parts of the world. When a major story breaks in a normally quiet and remote area, they must use the sometimes inadequate services of these men until an American-trained correspondent can reach the scene. Press association executives answer by pointing out that it is economically impossible for them to keep highly qualified men in every country. Improved air service makes movement of expert reporters to distant scenes of action much faster now than in the past.

Another criticism of the press associations is shared by the newspapers themselves—an alleged preoccupation with "crisis" reporting. That means trying to find conflict and excitement in every situation, to the point of distorting the news. In particular this charge has been made concerning the handling of political and legislative news. It is stated that too much emphasis is placed upon the routine partisan postures of the two major parties. This allegation results from the striving of each association to find sharp "angles" that induce telegraph editors to print its stories instead of its competitor's. Recently, however, both wire services have been broadening their coverage by offering more thoughtful, interpretative articles in such fields as religion, race, education, labor, and social problems. They are much less open to charges of "crisis" overemphasis than they were a decade ago. The news services are also criticized for not carrying enough foreign news, to which criticism they reply that their newspapers will print only a limited amount of such news, and there is no use in taking wire transmission time to give them what they won't use.

Actually, the conformity in presentation of national and foreign news by newspapers is less than might be expected. Checks of representative groups of newspapers receiving the same wire service show a surprisingly wide variation in the stories chosen from the telegraphed news report by editors for publication in their newspapers. Stories selected for prominent front page play by some editors may be dismissed by others with brief mention on inside pages, or omitted entirely. This is not surprising when we realize that the press association wire delivers far more dispatches than most newspapers can use, and the pressures of local news vary from city to city. So do the news judgments of the individual editors.

Another way editors have found to broaden their national and foreign news coverage is purchase of a supplementary news service, such as those offered by the New York *Times* and the Los Angeles *Times*-Washington *Post* Service. These services supply to their clients by wire a daily news report that includes dispatches on major Washington and foreign events, plus background dispatches under many datelines. They leave the hourly spot coverage to the press associations, but seek to round out the picture with news material that is exclusive in each client's territory. Because of the cost, supplementary services are used primarily by the larger newspapers.

section B # Limitations in Mass News

Before turning to specific areas of controversy in the sections that follow, it is useful to gain an understanding of news constraints to examine some of the so-called inherent limitations on the media news operations—inherent because by and large they grow out of the nature of the medium more than the effort to gather and report news. These problem areas will be discussed under four categories: newsgathering (actually getting the story); news reporting (presentation of the story); the story itself (content of story); and news reception (effects of the news on the home audience).

chapter 6 # Some Basic Limitations in Mass News

CHRISTOPHER H. STERLING

NEWSGATHERING

There are five key problem areas in newsgathering alone—lack of investigative reporting, reliance on others (nonmedia news people) for news, lack of access to some stories, media intrusion into news events, and cost factors in newsgathering.

Lack of Investigative Reporting

A particular element of reporting often drawing major criticism is the lack of solid investigative (as opposed to routine) newsgathering by both print and broadcast media. Below are some of the major issues involved.

Source of Complaints	Accused
Reporters, academics, some citizen groups, occasional public officials, some editors, and (most recently) the new regional press reviews.	Editors and publishers of print media; owners and news directors of broadcast stations.

Charges	Replies
Media are ritualistic in always reporting the same kinds of stories (events rather than situations, especially crises with little or no background presented).	Function of media is to report rather than make news. Reporters lack training and time (and it's too expensive).
Media rarely get out and explore important social issues (slums, pollution, race problems, etc.) until after others (public groups, crusaders, etc.) have opened issue up, ignoring media's ethical obligation.	Once issue is discovered, media do best job they can with it. Need to maintain balance and cover all news and feature areas rather than concentrate on just one.
The system (politically sacred, intellectually lazy, and functionally stingy), editors, and paternalistic seniority-ridden bureaucracies hinder creative reporting approaches.	Those most often "hit" by such reporting are major advertisers.

Possible Actions	Probable Reaction
Set up press councils or at least resident internal critics.	Ignore (or fire) them.
Set up local press review to air issue with professional and academic articles. (By public officials): Harass press with hearings, lack of cooperation and/or legislation.	Ignore (because of very small audience). Cite First Amendment freedoms as being under attack and focus lobbies against legislation and politicians.

Likely Results	
Recurring crisis for newsmen but lack of a sustained campaign.	Possibly make minor changes, but in essence keep reporting news as always and forget issue.

In no case, of course, are the problems as cut and dried as this—many reporters are apathetic about them; many publishers try to do something about them. Really good investigative reporting, however, is almost totally absent in television and radio, and few newspapers do a good job of it.

The lack of investigative reporting is a major cause of the second problem in newsgathering—the excessive reliance on outsiders for information. This is especially true of broadcast news operations which seldom have sufficient staff to properly cover news in their area. Probably 90 percent of national and international news comes to local news media from networks (for broadcasting) or wire services (for both broadcasting and print). Only the largest papers have their own reporters in major national cities, foreign capitals, or other news spots. Some papers, newsmagazines, and broadcast stations and networks maintain part-time reporters ("stringers") in likely news spots. The reliance on networks and wire services makes most local media sound the same—and makes the editorial decisions of national gatekeepers even more influential.

Another outside source of news is the public relations (PR) man hired by industry or government to get positive media coverage of his client's doings and events. This leads to the all too common "pseudo-event"—the meeting, demonstration, or political speech, which is planned primarily for the media coverage it will get. Such events are usually planned (often by PR men) to be most convenient for media coverage and this convenience factor in most cases means the story will get in the press or on the air simply because it was there and easy to cover. The more complex an issue or event, the more likely the media will make use of the public relations release at hand.

There is serious danger that news media will become too dependent on the wire or network services or the PR man's releases because of their convenience. For most of the period of American involvement in Vietnam, for example, military information officers (PR men) presented a daily five o'clock Saigon briefing which purported to tell all newsworthy events plus background so that reporters could theoretically stay in the relative safety of the capital and have the whole story to report back home. Those reporters who did get out in the field found much news that was not in those briefings and the briefings soon became known as the "Five O'Clock Follies," attended but not taken too seriously alone. Having overcome that trap of convenience, however, reporters fell into another one—only by complete dependence on the military transportation system could reporters get into the field to see individual soldiers and actions, thereby running the risk of seeing only those things that the military wanted seen. Reporters lost the important ability to choose what stories they would cover—and became, said many, mere pawns in a military game. Thus, one of the most serious limitations involved in Vietnam reporting was the reliance which must be placed on the group being reported.

The problem is the same stateside. When a reporter (usually for a network or wire service) is given a specialty "beat," he loses his critical judgment over time and begins to identify with the institution and people he works with daily, thus becoming in many cases, more proponent than critical analyst. The problem here is one of human nature combined with pressures of media reporting.

Lack of Access

Closely related to the problem of excessive reliance on news sources is the problem of limited access to some types of stories. The key issue here is the "free press–fair trial" debate now over three decades old. It is based on conflicting views of the First (freedom of speech) and Sixth (right to a fair trial) Amendments to the constitution. More specifically, it is based on disagreement over the American Bar Association's Canon 35, first promulgated in 1937 (and amended in the 1950s to include television) which states, in essence, that it is against courtroom decorum and ethics to allow picture taking, films, or televised records to be made of proceedings (the limitation extends to audio recordings except for official court use). The understandable concern of lawyers is for the rights of defendants and witnesses—the related and conflicting concern of newsmen is for the right of access to a public story. In fact, reporters are allowed to take notes (and artists to sketch the pictures we see on network news), but they can't use the modern tools of their trade to get a "realistic" view of what's happening. Constant tests of the Canon 35 rule in the 1960s were to no avail. Related to this courtroom coverage problem is the restriction often placed on coverage of pretrial events (evidence, arrests, implication, and speculation by the media, etc.) which has in the past been cause for overturned judgments and is now often subject to court-ordered restraint—another access problem growing out of the conflict of the people's right to know versus the individual's rights to a fair hearing, unbiased by journalistic speculation.

There are other types of access limitation on all levels of government. Most executive agencies of the federal government limit newsmen's access to possible stories. Legislative hearings or sessions on the federal and state level are often held in executive (closed) session barring the public and its reporter representatives, and the judicial branch on all levels has the limits already noted. Agencies and public officials often hold news briefings that seem to limit rather than to increase the flow of information. Some sessions are "off the record" (information for the reporter's background only with nothing to be reported publicly); others are termed "backgrounders" (the basic information can be reported but can't be attributed to any official source, thus taking away much of its validity); and still others limit the reporter to references to unnamed spokesmen. The limitations on these various briefings are upheld in the face of no cooperation from public officials and agencies if the restrictions are broken.

Unfortunately, such limited access leaves the press (and the dependent public) open for two government actions—the official lie and the unofficial leak. Countless examples exist of the federal government at least bending facts if not actually lying (the 1960 U-2 crisis; the 1961 Bay of Pigs invasion in which U.S. participation was vigorously denied at first; or the 1964 Gulf of Tonkin incident) to achieve a policy end. The news media, lacking access to all the facts, unwittingly carry the story to the people as truth. When, on the rare occasion that a reporter does have the full story (the *New York Times* was aware of most details of the Bay of Pigs invasion weeks before it came off), the government will pressure the reporter and his organization to stifle the story for a time "in the national interest."

The unofficial leak is a way government uses media to its own ends. One agency or public official may be fighting another and news information will be leaked early to a reporter representing a "friendly" paper or news service in an attempt to embarrass the other side. The competitive pressures of news will force the media to leap at every tidbit of information they get, thus often playing into the hands of political infighters.

Media Intrusion

Limited access in some areas may partially explain the third news-gathering drawback—media intrusion on many of the stories it can cover. The most commonly evident problem here is saturation or "herd" journalism where all media send every available man to cover the same story, leading to the common problem of seventeen microphones in a subject's face and ten questions shouted at the same time. Political conventions, weddings of presidents' daughters, and space shots seem to have suffered most in this regard lately. Media can almost take over events and heavily intrude into the incidents they are trying to report simply because of sheer numbers of reporters. Countless minor rumors (and candidates) at political conventions have had their moment of glory with the walkie-talkie carrying floor reporters passing on every bit— minor and important—to the waiting audience.

Broadcast reporters have two special problems of intrusion. First, and most important, is the intrusion brought about by the mere presence of lights, cameras, recording equipment, trucks, cars, and personnel. There is no way to get a sound TV picture story without being obvious about it. Many examples are on record of well-meaning TV crews arriving on the scene of one of the many race riots of the late 1960s only to have events get totally out of hand once the cameras were rolling. Demonstrators in ghettos and on campuses alike know that action is likely to get on the air—and action is what the TV crews get. This leads to distorted reporting (not to mention injuries and high police costs). At the end of the decade some stations experimented with small one-man camera units not requiring bright lights and traveling in unmarked cars. This helped a good deal but if the camera was spotted, people invariably played up to it.

The second broadcast-related intrusion problem is also based on equipment. Because it is cumbersome to get TV equipment on the scene (as one newsman put it recently, "In New York the problem is vertical— getting up to the right floor on time, whereas in Los Angeles it's horizontal—not running out of gas before you get there"), TV news crews are not always in the right place at the right time. This has led in several documented cases to "recreated" or "staged" news events where the same participants reenacted whatever was newsworthy (the incidents ranged from announcements to near-riots) so the cameras could record it. The danger in this practice (aside from the obvious ethical issue) is the thin line between filming what did happen and what *might have* or *should have* happened. Creation of fiction rather than reporting of news is the obvious problem here. A minor incident may lead to a major misconception by the audience. For example, one network TV crew, during the 1968 Democratic Convention, found a "Welcome to Chicago" sign, set it afire, and filmed it—leading to the conclusion by those who saw it that all Chicago was hostile, and some of it was burning.

Cost Factors

The fifth and last area of concern in newsgathering is the problem of economics—the cost of equipment and personnel. Again, the major "loser" here is television with all the expensive equipment (and technicians) required for adequate on-the-spot coverage. The press reporter can take a pad and pencil and he's set. All media are subject to varying degrees of labor regulations which can add to costs of events covered at odd hours or over long periods of time. Needless to say, these factors of cost have an effect on what is covered, for how long, and when.

NEWS REPORTING

There are four major problem areas here: time (for broadcast news), space (for print media), costs, and the newsman "star system" for all media.

Time Limitations

News is aired at a given time (or times) during the day, and regardless of the flow of news events in the real world, the newscast must appear as a finished "snapshot view" of important events at the moment of broadcast. A visualized television story will take longer to prepare for airing (and the news will thus be older), whereas a straight read story can be added during the newscast itself. In any event, the single thing lacking in broadcast news is time—there is never enough time to gather the story and there is too little in which to report it.

Television is fascinating; it *happens* to each of us almost daily. TV's portrayal of news, however, is necessarily colored by the medium's limitations, and TV is ephemeral yet rigid. Because of a fixed schedule of programs, news has to be reprepared for each newscast; once the show is over, the news is "old" and is either rewritten to get a new angle or incorporate new knowledge, or is forgotten.

Space Limitations

The related problem for print media is the limitation on space. With commitments of the sales staff for ads, and set amounts of space to be devoted to comics, departments, sports, and editorials, the news-staff has a limited "hole" for hard current news. On top of that limitation is a special factor of time for print media—the long lead time needed to get a story reported, set in type, printed, run off, bundled and transported to delivery or sales point, and into the readers hands. (Here we talk a matter of hours—while in broadcasting the measure is in minutes.) Before broadcasting, newspapers issued "extras" to cover late-breaking news; now they are no longer in the race to be first (broadcasting won that race years ago), but rather to be first with the depth report.

Cost Factors

The problem of cost arises again in news reporting. For print media, we are talking about the entire physical plant required to turn a witnessed news event into a printed story—presses, ink, paper, trained personnel, etc. In broadcasting, the studio, cameras (and/or microphones), control room, transmitter, and requisite personnel are all needed and expensive. These expenses in both cases become limitations on news by (1) limiting editorial budgets, and (2) increasing the pressure to sell news in a commercially competitive fashion.

The Newsmen

Finally, under newsreporting, we are faced with either the writer of the story or the station or network anchorman. This is the voice of the entire news organization, and through him all the news must pass. Because of the visual and talking situation, this man is far more important in broadcast news than in printed news where several people write the stories and usually aren't seen. What has been created in recent years is nothing short of a "star" who in broadcasting is more important than news itself. Network and local stations sell sponsors not on the news (after all, who knows it in advance?), and seldom on the strength of the news organization (a common practice in print media is to stress the team effort), but on the "pull" of the man. Looks, personality, and voice can (and have) come before news background in choosing and maintaining newsmen. Rather than letting the local researcher-reporter do an important story from abroad, one of the network's stars will fly overseas, get the story, record it for the cameras on location, and fly back with it—often in the space of days. The man lends credibility to the news and is paid highly for his credibility. Reporters, in the real sense of the word, are not often stars, and thus get paid a good deal less. The star system works commercially (even in print media, a major name will draw readers). Its effect on news is not fully known but is not likely to be positive.

THE NEWS ITSELF

The failings in actual news content are the most talked about. For ease of discussion they can be broken into two broad categories (which overlap somewhat)—the broad appeal of reports and the shallowness of them.

The broad appeal of American news media is based directly on the need to get the largest audience possible at all times. As noted above, this appeal has direct effect on news content in all media. News tends to be general rather than specific, that is, it offers a little bit about a lot of things over time. There is a lack of controversy in news in the sense that strong points of view are seldom taken on issues more complicated than shade trees, mended streets, or anti-litter campaigns. Too strong an editorial or too much news in one area tend to turn off segments of the mass audience needed by the media to sell advertisers and thus survive. There is a stress on the status quo and the establishment way of doing things; deviance from the accepted norm is reported as such—deviance as opposed to what may really be broad-based dissent. Finally, and most evident in all media, is the penchant for sensation, emotion, pictures, and action—a show-biz type of news reporting. TV news stresses fast brief reports ("Action" or "Eyewitness" news) and makes heavy use of visualized news—if you can't visualize it, the chances of getting it on the air are slimmer.

The problem of news visualization in television has been dealt with extensively in research and popular articles in the past. The gist of the problem is that pictures, especially those with movement and action, are the best ways of attracting and holding an audience. The old saw about a picture being worth a thousand words is all too true in television news selection. A story with still pictures has a better chance of airing than a story with no pictures at all, and film or video-tape has the best chance of air coverage. The most blatant examples of the film coverage problem were in the ghetto and campus disturbances of the late 1960s when night after night, viewers would see film clips of violent confrontation. Unfortunately there was little else presented—most ghetto or campus residents were not even taking part, and but for the small area of the demonstration, all was normal. TV is limited by the camera and the relatively small size of the home screen to show just so much of an event. In some ways television puts blinders on our eyes as we see only what the TV camera (and the man aiming it) select for us to see. It is often exciting film footage, and therein lies the problem of news distortion due to concentration on only the visual rather than on (in many cases) that which is important but perhaps not visual.

Similarly, newspapers are often more concerned about layout and pictures rather than solid news. This broad appeal emphasis is also demonstrated in heavy newspaper use of syndicated columns and cartoons, large amounts of space devoted to sports and society news, and heavy reliance on wire services for all but local news.

The second serious news content limitation is its lack of depth—mass news is shallow. Both print and broadcast media tend to report *events* rather than the more important and harder to discern *trends* which lead to the events. There is too little background and follow up in media (almost none at all in television with the exception of a few documentary presentations). Whole news areas are not covered or badly covered these days—the role of computers on society, trends in the arts, developments in law, breakthroughs and slower evolutionary discoveries in science. All these are ignored except for major isolated events. The sciences and related fields are harder to research and report as they require expertise; lacking that, most media ignore the topics entirely, thus doing a disservice to a society ever more dependent on technology. Many in the media feel that the audience not only isn't interested in such stories, but that most audience members aren't equipped to understand and deal with the issues presented.

This narrow, picture-stressing lack of depth leads to a negativistic emphasis in most mass news reports. With little background, news consists of a series of crises knitted together daily in newscast or newspaper. The items of importance nearly always detract from the peace and progress of the status quo (war, inflation, train and plane wrecks, crime in the streets, taxes going up, labor unrest, etc.) as witnessed by the "silent majority" establishment. News is a series of snapshots of crises rather than a film of trends showing both good and bad. As noted earlier, news is essentially what the newsman says it is—and most often he deems the negative aspects of life the most important and far reaching.

NEWS RECEPTION

The key factor in news reception is the context (or situation) in which media news reports are received. Most news reports are received in one's home directly from the media (though in rural areas or during working hours one's first knowledge of something important may be from another person. How, for example, did you first hear about the assassination of President Kennedy?). The intimacy factor comes into play here since when we are at home, most defensive barriers are down and we are relaxed.

Television gains its real impact from a combination of this intimacy in the home setting, and the delivery of the news by a visible, talking human—someone we can readily relate to, especially after a long period of watching. We naturally tend to accept the version of the news given to us in this person-to-person situation more than in the impersonal form of print media (which, in addition, is still somewhat limited in this country for those who can't read well or easily enough to get anything out of a newspaper). The problem comes when the televised newsman makes an error of fact or interpretation—his original statement is likely to have been readily accepted while the correction or restatement sets up a dichotomy many viewers try to avoid.

Like all mass communication, news communication is essentially a one-way process. There is little or no feedback as to how the audience accepted a story or commentary. Newspapers have letters-to-the-editor columns but they reflect only a small proportion of readers who are sufficiently moved to write letters. In press, however, at least other readers can find out what other audience members are thinking, thanks to letters-to-the-editor columns. In television, the feedback is even more limited and has no place in the medium to be expressed. This lack of ability to participate in the news reporting process leads in many cases to apathy on the part of viewers and readers.

CONCLUSION

Most of this discussion was related to newsgathering because it is in the initial steps of getting the story that the limitations of media are first apparent. The reporting, message, and reception categories merely magnify the basic limitations evident from the start.

None of these problems is impossible to solve. None of the specific controversies in part 3 is impossible to solve either. To overcome the limitations, however, will take an understanding of the system and its basis of commercial support, for in that support and its demands lies much of the cause of the trouble. Accepting that support system (as we do), change will have to be evolutionary and perhaps even limited. Awareness of the problems, however, is the first step.

part three **CONTROVERSIES IN MASS NEWS**

Introduction

Like politics, religion, and women's place in society, news is a continuing source of argument and discussion. It is easy to be swamped with a multitude of isolated issues and arguments, thus losing sight of the more important issues. It is impossible to give sufficient coverage here to every news issue (indeed, many presented here are worthy of a text), but it may be possible to suggest a mode of perception which will allow us to organize and isolate salient features which may deserve further thought and investigation. This necessitates breaking down certain arguments about mass news, and for this reason, we have developed a notion called the pattern of controversy.

CONTROVERSY

The grand issues facing the republic tend to remain the same throughout our history. Freedom of speech and the press, like our other constitutional rights, are global concepts which must be grounded in specific issues. But is every specific confrontation about the news media a classic freedom of the press issue? Advocates for the various positions often couch their arguments in such a way that to deny their validity is to threaten the very foundations of the republic. In fact, the argument is a part of a persuasive strategy of a network official or politician to effect or deter a change in the news media. Controversies about the news media are invariably emotional encounters with charge and countercharge obscuring the logic of the confrontation.

We have applied the notion of controversy to news rather than applying the conventional sociological term of a social problem. For the most part, this choice of terminology reflects more the reality of today's concern with the press as an institution.[1] For now, let us say that a controversy is a protracted *public* disagreement concerning a specific issue or issues having some presumed effect upon society's legal or social rights and privileges. In general, controversies rarely challenge an established constitutional privilege—usually both parties agree concerning the importance of one's constitutional rights. The disagreement emerges when one considers the specifics of the argument. Typically, these disagreements concern a conflict between normative behaviors and/or values. If one believes, for example, that the news should be fair and balanced, this value must be evidenced by some kind of *behavior.* Normative behavior is typically what one expects from oneself and others concerning the proper way of performing a given task. Often these values and norms, which evolve from past behavior, are poorly explicated in written form. In cases where the law requires a newscast to be fair and balanced (such as the American broadcasting regulations) volumes are filled attempting to delineate precisely what is meant by fair and balanced.[2]

Given this inherent ambiguity, it is easy to see why controversies are protracted in time and space. In a sense, none of the contesting parties is right; at best, one is perhaps more right than the other. Further, the contest occurs under the cloak of constitutional rights and privileges. This retards one party, given sufficient power (such as the Democrats or Republicans when in the White House), from exercising whims capriciously. The same would hold true for Congressional investigations—the conflict is protracted not because of any lack of power by the investigating committee or the accused television network, but rather because the conflict becomes dramaturgic, given the inherent constitutional rights of each party. Clashes between Goliaths in American broadcasting and Congress have occurred for more than thirty years, while criticism of print journalism undoubtedly began with the invention of the press.

1 Certainly the mass news media could become a classic social problem in the sociological sense of the term. But news has not attracted the deep concern surrounding mass media violence. Much of what follows is drawn from Otto Larsen's *Violence and the Mass Media* (New York: Harper & Row, Publishers, 1968), initial paradigm for casting violence as a social problem. At best, news is still in the initial stages of becoming a social problem. Consult any social problems textbook for a cogent summary of how an issue becomes a social problem.

2 In particular, see Edith Efron, *The News Twisters* (Los Angeles: Nash, 1971). Fair in whose sense and balanced by what criteria? How does one measure a lifted eyebrow, a damning modifying adverb?

It is possible to argue that there is a "natural history" of controversies. Apparently there is a pattern, an ebb and flow of charge–countercharge in most controversies. The process is as follows:

1. Someone perceives a need—lack or excess concerning news programming or coverage.
2. A counterproposal or ideal goal is postulated to correct the perceived shortcoming.
3. The reform is taken up by a group, or existing group accepts the reform as a part of its program.
4. Attempts are made to arouse public concern by drafting manifestos, model laws, action caucuses, and so on.
5. Law suits and/or hearings are instigated.
6. New normative behavior emerges either through laws, compromise, or private acquiescence by the attacked media personnel.

This is a rough guide of how a public controversy progresses. Certainly there are variations and often failures to achieve the sought after corrections. Also, a reform group may touch such a sensitive nerve in the public's conscience that many of the steps occur simultaneously. Or, the sought after reform may take years to achieve, requiring each concerned group to be so constituted to survive a fluctuating public and government concern for their issue.

At every juncture, the group under attack is responding with counterstrategies through press releases, introduction of its own legislation into Congress, or cease and desist orders. Certainly, in many cases, genuine issues of principle are concerned, but just as often the attacked party, be it the established media or Congress, tends to act instinctively, adhering to tradition and/or profit ratios.

Given a series of complaints that suggests a protracted campaign underway, it is helpful to establish where in the cycle the complaint occurs. A single citizen voicing his concern is different from a Congressional committee chairman subpoenaing the president of an American broadcasting network to appear before a committee to answer that citizen's complaint. Often a given speech, article, or news conference seeks no more than to arouse interest in a matter, and point toward the proper news organization for a fuller report. Thus, when hearing a charge against mass news, one should ask:

1. *Who makes the charge?* Does the individual speak for himself or a group? Have you ever heard of the group? Does it have substantial power through organization, money or public opinion to your knowledge?
2. *Are the charges specific and creditable?* Can malpractice have the possible effects which the speaker implies or suggests?
3. *Who or what is accused?* Is it possible for the practices to flow from the accused sector in the news bureaucracy? (This aspect is discussed in the readings in part two).
4. *What solutions are suggested?* Are they implied or explicit? Are the malpractices merely embedded in dire predictions concerning the fate of the republic or is the critic coherent about possible remedies?

5. *Keep track of how often you hear the charges and their source.* If you find
yourself learning more and explicit facts about the malpractice, you are
indeed witnessing a campaign; if there seems to be little variation in the
charges (or in the change of speaker) the issue is in its formative stages.

If there were a rule of thumb, it would be: The more hysterical the
charge, the less coherent the issue as a controversy. Let us take two
examples.

Consider Spiro Agnew's speech before the Des Moines audience. In
substance, he said that the news was biased in favor of liberalism. Further,
he went on, the few men in charge of the network news departments all
moved in a small provincial circle in Washington or New York and they
did not reflect the diversity of the country which, according to Mr. Agnew's
reading of the public and the polls, was somewhat more conservative. He
suggested the way to right this wrong was for listeners to express themselves to the appropriate authorities and to the networks themselves.

Certainly, Mr. Agnew sought to create a controversy, but he left the
actual organization and enactment to others. In the years following he has
returned to the topic of news bias a number of times. A strong right of
center political power group has never emerged to affect the media, although a few have made starts in that direction.[3] The question is, why did
Mr. Agnew's reform movement "fail"?

Compare this instance to a typical strategy of the consumer advocate,
Ralph Nader. First, it is necessary to formulate the charges and, in the
latter stages, accumulate information about and document the charges.
Suggestions for reform are made amid consistent efforts to enlist supportive public opinion. The whole campaign is orchestrated with an eye
for how power and publicity operate in American life. But perhaps the key
difference between Mr. Agnew and Mr. Nader is that the news is certainly
a less salient issue in comparison to tainted food, malfunctioning automobiles, or water pollution. Further, there are numerous ambiguities using
such terms as liberal and provincial. This is not to say that Mr. Agnew is
wrong; broadcast journalism is basically liberal but it is accidental liberalism—more a product of reporting norms than a conscious political bias
(we will return to this later). In the main, the vice president's charges are
difficult to document given the imprecision and ephemeral condition of
mass media stimuli.

Mass news will continue to engender complaints and controversy (one
rarely praises it) because news is a public act to be evaluated by anyone
who cares to devote some attention to it. Knowledge of the process by

[3] A number of groups do exist and a few books have been printed seeking to establish
his point, including an interesting study by Dennis T. Lowry, "Agnew and Network TV
News: A Before/After Content Analysis," *Journalism Quarterly,* 48 (Summer 1971),
205–10. During the Joe McCarthy era, certain right wing groups were incredibly successful in blackballing suspected communists. See John Faulk, *Fear On Trial* (New York:
Simon and Schuster, 1964). In all, the American press seems, for good or evil, to
have learned some valuable lessons in dealing with right wing attacks. The psyche of
American television is not dented by attacks or a hundred thousand letters when its
audience includes 40 million nightly viewers.

which the news is collected, edited, and disseminated can improve the precision of one's complaint. However, substantial *change* can come only when the bureaucratic features responsible for a news practice are changed.

In this introduction we have sought to establish a number of crucial distinctions. First, the specific content of an argument should be disengaged from the state of the controversy at which it occurs. A specific speech or attack occurs in a given social matrix. A charge of news bias at the beginning of a controversy is going to be much more general and emotional, than at the latter stages when a documented charge is lodged. Thus, we ask who is saying what, where is he saying it, and what sociological consequences will flow from the discussion. Thus, a politician's attack before a women's garden club is much different from a hearing held on his bill in Congress.

After identifying the locus of the charge, our next series of steps attempted to aid the reader in dissecting a particular charge. In a sense, we offered you nothing more than the old notion of how to analyze propaganda.[4]

In the sections to follow, we have selected but a few of the issues that trouble the institution of the press. For the interested student, this may serve as a springboard for further study.

THE ROLE OF LAW IN MASS NEWS

Before examining some of the current controversies over government's role in news, it is well to understand the legal and regulatory standards which now exist as controls on mass news content. The following two articles detail the major points of law for broadcast and print media which are the major sources of news for most Americans.

As the first selection by Burton Paulu of the University of Minnesota makes clear, broadcasting is a heavily regulated industry. Paulu traces the background and impact of radio-TV controls as he describes the most important Supreme Court decision affecting broadcasting in 25 years. He carefully describes the reasons for radio-TV regulation (regulations designed for a unique industry), and focuses on the FCC's "Fairness Doctrine" which has been in existence since 1949 (some say earlier), but has become a matter of major controversy in the past several years as the Commission attempts to find out how far the Doctrine should be carried.

The second selection, authored by Verne E. Edwards of Ohio Wesleyan University, details the problems of libel and slander and briefly explores the issue of free press–fair trial. Edwards deals with both print and broadcasting media, though the description is couched primarily in print media terms and examples.

[4] For those interested in pursuing the issue of propaganda analysis, see Larry Barker, *Listening* (Englewood Cliffs, N.J.: Prentice-Hall, Inc., 1970).

Readers are reminded that these two articles only touch the surface of the issues covered. Many items in the bibliography provide further details on regulation in general as well as specific coverage of free press, fair trial, and other issues. These two articles, however, give a notion of the complexity of existing regulations, and help provide a background for the third paper in this section by Eric J. Light, currently a Teaching Fellow at Trinity and All Saints Colleges in England. Although any number of other examples are possible, the issues surrounding the Pentagon Papers are typical of what transpires when an issue is taken to the courts. One is struck by the fact that most decisions are rarely clear-cut. Thus, the decision by the court may or may not be a victory for the press. Light's essay should be considered as a case study and should remind us of the inherent ambiguity that surrounds the concept of a free and unfettered press.

chapter 7 The 'Red Lion' Decision

BURTON PAULU

The decision of the United States Supreme Court in the case of the Red Lion Broadcasting Company versus the Federal Communications Commission announced on 9th June 1969 was a landmark in the history of radio and television regulation. On that date the court, by a 7–0 vote, held that the Fairness Doctrine and the related personal attack rules were a proper use of the authority of the Federal Communications Commission (FCC), and that they 'enhance rather than abridge the freedoms of speech and press protected by the First Amendment' to the Constitution.[1] The decision settled the question whether the FCC may legally prescribe certain programme policies and procedures for broadcasting stations without violating some of the freedoms guaranteed

Burton Paulu, " 'The Red Lion' Decision: A Landmark in American Broadcasting History," from *EBU Review*, No. 117B, September 1969. Reprinted by permission of the author and the publisher.

1 Two of the nine justices did not vote, Justice William Douglas because he missed the oral argument due to illness, and Justice Abe Fortas probably because his former law firm was involved in cases related to this one.

by the First Amendment to the American Constitution. Even more basically, it declared that the free speech concept long accepted for the printed press may be modified for application to the electronic communications media.

I

The Red Lion Broadcasting Company is the licensee of radio station WGCB in Red Lion, Pennsylvania.[2] On 27th November 1964 WGCB presented a programme in a syndicated series, 'Christian Crusade', by Billy James Hargis, the conservative American evangelist, which severely criticized Fred J. Cook, author of the book *Goldwater—Extremist on the Right*. Hargis stated that Cook had been discharged by a New York newspaper for making false charges against city officials; that he had worked for an alleged communist-affiliated publication; that he had defended Alger Hiss after the latter was convicted of perjury for denying certain communist activities; and that he had attacked J. Edgar Hoover, director of the Federal Bureau of Investigation. Now, said Hargis, Cook had written a book 'to smear and destroy Barry Goldwater', the unsuccessful Republican candidate for president in 1964.

When Cook asked for free time to reply under the Fairness Doctrine, the station denied his request.[3] Cook complained to the FCC, and the Commission ordered the station to give him time. When the station still refused, the matter was taken to the Court of Appeals in the District of Columbia, which in 1967 upheld the FCC's position as constitutional and proper. Thereupon the Red Lion Broadcasting Company appealed to the United States Supreme Court, which on 9th June 1969 sustained the decision of the lower court.

In 1967, after the *Red Lion* litigation had begun, the FCC issued an opinion and order outlining certain procedures to be followed by stations making personal attacks on persons or groups, or editorializing about political candidates.[4] The Radio and Television News Directors Association (RTNDA), an association of broadcast news directors, attacked these procedures as burdensome and vague in a brief to the Court of Appeals for the Seventh Circuit in Chicago, Illinois, which in 1968 held them to

[2] 89 *Supreme Court Reporter* 1797 (1969). The *Supreme Court Reporter*, Volume 19, No. 17, 1st July 1969, is published by the West Publishing Company, in St. Paul, Minnesota.
[3] The Hargis broadcast was carried in paid time, and Cook requested free time, although that was not an issue in the case.
[4] *Memorandum Opinion and Order. Amendment to Part 73 of the Rules to provide procedures in the event of a personal attack or where a station editorializes as to political candidates. Docket No. 16574.*

be unconstitutional abridgements of freedom of speech and press. When this decision also was appealed, the Supreme Court combined it with the *Red Lion* case because the same basic issues were involved in both.

In the United States, radio and television broadcasting are subject to control by the Federal government in Washington. The American Constitution, adopted in 1789, gave the Congress power 'to regulate commerce with foreign nations, and among the several states'. Since broadcasting is defined as a form of interstate commerce, the Congress from time to time has passed laws regulating it, including the Radio Act of 1927 and the more recent Communications Act of 1934. Among other things, the latter created the Federal Communications Commission whose seven members are appointed by the President, subject to confirmation by the Senate.

The FCC is authorized to license broadcasting stations, if 'public convenience, interest or necessity will be served thereby', although this phrase has never precisely been defined. Section 326 of the 1934 Act expressly denies the Commission 'the power of censorship over the radio communications or signals transmitted by any radio station', and also states that the Commission shall in no way 'interfere with the right of free speech by means of radio communication'. The only other notable portion of the law referring specifically to programmes, Section 315, requires equal treatment for all candidates for public office, although appearances on certain types of news programmes are exempt from these stipulations.[5] A recent amendment of Section 315 emphasizes the interest of Congress in having stations deal with controversial subjects by reminding them that they are 'to operate in the public interest and to afford reasonable opportunity for the discussion of conflicting views on issues of public importance'.

Ever since the Federal Radio Commission was created in 1927, the licensing agency has asked stations to provide certain programme information when it was deciding whether or not to grant licenses or license renewals (licenses are limited to three-year periods by law), and especially when choosing among competing applicants for the same channel. Many decisions, therefore, have involved programme judgments, although in the United States there is no comparable control of the printed press. Inevitably the question has arisen whether this is allowable under the First Amendment to the Constitution which reads in part: 'Congress shall make no law . . . abridging the freedom of speech or of the press'.

Chief Justice Marshall in 1803, in the famous case of Marbury versus Madison, wrote that the courts had authority to review acts of Congress

---

[5] Exempted are appearances by candidates on regular newscasts, news interviews, and news documentaries, as well as their appearances on any on-the-spot coverage of news events, including but not limited to political conventions and related activities.

and to declare them invalid if in conflict with the Constitution. Likewise, rulings by a Federal agency such as the FCC can be overturned if founded upon an unconstitutional law or policy, or if unconstitutional in themselves. In the *Red Lion* and *RTNDA* cases the court was asked to decide whether or not Congress had authorized the FCC to issue the Fairness Doctrine and related regulations, and if so, whether the actions complained of were unconstitutional abridgements of the freedoms of speech and press.

II

Basically, the Fairness Doctrine requires radio and television stations to be fair and impartial in treating controversial issues. Neither the Federal Radio Act of 1927 nor the Communications Act of 1934 contained such a stipulation. However, in addition to general insistence that stations serve the 'public interest, convenience, and necessity', both laws specified equal treatment of candidates for public office. As stated in Section 315 of the 1934 law: 'If any licensee should permit any person who is a legally qualified candidate for any public office to use a broadcasting station, he shall afford equal opportunities to all other such candidates for that office . . . '. But this clause does not apply to spokesmen for candidates or to controversial issues, being limited to the candidates themselves.

Back in 1929, the Federal Radio Commission (FRC) ruled that 'public interest requires ample play for the free and fair competition of opposing views, and the Commission believes that the principle applies . . . to all discussions of issues of importance to the public'.[6] In another case, at about the same time, the FRC used one of the arguments advanced by the Supreme Court in the 1969 *Red Lion* case:

> Since there is only a limited number of available frequencies for broadcasting, this commission was of the opinion . . . that there is no place for a station catering to any group, but that all stations should cater to the general public and serve public interest as against group or class interest.[7]

The Mayflower Broadcasting Company case in 1941 was another benchmark. The issue then was whether a station should be permitted to broadcast its own opinions—as can any newspaper, for example. The ruling was that 'the broadcaster cannot be an advocate'.[8] The Commission detailed its reasoning:

---

[6] 89 *Supreme Court Reporter* 1799 (1969).
[7] FCC, *Public Notice of July 1, 1964. Applicability of the Fairness Doctrine in the Handling of Controversial Issues of Public Importance,* p. 10426. Hereafter cited as *Fairness Primer.*
[8] ibid., p. 10426.

Freedom of speech on the radio must be broad enough to provide full and equal opportunity for the presentation to the public of all sides of public issues. Indeed, as one licensed to operate in the public domain the licensee has assumed the obligation of presenting all sides of important public questions fairly, objectively and without bias. The public interest—not the private—is paramount.

In 1949, in its report on 'Editorializing by Broadcast Licensees', the FCC reversed its position in the Mayflower case and lifted the ban on editorializing, but retained—and indeed strengthened—the requirement that stations serve all points of view.[9] Radio and television, it said, must be maintained

as a medium of freedom of speech and freedom of expression for the people of the nation as a whole . . . The Commission has consequently recognized the necessity for licensees to devote a reasonable percentage of their broadcast time . . . to the consideration and discussion of public issues . . . It is this right of the public to be informed, rather than any right on the part of the government, any broadcast licensee or any individual member of the public to broadcast his own particular views on any matter, which is the foundation stone of the American system of broadcasting.

In reply to the rejoinder that such requirements were in conflict with the First Amendment, and prophetically anticipating the issues raised in the *Red Lion* and *RTNDA* cases 20 years later, the Commission declared:

The freedom of speech protected against governmental abridgement by the First Amendment does not extend any privilege to any government licensees . . . to exclude the expression of opinions and ideas with which they are in disagreement. We believe, on the contrary, that a requirement that broadcast licensees utilize their franchises in a manner in which the listening public may be assured of hearing varying opinions on the paramount issues facing the American people is within both the spirit and letter of the First Amendment.[10]

The 1949 report required that time for the presentation of opposing views be provided free by the broadcaster if no sponsorship were available, and that if no dissenters requested time, it was the licensee's obligation to seek them out.

FCC policies were further detailed in its public notice of 1st July 1964, 'Applicability of the Fairness Doctrine in the Handling of Controversial Issues of Public Importance'; in the Memorandum Opinion and Order adopted 5th July 1967, already referred to; and in another Memorandum Opinion and Order issued 15th September 1967, 'Applicability of the Fairness Doctrine to Cigarette Advertising'. Taken together, these restated and extended the positions outlined above. In 1967 the Commission ruled:

9 ibid., p. 10422.
10 ibid., p. 10424.

When, during the presentation of views on a controversial issue of public importance, an attack is made upon the honesty, character, integrity or like personal qualities of an identified person or group, the licensee shall, within a reasonable time and in no event later than one week after the attack, transmit to the person or group attacked (1) notification of the date, time and identification of the broadcast; (2) a script or tape (or an accurate summary if a script or tape is not available) of the attack; and (3) an offer of a reasonable opportunity to respond over the licensee's facilities.

Furthermore, if a licensee in an editorial opposed or endorsed a candidate for public office, he must transmit such information to the candidate or to any other candidates for the same office, and offer time to reply.[11]

A few additional points may be cited at random. The fact that newspapers are one-sided (which they may legally be, since there is no Fairness Doctrine for the printed press), does not justify one-sided presentation by a broadcasting station. The requirement for fairness applies 'to a broadcast licensee irrespective of the position which may be taken by other media on the issue involved; and . . . the licensee's own performance in this respect, in and of itself, must demonstrate compliance with the Fairness Doctrine'.[12] However, exactly equal amounts of time need not be provided (as may be demanded by candidates for public office); the balance material does not have to be on the same programme; and the licensee himself may choose the spokesmen for other points of view. The Commission holds that stations carrying cigarette commercials must 'provide a significant amount of time to the other side of this controversial issue of public importance—i.e., that however enjoyable, such smoking may be a hazard to the smoker's health'.[13]

The reasons generally advanced in support of the Fairness Doctrine are indicated above. Opponents argued that such rules abridged the freedoms of speech and press guaranteed by the First Amendment. There are no such limitations on other media: a publisher may print his story, and a speaker say his piece, without any legal obligation to give space or time to other points of view. Broadcasters should be equally free. Furthermore, the fairness and personal attack rules are onerous, vague and difficult to apply.

Also involved is the fact that programme regulation may reduce profits. In addition to whatever administrative expenses may accompany the procedures required by the Fairness Doctrine, the need to develop more public service programmes, which is implicit in the whole concept, may

11 FCC, *Rules and Regulations*, Section 73.123. These rules did not apply to newscasts or news interviews; to attacks on foreign groups or foreign public figures; or when personal attacks were made by 'legally qualified candidates, their authorized spokesman, or persons associated with them in the campaign'.
12 *Fairness Primer*, p. 10419.
13 FCC, *Applicability of the Fairness Doctrine to Cigarette Advertising*, p. 13162.

have the effect of reducing income. Although this aspect of the problem is not used as an argument against the fairness rules, it is privately conceded as one reason for determined industry opposition to stricter government regulation.

Opposed to almost any regulation of programming, and especially to the Fairness Doctrine, has been the entire commercial broadcasting establishment—the National Association of Broadcasters, the Radio and Television News Directors Association, the networks (CBS, NBC, ABC, and Mutual), and most stations. A major reason for such determined opposition is the complexity of administering the rules. As the president of the Columbia Broadcasting System declared in 1968:

> The personal attack rules will pose particularly severe burdens for CBS in connection with some of its most highly regarded and informative public affairs programs. The rules do not in terms forbid such programs, but . . . the inhibitory effect of the rules on the commentators and program producers would have an insidious, if not totally destructive, effect upon many of these programs and the public confidence now enjoyed for the journalists who present them.[14]

Government censorship is a favourite theme. Thus, the president of the National Association of Broadcasters said that the Fairness Doctrine discourages the use of broadcasting for the expression of opinion, and thus abridges the broadcasters' right of free speech'.[15] He agreed—as do most critics of firm regulation—that a licensee does have an affirmative obligation to serve all points of view, but argued that 'the vast majority of broadcasters, if given freedom from government domination, would still provide balanced views on important matters'.

The keynote address given at the 23rd annual conference of the Radio and Television News Directors Association in Los Angeles on 20th November 1968 was even more outspoken:

> If we support the right of government to determine the propriety of our copy after it is aired—and that's what the Fairness Doctrine is all about—what is wrong with an even more foolproof system; the installation of a censor in your news rooms who will view the copy *before* it is aired, pass judgment on it, and thus keep you and your management from all those FCC troubles.[16]

At any rate, in the *Red Lion* case, RTNDA, CBS and NBC all submitted briefs to the court opposing the FCC's position. *Broadcasting* magazine commented that *Red Lion* 'was the culmination of an all-out industry

---

[14] Richard W. Jencks, *The FCC's 'Personal Attack' Rules: How to Throw the Baby Out with the Bath Water*, pp. 3–4.
[15] Vincent T. Wasilewski, as reported by the Associated Press, 6th March 1968.
[16] Richard Cheverton, *A Censor in Your News Room?*

effort to knock out the rules and, if possible, undermine the doctrine itself. NBC, in its brief, had made a frontal attack on the doctrine'.[17]

The issue in these cases, then, was not just the Fairness Doctrine, but the whole principle of whether the government can legally impose different or stricter performance standards for broadcast licensees than, say, for speakers on a public platform or newspapers and magazines. If the court had held the Fairness Doctrine unconstitutional, the way would have been open for a challenge of Section 315 of the Communications Act of 1934, requiring equal treatment of candidates for public office, as well as of any consideration of programme performance as a criterion for the FCC and its work.

III

The opinion in the *Red Lion* case, written by Associate Justice Byron R. White, dealt with three issues: the scarcity of frequencies; congressional authorization for the rules under attack; and the constitutionality of the Fairness Doctrine.

As to the first, the decision pointed out that, because of the lack of government authority to allocate frequencies before the Federal Radio Act became effective in 1927, 'the result was chaos'.[18] One of the main reasons for setting up the Federal Radio Commission was to allocate frequencies to competing applicants. There still are some competitive hearings; the highly desirable VHF television channels are almost entirely occupied in the nation's major markets; 'existing broadcasters have often attained their present position because of their initial government selection in competition with others'; and, even if there is no technological scarcity of frequencies, there is economic scarcity, since the Commission could limit entry on the grounds that it will not license more stations than a market can support.[19]

Because frequencies are so limited in number, they must be regarded as a public trust. A recent Senate committee report stated: 'Every licensee who is fortunate in obtaining a license is mandated to operate in the public interest and has assumed the obligation of presenting important public questions fairly and without bias'.[20] Replying to the argument that the First Amendment rules out programme service as a basis for choice among competing applicants, the court stated: 'Where there are substantially more individuals who want to broadcast than there are

---

[17] 16th June 1969, p. 23.
[18] 89 *Supreme Court Reporter* 1799 (1969).
[19] ibid., 1810–1812.
[20] ibid., 1803.

frequencies to allocate, it is idle to posit an unabridgeable First Amendment right to broadcast comparable to the right of every individual to speak, write, or publish'.[21] Since so few stations must serve a nation of 200 million people, the government might have divided up air-time among far more stations than it did. It has not done so; but certainly there is justification for requiring each licensee 'to make available a reasonable amount of broadcast time to those who have a view different from that which is already being expressed on his station'.[22]

On the question whether these rulings were in accordance with congressional intention, the court stated:

> The history of the emergence of the fairness doctrine and of the related legislation shows that the Commission's action in the *Red Lion* case did not exceed its authority, and that in adopting the new regulations the Commission was implementing congressional policy rather than embarking on a frolic of its own.[23]

Congress authorized the Commission, 'as public convenience, interest, or necessity' required, to make 'such rules and regulations and prescribe such restrictions and conditions . . . as may be necessary to carry out the provisions of this chapter. . .'.[24] Furthermore, from the beginning, Section 315 of the Communications Act required equal treatment for all candidates for public office, and when Congress amended this portion of the law in 1959 it reiterated 'the obligation . . . to afford reasonable opportunity for the discussion of conflicting views on issues of public importance'.[25]

The court further pointed out that the intention of Congress in requiring fair treatment for all candidates for public office could easily be circumvented were it not for the Fairness Doctrine. Section 315 applies only to appearances by candidates, and not to spokesmen for them. In the absence of the Fairness Doctrine, therefore, a licensee could ban all candidates from the air, and devote his station entirely to the supporters of one slate of candidates. 'It is the fairness doctrine as an aspect of the obligation to operate in the public interest, rather than Section 315, which prohibits the broadcaster from taking such a step.'[26] Therefore, concluded the court, 'we think the fairness doctrine and its component personal attack and political editorializing regulations are a legitimate exercise of congressionally delegated authority'.[27]

21 ibid., 1806.
22 ibid., 1807.
23 ibid., 1799.
24 ibid., 1801.
25 ibid., 1801.
26 ibid., 1803.
27 ibid., 1804.

The court then addressed itself to the basic question: do the Fairness Doctrine and related rules abridge freedom of speech and press as guaranteed by the First Amendment? The contention of the broadcasters, said the court,

> is that the First Amendment protects their desire to use their allotted frequencies continuously to broadcast whatever they choose, and to exclude whomever they choose from ever using that frequency. No one may be prevented from saying or publishing what he thinks, or from refusing in his speech or other utterances to give equal weight to the views of his opponents. This right, they say, applies equally to broadcasters.[28]

Obviously, broadcasting does have a 'First Amendment interest'.[29] But the new technologies require new interpretations. It is no denial of freedom of speech for the government to ban noisy loud-speakers, and the FCC may and does limit the use of broadcasting equipment. Only a few people can be licensees of broadcasting stations, although every man has the 'right' to license such a station. Just as the First Amendment does not prevent the government from limiting the number of licensees in order to eliminate interference among stations, so a 'licensee has no constitutional right . . . to monopolize a radio frequency to the exclusion of his fellow citizens. There is nothing in the First Amendment which prevents the Government from requiring a licensee to share his frequency with others . . .'.[30]

With more eloquence than usually is found in a court opinion, Justice White proclaimed:

> It is the right of the viewers and listeners, not the right of the broadcasters, which is paramount . . . It is the purpose of the First Amendment to preserve an uninhibited market place of ideas in which truth will ultimately prevail, rather than to countenance monopolization of that market, whether it be by the Government itself or a private licensee . . . It is the right of the public to receive suitable access to social, political, esthetic, moral, and other ideas and experiences which is crucial here. That right may not constitutionally be abridged either by Congress or by the FCC.[31]
>
> In terms of constitutional principle, and as enforced sharing of a scarce resource, the personal attack and political editorial rules are indistinguishable from the equal-time provision of Section 315, a specific enactment of Congress requiring stations to set aside reply time under specified circumstances and to which the fairness doctrine and these constituent regulations are important complements.[32]

[28] ibid., 1804–1805.
[29] ibid., 1804.
[30] ibid., 1806.
[31] ibid., 1806–1807.
[32] ibid., 1807.

During the trial it was argued that if the FCC required too much free time to be allocated to dissenting speakers, stations 'will be irresistibly forced to self-censorship and their coverage of controversial public issues will be eliminated or at least rendered wholly ineffective'.[33] The court doubted that this would happen, but observed that if it did, Congress and the Commission could insist that license renewal depend upon giving 'adequate and fair attention to public issues'. The court also brushed aside claims that the regulations were too vague. There was nothing at all vague, it said, about the ruling that Fred Cook be given a chance to reply to the attack by Hargis.[34]

Justice White concluded by saying:

> In view of the prevalence of scarcity of broadcast frequencies, the Government's role in allocating those frequencies, and the legitimate claims of those unable without governmental assistance to gain access to those frequencies for expression of their views, we hold the regulations and ruling at issue here are both authorized by statute and constitutional.[35]

The broadcasting 'industry', as it often calls itself, was much upset by *Red Lion*. Other recent decisions relaxing controls over the communications media—for example, pertaining to pornography in the cinema and in publishing—had led the broadcasters to anticipate a 'favourable' court. The disappointment was the greater in view of the 7–0 division, since so many important cases are settled by a margin of only one or two votes. With such unanimity, the chances of reversal on another try are negligible.

Broadcasting ('The Business Weekly of Television and Radio'), which consistently takes an anti-government position on all matters pertaining to regulation, surely spoke for many if not most broadcasters when it headlined its report, 'A bleak benchmark in regulation', and asked in a subhead: 'Will FCC impose as much control as high court says it has over programs?'[36] The story began:

> Broadcasters who had long opposed government intrusion into their coverage of controversial issues and who had considered themselves the electronic equivalent of print-media journalists are shaken and stunned. They have had their long-awaited confrontation with the government in the US Supreme Court on these contentions—and have lost.
>
> They may even have lost more than they had thought possible. For in the wreckage of their hopes for greater freedom from government control can be found Supreme Court support for tougher government regulations of programming generally, if the FCC chooses to use it.

[33] ibid., 1808.
[34] ibid., 1809.
[35] ibid., 1812.
[36] *Broadcasting*, 16th June 1969, p. 21.

The accompanying editorial, headed: 'Highest court, lowest blow', said in part:

> The basic position of the court is that the First Amendment accords a lower order of protection to broadcasting than to, say, the printed press. Because radio and television stations are licensed, the reasoning goes, the government has a right to demand from them a standard of performance that it may not extract from unlicensed media. This is the reasoning that has been used by every regulator who wished to impose his private standards upon the US broadcasting system. Now that it has been endorsed by the court of last resort, it will be both the excuse and the incentive for future regulations . . . This and other language like it in the decision could provide the legal underpinning for the construction of an apparatus of program control far beyond anything the FCC has yet attempted.[37]

Having followed thus far a self-imposed 'Fairness Doctrine', I now offer my own editorial. Though not a lawyer I always have regarded the Fairness Doctrine and Section 315 as both desirable and constitutional, and am pleased that the high court ruled as it did. There always is the danger that a regulatory agency may exceed its powers; and clearly we must avoid government domination of such sensitive and vital democratic instruments as the information media. But I fear abuse by private entrepreneurs more than by the FCC, although we must constantly scrutinize the regulators (that is, the FCC) to assure their integrity and objectivity.

We cannot assume that all broadcasters will be fair, if they do not have to be. It is true that the code of the National Association of Broadcasters stresses fair and objective coverage of important and controversial issues, and there undoubtedly are networks and stations that do that. But only a minority of stations subscribe to the code; and in any case, it has no legal weight. Inevitably there would be many large and powerful broadcasting stations, just as there are many newspapers, which would not be fair and balanced; and that is the reason a government mandate is essential.

The decision surely will encourage those both in and out of government who favour stricter regulation. The Commission may require more educational, cultural and public affairs programmes. Organized groups will find their bargaining power greater when they pressure stations directly, or through the FCC, to develop public service programmes. Movements against commercial excesses will be encouraged. The decision should prompt the FCC to look more critically into programme performance when considering license renewal applications.

The decision should end the debate as to whether the FCC has the legal right to use programme performance as a criterion in its decisions.

[37] ibid., p. 86.

It has been argued that those provisions in the Communications Act of 1934 which suggest that the Commission may properly concern itself with programmes were nullified by other provisions withholding the right to censor, and that the First Amendment made invalid any attempts by the FCC to be more than an electronic policeman. Such concerns have been resolved. In fact, if the court were asked now for an opinion, it certainly would uphold the constitutionality of Section 315, requiring the equal treatment of candidates for public office.

However, the decision does not provide the FCC with a basis for direct control of programme content, as some critics of the Fairness Doctrine have claimed. The Fairness Doctrine does not prohibit licensees from carrying programmes they regard as desirable; nor does it specify what controversial issues should be covered, what programme formats should be used, or what speakers should be presented (except for the personal attack rule, which provides that a man may reply personally to an attack on himself). The *Red Lion* decision does not give the United States government authority to take over or control the programmes of America's broadcasting stations.[38]

The Supreme Court finally has faced squarely the problem of broadcasting and the First Amendment. The differences between the broadcast and the printed media, as reviewed in the court's opinion, justify different regulatory procedures. This concept, although suggested in some earlier decisions, now has firm legal sanction.[39]

In the *Red Lion* case the First Amendment was applied affirmatively to authorize the government to require broadcasters to adhere to the Fairness Doctrine, rather than negatively to protect someone against abuses of government power. The right and obligation of the courts to provide such protection when necessary, of course, remains. But the Supreme Court felt that the current problem is not so much to protect the public against the government, as to have the government guarantee certain rights to the public.[40] Therefore, *Red Lion* identified 'the purpose of the First Amendment [as being] to preserve an uninhibited market

[38] If the broadcasters had won, and hence were under no legal obligation to follow any sort of Fairness Doctrine, the Commission, perhaps stimulated by congressional concern over editorializing, might have moved vigorously to break up multiple ownerships, reasoning that the potential dangers of concentrated control would have been increased by the absence of any fairness requirement. So the broadcasters may have won at least something from *Red Lion*.

[39] Because one of the reasons advanced by the court for the Fairness Doctrine was the scarcity of channels, and since it could be argued that it is equally important to apply similar rules to the print media, it is possible that in the future the court might accept an extension of the Fairness Doctrine to the printed press.

[40] For an historical review and discussion of this concept see Jerome A. Barron, 'An Emerging First Amendment Right of Access to the Media?' *The George Washington Law Review*, Vol. 37, No. 2, March 1969, pp. 487–509.

place of ideas in which truth will ultimately prevail, rather than to countenance monopolization of that market, whether it be by the government itself or a private licensee'.[41]

Finally, the court recognized the very broad aspects of mass communications: 'It is the right of the public to receive suitable access to social, political, *esthetic, moral, and other ideas and experiences* which is crucial here. That right may not constitutionally be abridged either by Congress or by the FCC'.[42] The public should be assured of exposure, wrote Justice White, not only to social and political issues, but to all things of the mind and the spirit.

[41] 89 *Supreme Court Reporter* 1806 (1969).
[42] ibid., 1807. Emphasis supplied.

chapter 8 Some Legal Pitfalls

VERNE E. EDWARDS, JR.

Among the more than half-a-dozen legal categories which directly impinge on journalistic work, the most important—and most complicated —is that of civil libel. Understanding some of the rudiments is important to lay citizens in proper assessment of press performance. Reporters and editors should study the subject, both to protect the press from needless suits and to enlarge their reporting and commenting by recognizing what is safe under the law.

A public speaker who defames an individual may be sued for slander. The publisher or broadcaster who reports the speaker's allegations may be sued for libel—the more serious species of defamation. (Although the "oral" aspect of slander might appear to belong to broadcasting, court decisions have tended to equate broadcasting with publishing because of the mass audiences involved.) Rarely, the same publication or broadcast brings both a criminal-libel indictment and a civil-libel suit. Criminal-libel actions, which have been infrequent, are employed when prose-

Verne E. Edwards, Jr., "Some Legal Pitfalls," from *Journalism in a Free Society,* pp. 196–206, 1970. Reprinted by permission of Wm. C. Brown Company Publishers.

cutors believe that a defamation threatens law and order. This may in- volve alleged defamation of a government official (as in the *Brooklyn Daily* case mentioned in Chapter 2) or defamation of a dead person (not normally subject to civil-libel action) or any defamation "inciting to vi- olence"—e.g., allegations that might so enrage the victims as to inspire them to attack their foes.

Most libel actions, as we have said, involve civil suits—an individual seeking damages from a publisher or broadcaster for having allegedly harmed his reputation illegitimately. Confusion about civil libel stems from several factors—wildly conflicting court decisions, the fact that many victims ignore libels, the fact that many potential cases are settled outside courtrooms, and ignorance of such factors as "privileged" communication. A brief look at the major defenses against libel damages should provide some understanding. These categories overlap each other, of course, and most libel cases involve elements of several defenses.

MAJOR LIBEL-SUIT DEFENSES

1. *Privilege.* Let us take a hypothetical situation with the fictional Senator J. M. Rail from Chapter 4. If Rail carried out his threat and charged in a Senate speech that D. R. Forp, a State University professor, was a Communist, the fictional professor—no matter how innocent— could not successfully sue Rail for slander. Nor could he successfully sue any publisher or broadcaster who accurately reported what the senator charged. The senator enjoys "absolute privilege" in performing his duties as an elected official—on the Senate floor or in any duly constituted of- ficial Senate proceeding. Publishers and broadcasters cover news of such proceedings with "qualified privilege." That "qualified" means that re- ports must be accurate and fair. (It is theoretically possible that Forp might win damages if he could show that a given publication or station had blatantly ignored significant, related defenses of his loyalty, or had pursued him with distorted coverage indicating malice toward him. If the plaintiff could sustain such charges, the defendant could escape only by proving that Forp was indeed a Communist.)

However, if Rail calls Forp a Communist during a press conference or in some speech outside a duly constituted Senate proceeding, he is open to a slander suit, and any medium which reports his allegation is open to a libel suit. Proving the truth of the charge would offer the only defense for either Rail or those who spread his charge.

Absolute privilege is accorded to official participants during official judicial and legislative proceedings and to "important" government executives in the line of duty. In fact, it means that even individuals wrongly accused of heinous crimes—through gross error—cannot recover damages for such abuse. That special exemption is considered essential to sound government and based on the premise that the common good overrides individual interests in these limited circumstances. Congressional investigations, like that of the Teapot Dome scandals in the 1920s, might be seriously hampered if the investigators were subject to normal slander and libel threats. Judges, lawyers, and witnesses in court sessions must be free of defamation restraints if truth is to be pursued vigorously in the courtroom—where fair-play rules are supposed to be rigidly enforced to protect all participants. And citizens must be able to follow those vigorous pursuits in detail through their press. (Legislators who abuse this special privilege may be censured by their colleagues, for whatever satisfaction that may give their victims. Courtroom witnesses who knowingly lie may be indicted for perjury by the state, but the victims of their lies have no means of recovery.)

So that the public may know what its government does, news reports of such proceedings are also protected, but not absolutely. A newspaper printing complete, verbatim testimony of a trial could acquire almost perfect privilege. Actually, few instances of successful libel suits have occurred when the basic derogatory matter came from absolutely-privileged sources. But legal, as well as ethical, considerations suggest that news media which reported a man's drunken-driving conviction must report his successful appeal of that conviction.

One travesty of civil libel involves the arbitrary gradations of qualified privilege according to government level. It should be as safe to report accurately city-council proceedings as those of a state legislature, but the government-closest-to-the-people myth bends in libel-law records. A New England newspaper was successfully sued for libel after it reported a Council meeting during which a lawyer hired by the village council had been called a "city slicker" for allegedly overcharging the village for legal services. Probably, failure of smaller media to appeal such judgments to higher courts accounts in part for such diluting of qualified privilege at local levels. Some defend the difference as proper protection against the relatively unsophisticated behavior of small-town council members and county commissioners, whose governmental commitments are less than those of their higher-placed counterparts. Privilege in the executive branches ranges from 100 per cent for a presidential press conference to utter confusion down the line.

During the heyday of U.S. Senator Joseph McCarthy's free-swinging attacks on "traitors" in government, many of his defenders said his charges "must be true since he hasn't been sued for libel." Whether they, or McCarthy's Senate colleagues who censured him in 1954, were correct, the not-sued-for-libel argument was erroneous, as an understanding of "privilege" shows.

2. *Fair comment.* The right to criticize duty performance of government officials, the qualifications of political candidates, and the professional competence of authors, actors, and athletes is among the press's most important libel protections. It is essential to cover news of political controversy and to comment with any forcefulness. Except for the Sedition Act of 1798 and a few limited war-time lapses, the United States has adhered to a fair-comment principle quite religiously.

Even so, a great leap forward was made in 1964 when the U.S. Supreme Court unanimously reversed a $500,000 libel judgment against the *New York Times* and four Negro ministers. That landmark decision involved a full-page advertisement (March 29, 1960) which denounced behavior of Montgomery, Alabama, officials in dealing with civil-rights demonstrators. The *New York Times vs. Sullivan* decision in effect knocked out the old "strict rule," which had held that any factual errors, on which strong criticism was based, destroyed the fair-comment protection. Only when errors are made with "malice"—i.e., with knowledge that they are errors, or *with reckless disregard* for accuracy—does the fair-comment defense collapse in an action brought by a public official, the court ruled.

In a sense, the court could be said to have extended to the private citizen a right of political criticism rivaling the "absolute privilege" of government officials. The opinion specifically cited the protecton of officials from "the threat of damage suits," and declared: "Analogous considerations support the privilege for the citizen-critic of government. It is as much his duty to criticize as it is the official's duty to administer." (The defense of fair comment here, as in many cases, involved an element of privilege as well.)

In later decisions, the court extended the newly enunciated protection to cover criticism of "public figures" as well as government officials. The extension came when the court in 1967 reversed a $500,000 libel judgment against the Associated Press for having reported that retired Major General Edwin A. Walker of Texas had "led a charge of students against federal marshals" during integration riots at the University of Mississippi in 1962. Lower courts had ruled for the plaintiff because the AP was unable to substantiate its reports of the general's actions during his presence in Oxford, Mississippi.

Unprovable allegations are not, however, always safe press practice in such cases. The Supreme Court in 1967 upheld damages awarded to Wallace Butts, who as University of Georgia athletic director had been accused in a *Saturday Evening Post* article of having passed Georgia football plans to an upcoming opponent. An important difference between the Walker and Butts cases was the factor of time: A press association serving broadcast outlets and dailies has less opportunity to verify details of a running story like the Mississippi campus riots than does a magazine publishing articles of wider choice at a slower pace. If Walker had not made himself a public figure by speaking out on political matters and if he had not been in Oxford, Mississippi, during the rioting, the defendant's appeal might well have lost.

Fair comment does not extend to criticism of the artist's or public figure's personal life or a charge of criminality. Commentators may accuse a governor of "recklessly spending the taxpayers' money" under the fair-comment umbrella, but any charge of embezzling public funds would need to be provably true in court or an accurate report from an absolutely privileged source (a formal indictment or an accusation in the legislature). A reviewer may safely call an author's work "juvenile" even if all better-qualified reviewers hail its "maturity," but an accusation of "plagiarism" is libel per se and would have to be proved in court if the author sued for libel. A critic may safely call a handsome actor "too ugly" for the romantic lead, but dismissing his stage appeal "because he beats his wife" would require another libel defense.

Criticism of public figures, public institutions (like schools), artists, and performers can be caustic—even exceeding the bounds of good taste —but it must be based on substantially accurate facts and it must concern performance offered to the public. The more private the subject's dealings, the less likely fair comment is to cover criticism. Fair comment does not, for instance, extend to criticism of performance by a private doctor or lawyer or retail merchant, as it does to that by a state college's health director or the county's district attorney or an armed services post exchange. One Western college newspaper editor thought fair comment covered editorial charges that a photographer's "prices have steadily risen as his services have steadily declined; his only merit would appear to be his location near campus." The ensuing libel suit was settled out of court for several thousand dollars. Had the case come to trial, the publisher would have had to prove that services had "steadily" declined and that the photographer's "only merit" had been his convenient location.

Had the editor criticized the artistic quality of the plaintiff's photographs voluntarily displayed in the student union building, the defense of fair comment would have been pertinent.

3. *Truth.* Often called the best defense, truth has been left till last because laymen—and some journalists—are often naïve about its application. Actually, a fair and accurate report of a lie made under privileged

conditions may be easier to defend than a story the reporter knows to be true. Unless the libel defendant can prove his allegations in a court of law, they cannot be considered "legal truth." The plaintiff may produce more and better witnesses, or the defendant's damning evidence against the plaintiff may not be admissible in court. Just as a prosecutor may legitimately delay seeking an indictment against a known criminal until he has convincing evidence, so a press unit may take time to dig up evidence before exposing scoundrels. The prosecutor knows a poor case may result in "double jeopardy" protection of his quarry, acquitted for lack of evidence. And responsible newsmen know that a successful libel suit against their premature attack may elevate the scoundrel in public esteem, as the vindicated victim of a bullying press.

The worst misunderstanding among laymen has to do with which truth serves as a defense. In those cases where privilege and fair comment are not defenses, truth must cover *both* the allegation and the source of the allegation, if any. For example, in reporting the fictitious Senator Rail's nonprivileged charge (see second paragraph under "Privilege"), defense against a libel suit by Forp would require proving that Rail made the charge *and that Forp was a Communist.*

A video-taped interview, certified as accurate by the defamer, provides grounds for libel damages against the broadcaster unless he can prove the third party's defamatory remarks are true. A radio station in the Northwest wisely decided not to air its recording of a state legislator's speech because a lawyer defamed in the speech said he would sue the station if it broadcast such defamation. A notarized letter-to-the editor or a paid-for advertisement still leaves the publisher or broadcaster liable for libel damages. Even if the defendant has taken editorial exception to the defamatory remarks, further indicating that they are not his, his publishing or broadcasting of the defamation is still his responsibility. The fact that the defendant can prove that someone else said it is not a sufficient defense of truth. [The only exception in all this covers broadcast campaign speeches, which cannot be censored by the station. Significantly, news coverage of such speeches does not carry the immunity.]

The key to understanding publisher-broadcaster liability lies in recognizing the relative degree of damage delivered by the original defamer and that delivered by the agency which spreads the defamation. The remarks by the aforementioned legislator were heard by 150 persons in one room; the 5,000-watt station would have carried them to thousands over a three-state area. A defamatory letter may be read by an editor and his secretary; publication can lay it before hundreds of thousands and preserve it in the microfilm or bound-volume files of libraries.

All of which is intended to say that truth is not an easy defense. It is, however, an important defense. The *Chicago Tribune* once called a city alderman a "gangster." When he sued for libel, the *Tribune* proved to the court's satisfaction that the plaintiff was a gangster in the accepted meaning of that word.

Responsible journalists look beyond libel risks in deciding whether to report or comment in given situations, of course. Some sensational derogatory statements, well protected by privilege, may be ignored. Unprovable "truths" are put forward with courage on occasion.

OTHER LIBEL CONSIDERATIONS

Not naming persons defamed in news reports or editorials is a dangerous means of trying to avoid libel suits. A plaintiff may be able to show that many readers or listeners identified him as the unnamed "culprit." This has happened accidentally, both with the person alluded to and with some person not even thought of by the writer. (The "sophomore resident of Stokely Hall who was expelled for cheating" might accidentally point to a sophomore who left school about the same time because of family illness.)

Consent—formal or informal—may protect journalists in reporting derogatory material. (But the willing victim of being lampooned in a lodge paper could successfully sue the station which broadcasts the contents beyond lodge circles.) If B responds to A's attack in kind, the balanced report is safer than either attack by itself. Provocation and the right of reply are important factors.

Headlines present a special problem in libel. Court decisions have ruled both ways—that headlines must be judged by their content alone, and that defamation depends on considering both the headline and story text. Good copy editors look to the former. They sacrifice the specificity of "Burglar Nabbed/In Widow's Home" for "Police Arrest/Burglary Suspect." Both ethics and libel law dictate that he is only a suspect until final court action.

Corrections and retractions present special problems. Where error is clear, both ethical and legal common sense dictate that prompt correction should be made. However, automatic retraction on any demand (as practiced by some media) is editorially debilitating and sometimes legally dangerous. A hasty retraction, as required by some libel-insurance policies, can interfere with other defenses. Thus the prospective defendant may ruin a defense of truth in order to establish mitigation (reduction) of damages. On the other side, refusal to retract may help prove malice on the defendant's part.

Although the general public hears more about dramatic direct-confrontation libel suits like that of Quentin Reynolds against columnist Westbrook Pegler (see Louis Nizer's *My Life in Court,* "Suggested Reading") and *Sullivan vs. New York Times,* the vast majority of actions involve unimportant issues and unknown plaintiffs. They stem from simple errors—sometimes careless, sometimes almost unavoidable. A reporter's copying the wrong line in a police report or composing-room transposition of picture captions can lead to court. An interviewee's ad lib remark during a live broadcast could bring lengthy litigation.

MISCELLANEOUS LEGAL PITFALLS

Invasion of privacy is recognized as a journalistic offense entitling victims to damage claims. Newsworthy persons are entitled to less right of privacy than others, and the right does not protect any participant in the news, willing or otherwise, from reasonable coverage. Trouble arises when journalists begin probing into family affairs and remote connections of persons whose names have been in the news perhaps briefly. Or when "anniversary" features are unearthed to rework details of some tragedy, with unwelcomed reports on what the principals' survivors "are doing now." A particularly loathsome invasion is that involving the unauthorized use of a person's picture to advertise some product or service. Generally, the highest courts have been most lenient with the press when suits involved stories at all connected with legitimate public interest. Thus *New Yorker* magazine successfully defended against a former child prodigy's suit for damages after they interrupted his later obscurity by profiling his life. Exceptions, however, are on record, and confusion may develop even further in this special area than it has in general civil libel. Truth is not an automatic defense, since damage claims are based on invading the plaintiff's wish to be let alone. A story about a plumber's interrupting a housewife in her bath is not of public concern unless she has him arrested in connection with the incident.

Postal regulations concern publishers, though not as much as Federal Communications Commission rulings affect broadcasters. Rules on percentage of space devoted to advertising, rules against promoting lotteries, and wavering restrictions on "obscenity" all impinge on publishers. Magazines, which depend upon second-class mail for about 70 per cent of their distribution, are most concerned. Even with less than 10 per cent dependence, dailies must observe restrictions. As absolute overseer of broadcasting's delivery system, the FCC has vaster regulatory power, which it has so far used with great restraint.

Statutes regulating advertising and copyright ownership are among other legal concerns of journalists. Pirating of newspaper stories by radio stations has been held in violation of "common law" copyright, for example.

CONTEMPT OF COURT

Once ranked under "miscellaneous" in listings like this chapter's, contempt of court threatens to become a bigger issue in this last third of the twentieth century. Simple citations for disturbing courtroom decorum with photographers' shenanigans or reporters racing for telephones have largely faded into history. Bottles between the bench and press over picture-taking "near" the courtroom may continue. So will occasional contempt citations for reporting testimony stricken from the record and other defiances of judges' orders. The press's right to criticize judicial performance, though well established by precedent, will continue to be challenged here and there. Two special aspects, however, appear headed for major debate.

One involves a journalist's obligation to reveal sources of information on criminal activity. University of Oregon graduate Annette Buchanan lost a long fight in 1968 against a $300 fine for contempt in such a situation. She had reported in Oregon's *Daily Emerald* on student use of narcotics. Her refusal to identify students who had given her the information in confidence led to the contempt charge. A minority of states grant reporters and their sources a right of "privileged communication" like that accorded a lawyer and his client, a physician and his patient, or a priest and his communicant. Even journalists are divided on whether they should be free to report scandalous allegations without being held accountable for particulars. Opponents argue that such exemption would enable irresponsible journalists to smear public servants and others. Proponents insist that contempt-citation threats discourage the kind of full disclosure necessary for a watchdog press in a democratic society. Alerting the people to collusion between racketeers and dishonest officials, for example, may be possible only if the press can protect the anonymity of its sources.

By far the biggest contempt-of-court issue facing heated debate is that related to the "Free Press-Fair Trial" controversy. Concern over "trial by the press," which had been growing for decades, reached a climax in the Warren Commission's 1964 report on the assassination of President John F. Kennedy a year earlier. The report cited "irresponsibility and lack of self-discipline" by the press in covering the assassination's aftermath. Typical of stories which bother those concerned with fair trials was this one, which appeared two days after President Kennedy was killed:

DALLAS (UPI)—Police said Saturday night they have an airtight case against pro-Castro Marxist Lee Harvey Oswald, 24, as the assassin of President Kennedy, including photos of him holding the rifle.

Police were reported showing the photos to the sullen ex-Marine from suburban Irving, Tex., who has steadfastly maintained his innocence and has also denied slaying a Dallas policeman.

The photos, police said, show him with both the rifle used to kill President Kennedy and the pistol used to kill pursuing Patrolman J. D. Tippitt shortly after the assassination.

"This case is cinched," said Homicide Chief Capt. Will Fritz.

When he was brought down from a cell in city jail to a room where he was shown the photos, Oswald was the picture of confidence, smiling and loudly complaining about prison treatment. When he was taken back up to his cell he looked frightened. . . .

Such prejudiced reporting, it is argued, makes a fair trial difficult for a defendant. The fact that Oswald was "found guilty" by the Warren Commission's investigation after Oswald was slain by Jack Ruby (the same day that story appeared) did not detract from the fact that prejudice against the suspect had been built up unfairly among prospective jurors, critics maintained. Perils include both difficulty in convicting the guilty and the danger of convicting the innocent.

The American Bar Association soon thereafter appointed a committee, headed by Massachusetts Supreme Judicial Court Justice Paul C. Reardon, to recommend pretrial safeguards against prejudicial publicity. In 1968, the ABA adopted, by a more-than-two-thirds majority, four recommendations of the Reardon Report. Briefly, these would forbid lawyers, court officials, and police from releasing other than a suspect's vital statistics and the arrest circumstances. No reports of confession or previous criminal record, etc., would be allowed, and no statements like that of the Dallas homicide chief in paragraph 4 of the foregoing example. No interviews or picture-taking of the person in custody would be permitted without his written request. Most controversial from the press's point of view are recommendations for excluding the public and press from various preliminary hearings and encouragement of using contempt powers to protect the defendant from unfavorable publicity. Judges would be encouraged to cite the press for any report a judge considered aimed at influencing the trial's outcome or for reporting any information from closed proceedings—no matter how obtained.

As each of the fifty states decides—in its bar association, legislature, and court system—whether to follow the ABA recommendations, the contempt-of-court pitfall will be profoundly affected for all of the media. Meanwhile, as in every legal-problem area, press performance can help reduce or widen that pitfall.

chapter 9   Censorship: The Pentagon Papers and a Free Press

ERIC J. LIGHT

Congress shall make no law . . . abridging the freedom of speech, or the freedom or the press. *First Amendment, U.S. Constitution.*

I can only say . . . that to me it is equally obvious that "no law" does not mean "no law". . . . *Erwin Griswold, Solicitor General, United States Department of Justice.*

The issue of press censorship is not a new one. The Supreme court itself has ruled against prior restraint on other occasions; most notably the 1931 landmark decision of *Near vs. Minnesota.* What was different, four decades later, about cases 1873 and 1885 was the nature of the participants and the information whose publication created the confrontation.[1] The

Eric J. Light, "Censorship: The Pentagon Papers and a Free Press." Published here for the first time by permission of the author.

[1] "Vietnam Archive: Pentagon Study Traces Three Decades of Rising United States Involvement," the *New York Times* (June 13, 1971) I:1, 35–40. the *New York Times*, Petitioner, vs. The United States and The United States, Petitioner, vs. The *Washington Post. U.S. Supreme Court Reports,* 29, No. 4; Lawyers Edition, Second Series (August 1, 1971), 882–97.

litigants included on the one side the executive branch of the Federal government. The defendants were two of the nation's foremost newspapers. The information was contained in documents, labelled top secret, that were an historical record of the Vietnam war. By a vote of 6 to 3 the United States Supreme Court blocked the Federal government's attempt to stop the publication, in *The New York Times* and the *Washington Post,* of the Pentagon study of the Vietnam war. Many journalists have cited the case as a clear example of the sanctity of the First Amendment. On the surface, the ruling would appear to be so. However, the complex issues and the way they were resolved might leave room for re-evaluating that way of thinking.

THE PAPERS APPEAR

The momentous fight began with the Sunday, June 13 issue of *The New York Times.* The story was introduced in a low-keyed manner that attracted very little reaction[2] until the Attorney General obtained a temporary restraining order two days later which stopped the series and charged the *Times* with making disclosures that would "cause irreparable injury to the defense of the United States.[3]

The information for the articles was drawn from a massive Pentagon study apparently turned over to the *Times* by Daniel Ellsberg, a former Pentagon analyst and one of the researchers for the study. The documents were given to Neil Sheehan, then a Washington reporter for the *Times,* but at one time assigned to covering the Vietnam war. James L. Greenfield, foreign editor for the *Times,* was named as director of the project and Gerald Gold, assistant foreign editor, was assigned to work with Sheehan on turning such a massive study into a series of articles.

From the start of the project until the study's first appearance in print,[4] utmost secrecy was maintained. Gold joined Sheehan in Washington where they began to evaluate the material. They assembled a collection of books, magazines, and articles to help determine what had and what had not already been published about the U.S. role in Vietnam. After two weeks, they informed the managing editor, A. M. Rosenthal,

2 Neither the broadcast networks nor the wire services mentioned the story until almost a day after the papers were initially published in the *Times.*
3 Text from a telegram sent to the publisher of the *New York Times* by Attorney General Mitchell, as published in the *New York Times,* (June 15, 1971) I:1, 18.
4 Neil Sheehan allegedly obtained the Pentagon Study from Daniel Ellsberg during the first week in April. He was joined in Washington by Gerald Gold on April 5. Two weeks later, tentative permission had been granted for the series of articles and the project team had been moved to New York. In all, seven weeks elapsed between Sheehan's obtaining the documents and their appearance in print.

of their results and he in turn spoke to the publisher of the *Times,* Arthur Ochs Sulzberger, who gave his initial go ahead for the articles.

Because of the magnitude of the project Sheehan, Gold, and all their books and magazines were moved to New York and a suite in the Hilton Hotel where they were watched over by *Times* security guards. Added to the project team were newsroom secretary Muriel Stokes and another assistant foreign editor Al Siegal, the first of up to 75 *Times* personnel who were to be removed from regular assignments to work on the project. Sheehan and Hendrick Smith and E. W. Kenworthy, also from the Washington bureau, were the principal writers of the articles. They were assisted by Fox Butterfield, currently covering New Jersey for the *Times,* but formerly reporting from both North and South Vietnam.. All of these writers were instructed to leave the hotel as little as possible and, if they did, not to go near the *Times'* offices. Their only contact was to be through Greenfield, who shunted back and forth between the offices and the Hilton supervising.

As the target date for publication approached, a trusted composing crew was assembled and sworn to secrecy. They were informed of the project and then set up in a special composing room to await the copy from the Hilton. On Thursday, June 10, the finished copy started to arrive. Under tight security type was set, proofs were taken, and pages were made up. On Friday, publisher Sulzberger gave final approval for the story. On Saturday, June 12, page one was laid out with a large gap at the top and sent to the main composing room. A short while later, the type for the Pentagon study was brought down from the project composing room and added to the page. The page was then locked and sent to press.

Before editing, the study included 4,000 pages of documentation and 3,000 pages of analysis, most of which was classified either secret, top secret, or top secret-sensitive. The study, quickly dubbed the "Pentagon Papers" by the press, was started in 1967 by the then Secretary of Defense Robert McNamara. Growing disillusioned with U.S. involvement in Vietnam, and wanting to prevent such involvement from occurring elsewhere again, McNamara decided to compile an historical evaluation in hopes that historians and future planners might learn from a record of past mistakes. The study covered data as far back as the late Roosevelt administration but concentrated, because of McNamara's involvement and the war's build-up, upon the decision making processes during the Johnson administration. Its information was especially incriminating to Lyndon Johnson and his advisors, implying that they had planned the major 1964–65 escalation long before it took place (supposedly spontaneously) and had lied or withheld information about it from both the public and Congress. Charges that the study was misleading, selective, and presented out of context got lost as the suspicions it evoked were played up in headlines and broadcasts all across the country.

THE GOVERNMENT REACTS

If the printing of the Pentagon Papers did not arouse much attention at first, the eventual reaction of the Nixon administration did. It was an unprecedented attempt to legally prevent a newspaper from printing a story. Most of the administration, the President included, were not even aware of the study's existence. The reason for the move toward prior restraint was a feeling within the administration that the publication of the Papers was a direct attack upon the operation of government and its ability to conduct foreign affairs properly and discreetly.

The restraining action was initiated by the Justice Department, first in the form of a June 14 telegram to the *Times,* asking the publishers of the paper to voluntarily stop printing the articles. When the cooperation was not forthcoming, the Justice Department sought to obtain a temporary restraining order against the *Times.* The *Washington Post* also had a set of Pentagon Papers and began running its own series of articles on Friday, June 18, the day the *Times* was due in court for its injunction hearing. With news services carrying synopses of the *Post* stories, the arguments of the *Times* lawyers dealt not with the issue of prior restraint, but with its readers being unfairly denied news others were publishing if the restraining order was allowed to stand. This defense on the part of the *Times* forced the government into broadening its attack and seeking a temporary restraining order against the *Washington Post* as well. It soon became apparent that this tactic also had its difficulties as one after another, the *Boston Globe,* the *Los Angeles Times,* the *Chicago Sun-Times,* the *St. Louis Post-Dispatch,* and the eleven papers of the Knight news chain each came out with articles on the papers. A pattern soon developed. On the first day, a newspaper would print the story. The next day, the editor or publisher would be contacted by the Justice Department and politely asked to stop printing their articles. The newspaper would refuse and the Justice Department would go to court seeking a temporary restraining order forcing the paper to stop.

This broadened attack quickly landed the government in trouble and clouded the issue still more. While New York Judge Murry Gurfein, a Nixon appointee in his first day on the bench, saw fit to grant the Justice Department a temporary restraining order against the *Times,* Washington Judge Gerhard A. Gesell labelled the case an attempt at censorship of "essential historical data" and refused to grant an injunction, temporary or otherwise, against the *Post.* With the *Times* case still pending, the Justice Department was forced to hastily throw together an appeal on the *Post* case and bring it before a Federal Appeals Court in Washington, where it was able to obtain a two-to-one decision preventing the *Post* from printing any further excerpts.

The confusion created in the process of the government's obtaining restraining orders seemed to some observers to demonstrate the futility of its position. There were no precedents for the support of prior restraint, only precedents against it. The Justice Department was engaging in a procedure long viewed to be beyond the perview of American law: the prior restraint of the American press. Indeed, this very question was raised by the Hutchins' Commission on Freedom of the Press when, in 1946, it said:

> . . . Every modern government, liberal or otherwise, has a specific position in the field of ideas; its stability is vulnerable to critics in proportion to their ability and persuasiveness. A government resting on popular suffrage is no exception to this rule. It also may be tempted—just because public opinion is a factor in public livelihood—to manage the ideas and images entering public debate.
>
> If the freedom of the press is to achieve reality, government must set limits on its capacity to interfere with, regulate, or suppress the voices of the press or to manipulate the data on which public judgement is formed.[5]

With no such limitations to be found, it was apparent that the issues would have to be solved in the Supreme Court.

THE COURT DECIDES

The Supreme Court, a body known for its lengthy and deliberate considerations of issues, was unusually swift in acting. Oral arguments were scheduled June 26, 1971, a day after the court agreed to hear the cases. The court extended its spring term so that the decision could be handed down quickly.

It was part of the arguments of the lawyers for the *Times* and the *Post* to concede that there could be occasions where the First Amendment might be overruled. This principle had already been established in the *Near vs. Minnesota* Supreme Court decision of 1931. But the lawyers extended the decision by arguing that it was up to the government to prove that there was a need for such a suspension. They contended that the government had never proved its allegation that the publication

[5] *A Free and Responsible Press: A General Report on Mass Communications: Newspapers, Radio, Motion Pictures, Magazines, and Books* (Chicago: The University of Chicago Press, 1947), pp. 7, 8.

of the Pentagon Papers would have a detrimental effect upon the national security. The Justice Department countered, arguing that the government had the authority to censor based upon the unwritten, "inherent" powers of the president as the formulator of the nation's foreign policy.

With the issue such a momentous one, it was not surprising that each of the judges had written a separate opinion. In an attempt to rule as quickly as possible, there was little time for the Justices and lawyers to examine all the documents or research all the previous decisions related to the case. Somehow, despite a sense of rushing to a verdict, the Supreme Court's six to three ruling against the government (handed down on June 30, 1971) has been viewed as a clear reaffirmation of the First Amendment guarantee of freedom of the press.

The praise came from sources beyond the press. Politicians applauded the Court, saying that it had served "its most valuable service."[6] The decision also served to bolster the House and Senate doves and their support of the idea of the "public's right to know." Yet among all the praise, there were some notes of dissent. The most notable of these could be found within some of the majority opinions of the Supreme Court decision. A careful examination of the nine opinions quickly indicates that the triumph of the press was not completely unqualified. Only two of the nine justices held that the First Amendment was an absolute guarantee against censorship under any conditions while four of the justices thought that it might be proper for criminal proceedings to be used against the press if it reported information deemed detrimental to the national security. There was, however, an even more considerable questioning of the government's right to set itself above the boundaries of the First Amendment.

Justices Douglas and Black staunchly held the First Amendment to be absolute in its guarantee of the freedom of the press. In the words of Justice Black:

> I believe that every moment's continuance of the injunctions against these newspapers amounts to a flagrant, indefensible, and continuing violation of the First Amendment.
> The press (in the Founding Father's view) was to serve the governed, not the governors. The government's power to censor the press was abolished so that the press would remain free to censure the government . . .[7]

Douglas indicated that if Congress passed a law permitting prior restraint it would be unconstitutional. It was this point that distinguished

---

[6] *Newsweek* (July 12, 1971), p. 17. Quoting Hubert Humphrey.
[7] Op. cit, *U.S. Supreme Court Reports.*

his opinion from that of Thurgood Marshall. Justice Marshall viewed the First Amendment as absolute but felt that Congress could pass a law that might legally permit prior restraint of the press. However, he goes on to point out that since Congress had not passed such a law, and since it was not the function of the Supreme Court to do so, there were no grounds at that time for the government's prior restraint. Justice William Brennan indicated that a law was not necessary if the government could substantiate a claim that "publication must inevitably, directly, and immediately cause" some danger to the nation during a war.[8] Justice Brennan did not feel that the government had done anything more than make an allegation. There was no evidence for support of its claims.

Justices Potter Stewart and Byron White both viewed the printing of the documents as having a detrimental effect upon the government. Both felt however that this effect must be weighted against, in the opinion of Justice Stewart:

> . . . an informed and critical public opinion which alone can here protect the values of democratic government . . . For without an informed and free press there cannot be an enlightened people.[9]

But in weighing the two sides, Justice White felt that:

> . . . The United States has not satisfied the very heavy burden which it must meet to warrant an injunction against publication in these cases.[10]

White also felt that some Congressional guidelines were needed in order to ensure the proper balance:

> . . . to sustain the government in these cases would start the courts down a long and hazardous road that I am not willing to travel at least without Congressional guidance and direction.[11]

The three Justices voicing the minority opinion favoring the government position, Justices John Harlan, Harry Blackmun, and Chief Justice Warren Burger, felt that the major issue confronting the court was one of rushing into a decision without the proper time to examine all the issues and deliberate the answers properly. Justice Harlan saw the Court acting irresponsibly:

> . . . It is a reflection on the stability of the judicial process that these great

8 Ibid.
9 Ibid.
10 Ibid.
11 Ibid.

issues—as important as any that have arisen during my time on the court—should have been decided under the pressures engendered by the torrent of publicity that has attended these litigations.[12]

Chief Justice Burger was just as explicit in his condemnation of the proceedings:

> In this case, the imperatives of a free and unfettered press comes into collision with another imperative, the effective functioning of a complex modern government . . . Only those who view the First Amendment as an absolute in all circumstances—a view I respect, but reject—can find such a case to be a simple one.
> This case is not simple for another and more immediate reason. We do not know the facts of the case . . . I suggest we are in this posture because these cases have been conducted in unseemly haste.[13]

There was one point that did draw common support from both the majority and minority. That was the question of possible criminal prosecution. In a sharply worded statement supported by Justices Stewart, Blackmun, and Chief Justice Burger, Justice White said:

> . . . failure by the government to justify prior restraints does not measure its constitutional entitlement to a conviction for criminal publication. That the government mistakenly chose to proceed by injunction does not mean that it could not successfully proceed in another way . . . If any of the material here at issue is [covered by Federal espionage laws], the newspapers are presumably now on notice of the position of the United States and must face the consequences if they publish.[14]

Attorney General John Mitchell, on the day after the decision was handed down, vowed to take this "other way." He announced that he would prosecute all those who had violated Federal criminal laws in connection with this matter. The real direction of Mitchell's announcement was at the newspapers, informing them that they were subject to prosecution for any violations, past or future. As one government lawyer said: "I would hope that the Court's opinions will persuade the papers to put some restraint on themselves."

ROLE OF THE "PAPERS" CASE

The Supreme Court's ruling against prior restraint of the press added little that was new to the existing precedents. It only served to reinforce

12 Ibid.
13 Ibid.
14 Ibid.

earlier decisions. The issues raised by the publication are still unresolved. The fact that the government sought and obtained a restraining order leaves the press facing the prospect that, despite the Supreme Court decision, the government might seek further restraints in the future. The Court has said that if publication would directly cause a threat to the naional security, the government may restrain a paper from printing. The government says that in the case of the Pentagon Papers, there was such a threat. The Supreme Court did not dispute this allegation, it only said that it was not sufficiently proved. The *Times* and the *Post* contended that most of the material was not new, that it had been printed before, and that because the information printed concerned events prior to 1968, there was no threat to the present national defense. The Court never commented on this line of argument. The Court did state that there might be grounds for criminal prosecution of the newspapers under the Federal espionage acts. However, these acts govern situations only during a period of declared war. What has been (and is) going on in Vietnam has never been officially declared a war. The Court did not comment as to how this would effect the application of the espionage acts.

The question to be answered is whether the "public's right to know" has been served by the printing of the Pentagon Papers. The Papers did little more than add a bit of farther documentation to allegations that had been made (and believed by many) for years. Much of the American people had already rejected continued involvement in the Vietnam war long before the Papers' printing. They had become paralyzed, unable to react to a war that they had been watching on television for years. Any shock value or vindication to be obtained by pointing another finger was offset by the realization that the American people could be easily lied to.

The only conclusive results of their publication seems to have been in increasing the threat of injunction and criminal prosecution to prevent from being published anything that the government does not want to see in print.

The decision of the Supreme Court was not quite the victory for the press that it has been made out to be. Three of the affirmative votes contained qualifications which, under different circumstances, might have led to an adverse decision. The Court itself has said that it is not the body to determine the limitations to be placed upon the liberties of the press. It said that it could not act against the newspapers because there were no Congressional guidelines to guide it. One of the most important events in relation to the cases is that since the decision, the composition of the court has changed—and it will continue to change. With a change in its make-up might also come a change in the Court's attitude toward freedom of the press.

Freedom of the press depends upon how that freedom is used. Indeed, the press (whether broadcast or journalistic) must be free to develop and function within its own concept of service. This carries with it the implication that the press must be accountable to the society in which it exists for meeting the public's needs and maintaining the society's rights. In the instance of the Pentagon Papers, although the freedom might not have been abused, the obligations of that freedom might have. The action of the publication within the context of the "public's right to know" without considering the public's "need to know" (for indeed, the public has long been in possession of most of the Pentagon Paper data) has placed the freedom of the press under a sword of Damocles. That sword is the possibility of farther court action in the form of criminal prosecution. The act of publication seemed to disregard the implications of the consequences.

section C # News: The Ambiguous Tautology

At its core, news is a metaphysical concept. Like a theologician discussing the nature of God, one knows news on faith alone. One is reminded in many discussions about news of those earlier arguments concerning how many angels can stand on the head of a pin. Journalism textbook authors often argue, "One has a nose for news," or "He is a born reporter." Certainly statements like these do not encourage the search for an "essential" definition of news. Rather, the whole notion of defining news resembles an attempt to find the core of an onion; one peels away the layers or arguments to a nonexistent center. One can say that, in the final analysis, any definition of news is going to be a tautology.[1]

---

[1] There is no need to belabor the point that news is what journalists say it is. For those who wish, an excellent discussion film is available from the Indiana University Audio-Visual Center, Bloomington, IN 47401, entitled *The Whole World Is Watching*. This film presents a discussion of what is news amidst scenes of the Chicago Democratic convention of 1968. Another film in the series worth considering is *Journalism: Mirror, Mirror on the World*. This film selects one event and then gives the coverage of the event by the press and television networks—an excellent demonstration of the effects of compression and objectivity upon the "reality" of an event. (Before ordering, check your state audio-visual center to see if they have the films. They are usually the most inexpensive source of 16 mm films.)

In this reader we have attempted to stress this concept by dwelling on the business organization and how it produces news. Therefore we say that news is the output of an organization labelled newspaper, television, or wire service. It is the product of men and bureaucracy; an interaction of individuals, rules, technological constraints, and obligations to a variety of interdependent mass society institutions.

In the following article, Frank Stanton addresses himself to a recurring issue of news and violence. First, consider what he defines as news and then what constitutes his test of newsworthiness. Also note what comprises the essential nature of the television medium in regard to its journalistic function. (Ask yourself why there must be compression and selectivity. Why must a news program be 30 minutes long? Why commercials? Why film clips rather than extensive interviews with participants? Why must television "involve" the viewer in the news as if the institution of journalism must meet dramaturgical standards?)

Many of the questions raised above can be answered economically. Television and print need large audiences to attract and maintain advertising. Like it or not, mass news interacts with a variety of constraining institutions. But there is also no grand conspiracy. The advertiser does not shape the news or directly meddle with editorial judgments.[2] Rather, the organization and the men that work each day at collecting the news perform their daily rituals. It is for this reason that we reprint a salient section from Edith Efron's *The News Twisters.*

It should be stressed that one could write a book about newspapers and ask the same question Miss Efron asks: Do "they" know what they are doing? If the question means do newsmen evaluate and analyze their labor over a period of time, then the answer, in many cases, is no. In fact, there is little self-analysis and appraisal by journalists of their performance. (Those "new" forms of appraisal such as press reviews and press councils will be discussed later.)

We include here the major portions of a study by Bailey and Lichty, following one story from its conception to its dissemination. The point is that almost everyone involved in the processing of the story shares similar values and norms. In a sense, it is right to assert that an organization "edits" a story. There is a mindless automation operating in the way a story is selected and in which it follows standard procedures as it passes through the organization. Editing decisions are few. News values and news judgments are embedded in the socialization process—learned on the job and reinforced through years of exposure to one's peers and supervisors.

This perhaps explains why outsiders criticizing the mass news media are perplexed by the rhethoric of objectivity. The journalist moves in a hall of mirrors, seeing himself and a small group of intimates. The real

---

[2] Two articles from the journalist's point of view on this related issue are Reuven Frank's "The Ugly Mirror," *Television Quarterly* (Winter 1969), and "An Anatomy of Television News," *Television Quarterly* (Winter 1970).

audience is not the public, but the editor and his peers. Studies have shown that editors are poor predictors of the public's tastes and evaluation of news items.[3] The following three articles should give some needed background so that we can return to these issues shortly.

3 An example of these studies is L. Erwin Atwood, "How Newsmen and Readers Perceive Each Others' Story Preferences," *Journalism Quarterly* (Summer 1970). The indifference of the journalist to the "effects" of the news upon the public is summed up in the following articles: Walter Cronkite, "What It's Like to Broadcast News," *Saturday Review* (December, 12, 1970), and Irving Fang's reply, "It *Is* Your Business Mr. Cronkite," *Saturday Review* (January 9, 1971).

chapter 10 Violence and the News

FRANK STANTON

From the International Press Institute offices in Zurich, Ernest Meyer said something last month that could well serve as the theme for this morning's panel discussion on violence. For 18 years, as Mr. Meyer put it, the IPI has been waging an unremitting campaign against direct government regulation of the press. Now the time has come, he said, to broaden the old Jeffersonian idea of press freedom being merely the absence of tight government control. In today's increasingly complex and troubled world, there are many equally insidious pressures that modern journalists must guard against—not the least of which is a much subtler, more indirect, though often no less effective, government restraint through intimidation. In no area of American journalism is this pressure more manifest than in the reporting of violence in the news—the subject on which I have been asked to speak this morning.

Today the three major areas of violence in the news—and without doubt three of the most important continuing news stories in my country

Frank Stanton, "Violence and the News," from *International Press Institute Speech*, Ottawa, Ontario, June 11, 1969. Reprinted by permission of the author.

and the world—are violence on the campus, violence in the city and violence on the battlefield. Though speaking from the experience of a single broadcaster from a single country, I think it is safe to say that nearly all of you here today must deal—in one degree or another—with the same three areas of violence.

Violence and how journalists should cover it is—I am sure we all agree—an extremely sensitive subject. The problem, of course, is that no one likes bad news, and the public tends to blame the press for whatever bad news it reports, if only because the press publicizes the news and helps to focus national interest and attention on it. This happened 35 years ago during our Great Depression, and it is happening today with the ghetto disturbances, the campus turmoil and even—to a certain degree —with the war in Vietnam.

The reaction is even stronger in the case of television, because of the necessary compression and selectivity of the medium and—on a broader level—because of its sheer impact and immediacy. In some ways, this is understandable. The face of violence is never pleasant to look upon, and its stark reality is frequently more disturbing in the peace and quiet of our living rooms than it is on the actual scene of the event itself. But the fact remains that we in our living rooms are no less involved in these conflicts because of our physical distance from them. And this involvement—however indirect—goes straight to the major value and function of modern journalism in a modern society. Decisions made in our local and national governments and culminating on the college campus, in the city or on some remote battlefield in Vietnam begin in our living room and end there. And because the final responsibility for those decisions rests with the people, they must have the facts—the bad as well as the good, the unpleasant as well as the pleasant.

In reporting this violence, journalism faces perhaps the greatest philosophical and intellectual challenge in its history. Philosophically, we must ask ourselves which elements of the news we will cover. Then intellectually, we must ask ourselves how we will cover them—how we can best convey the news to the public. The great problem is that amid the stresses, strains and very deep complexities of our modern world, today's news happening is often, in itself, of little importance. What matters is the meaning of what happens and its comprehension. What matters is some larger sense of proportion, perspective and balance. One of our CBS News directives—issued to our news personnel just before the civil disturbances that swept the United States in 1967—summed it up very well. "The best coverage," the directive read, "is not necessarily the one with the best pictures and the most dramatic action. By focusing on a handful of violent activities in a large area occupied by thousands of people, we may give the impression that that's the way it is all over.

We must always try to get this in context and explain the whole picture and just how widespread the violence is—or is not. Above all," the directive stressed, "we should try to get something of the root causes—and the effects—in a community." This holds true in reporting any situation of group violence—whether a student crash-in at Columbia University, a Black Panther ambush in Detroit or a battle in Vietnam's Central Highlands.

We also recognize, unlike some of our critics, that news is just that— what is new or unusual. We feel, therefore, that the test of newsworthiness must not be whether we or the government or anyone else approves of the event or agrees with the individual whom we are covering. The test must be whether the event or individual is legitimate news and whether it somehow reflects, symbolizes or has some important impact on, or meaning for, the total flow of events that we are trying to portray.

To help guarantee that the presence of newsmen, with cameras and microphones, does not contribute to the violent mood of a moment and thereby alter the basic character of the event being covered, our news personnel follow a strict set of guidelines. In the case of a campus or urban disorder, with few exceptions, they use unmarked cars. They are cautious with television lights, since lights draw crowds. They obey all police instructions instantly and without question—even in the occasional cases where those orders may seem unreasonably harsh. In general, they also avoid "live" coverage, to give us more time to establish that all-important perspective.

As part of that perspective, we follow up our news reports with other special broadcasts. This past month, for instance, *Face the Nation* carried an interview with the national secretary of the Students for a Democratic Society, the organization behind much of today's campus unrest. Nine days later, the first of three *CBS Reports* examined the larger problem of the generation gap and where it fits in. And last Sunday, New York Governor Nelson Rockefeller, appearing on *Face the Nation*, discussed his recent Latin American fact-finding trips for President Nixon, comparing student protest in Latin America with what we are encountering in my country today.

We strive for the same breadth and dimension in our special broadcasts on racial problems. To illustrate, last summer, the CBS Television Network broadcast a major, seven-part CBS News series called *Of Black America*. This series, in prime time, explored the evolution of the black American from his roots in Africa through the American Revolution and all the way down to the modern day.

In our reporting of the war, we strive for the same balance and perspective. Because no war is fought in a military vacuum, we have tried to place our battle scenes in a social, economic and political context.

This means showing the melancholy plight of the noncombatants, the efforts to repair the homes and broken lives of civilian victims, and more generally the long, slow, torturous attempts to achieve social progress, economic reform and human dignity. We have also tried to report both the support and dissent surrounding our public policy—not to persuade, but to stimulate thought and to provoke discussion. We may or may not all of us agree with some of the press coverage of the war in Vietnam. But it must be acknowledged that the American press, including the broadcast press, has played a major and meaningful role in forming or changing the American attitude toward the war. It is also worth recalling that President Kennedy once told Turner Catledge of the *New York Times* that if the *Times* had printed all it new of the Bay of Pigs invasion before the fact, it would, as President Kennedy phrased it, "have saved us from a colossal mistake."

In covering these three broad areas of violence—on the campus, in the city and on the battlefield—broadcast journalists have tried to exercise high standards of objectivity and taste. And, on the balance, I think we have succeeded, considering the unprecedented nature of the times and the events. After the urban violence that broke out in the United States two years ago, the National Advisory Commission on Civil Disorders—more commonly called the Kerner Commission—looked into broadcast coverage of those disorders, and concluded that our reporters "made a real effort to give a balanced, factual account" of the news.

While we welcome these words of praise, however, the fact that a government commission saw fit to investigate our news judgment points to a trend that is not nearly so welcome. That is a trend toward closer government scrutiny of our news operations and why we make the news decisions that we do. In years past, of course, there has always been a tendency to criticize or attack the press in almost direct proportion to the fault that we find with our times—probably because the press, both print and broadcast, is so much a mirror of our times. We saw it in my country in 1947 when the Commission on the Freedom of the Press—the Hutchins Commission—warned of the uncertainties of the new industrial and international age, then in the same breath criticized the press for its inability to probe those uncertainties.

More recently, the uncertainties have multiplied, and so too has the criticism of the press. In 1967, President Johnson created the Kerner Commission to look into America's growing racial troubles and the role the media play. Last year, he followed that up with the National Commission on the Causes and Prevention of Violence, and ordered it also to investigate how much, if at all, the media contributed to violence. Today, many of our critics feel that the times now demand some type of formal restrictions or guidelines either on the overall news media or at least on broadcast journalism—if only to insulate the public from what these critics consider to be the unwholesome and unhealthy quality of today's increasingly violent news. As presently discussed, these restrictions would take the form of a code, administered—either directly or indirectly—by the government through a Federal agency, through a group of civic-minded citizens or possibly through industry officials appointed by the government.

We at CBS categorically reject any such idea. If the agency were related to the government—no matter how distantly related—honest journalism simply could not long survive. Broadcast journalism would be particularly vulnerable, since the renewal of broadcast licenses, in the United States, is at the discretion of government officials every three years, and these officials would now be armed with a set of rules that, at the very least, would act as a Damocles sword. Inevitably, the licensee would tend to play it safe to avoid endangering his license—and his very livelihood. The result could be only an homogenized version of the news— bland, sanitary and utterly devoid of any social significance or purpose.

Even if some way were found to create an agency completely independent of the government—and I fail to see how this could ever be achieved —I would have the same fears. By its very nature, effective surveillance* would influence news judgments by the media. The effect of such influence—no less than of official censorship—would be to split responsibilities which are inherently indivisible. And the most fundamental fact of democratic life is that the press cannot share its responsibility for news judgment and still fulfill its basic role. In a democratic society, the great strength of the journalist is not that he is committed to particular policies or issues, but that he is not. He is a free agent, with an obligation to fact and truth that is rooted in centuries of tradition. And he, the public and, most importantly, the government whose job it is to protect our rights under the Constitution, must all guard against any threats to this freedom to report.

This is not to say that newspapers or broadcasters should be free of external influence and criticism. Again, the Hutchins Commission was quite correct when it said: "A free press is free of compulsions from whatever source . . . not from pressures, except in a moribund society empty of contending forces and beliefs." Today, the media—and especially broadcasting—are feeling healthy, outside pressures of an unprecedented variety and volume. More than 2000 publications cover some phase of television. The major daily newspapers, wire services, weekly news magazines and

* Surveillance is defined by Webster's New International Dictionary as "close supervision; now, usually, constant guard; close watch; as, a suspected person under police surveillance."

journals of opinion all regularly criticize broadcast programs and comment on the economics of broadcasting and other aspects of the industry. Radio and television journalism is regularly analyzed at some of the country's best academic institutions. The White House, the Congress, the Judiciary and the Federal Communications Commission all review our performance. So do private citizens' organizations. And so do individual viewers—many of whom take the time to sit down and write us their opinions.

We believe that broadcasting can only gain from more and better informed criticism of this free, open and public nature. And to encourage more of this criticism, CBS is now screening, for critical review by the media, both television news broadcasts and entertainment programs which are produced sufficiently in advance of air date to make this feasible. Viewers, we believe, will find this advance criticism far more useful than after-the-fact reviews. Such advance criticism should also encourage new standards of excellence and conscientiousness in broadcasting—and thus help preserve and encourage the pluralism that is the cornerstone of our democracy and society's best defense during periods of violence and uncertainty. As John Stuart Mill said many years ago: "If all mankind minus one, were of one opinion, and only one person were of the contrary opinion, mankind would be no more justified in silencing that one person, than he, if he had the power, would be justified in silencing mankind."

The public cherishes the same pluralism and freedom of expression. At a time, in fact, when broadcast journalists are under sharp attack from their critics, the latest Roper survey covering U.S. attitudes shows that among the public—the people, after all, who really matter—television's credibility as a news medium stands at an all-time high. The same study also indicates that television coverage of urban disorders and campus violence ranks far down the public's list of possible causes of increased violence. At the same time, a survey question on possible government involvement with television news broadcasts drew a strong anti-control vote. Seventy-six percent of the overall sampling said the government should have no control of television news. In the college-educated group, the vote was 92 percent in opposition.

What this nationwide sampling tells us is very important. It tells us that the public recognizes what many government officials and other critics either ignore or overlook—the fact that violence is part of our culture and our civilization, and that no matter how much we all abhor it, violence will more than likely always be with us. It tells us that the public also recognizes the inseparable bond between journalism and the highest purposes of our civilization and, therefore, journalism's responsibility to report and comment on violence—so long as it maintains the highest standards of fairness and óbjectivity. Far more fundamentally, it tells us that the public itself is concerned about government intrusions into the news.

And that, in the end, is what gives such urgency to the goals of the International Press Institute—and to these particular times in our world history.

chapter 11   # Do The
Networks
Know What
They Are Doing?

EDITH EFRON

To what degree are network newsmen aware of bias in their own newscasts? And is it deliberate? There is no single answer to this question—and above all there is no collective answer that applies to all individuals.

It is fairly apparent that awareness ranges from abysmal confusion to a high degree of understanding. There is unquestionably genuine confusion on this issue at all three networks. The evidence of such confusion takes several different forms.

One is sheer illiteracy on the epistemological issues involved in the nature of bias and in news coverage itself. The gibberish which emerged from the mouths of Walter Cronkite and former CBS news president Fred Friendly when they were seeking to analyze "objectivity" and "fairness" . . . illustrates this point painfully well.

Similarly, only a severe defect in understanding that value judgments underlie acts of selectivity could lead ABC's former news president James

Hagerty to say: "We're trying to be objective . . . we are reporters! We get interpretations from *other* people and present them. If anyone on this network is expressing his own opinion—well, if I catch him I won't permit it." And only a refusal to acknowledge the phenomenon of selectivity at all can explain the astonishing claim of CBS news president Richard Salant, published in *TV Guide* on April 11, 1964: "We believe in objective coverage. Our reporters do not cover stories from *their* point of view. They are presenting them from *nobody's* point of view."

The concept of news itself is a source of massive confusion at the networks, where—in a political crisis—management invariably pretends that "News," like a platonic archetype, has an immutable, independent existence and that neither human choices nor human evaluations nor human acts of selectivity or exclusion have anything to do with the phenomenon.

Thus NBC president Julian Goodman, in a speech to broadcasters made on June 23, 1970, said: "There are many viewers—and some public officials—who feel that television, if it were handled properly, could make bad news good, and who charge that, through some kind of ill will, television insists on making good news bad. *The fact is, of course, that any responsible television news organization does not make the news at all. It reports the news.*" (italics mine)

Mr. Goodman had not consulted with his star reporter, David Brinkley, who says: "News is what *I* say it is. It is something worth knowing by my standards."

Again: Mr. Goodman told the broadcasters, "television is not a political instrument or a social theory—it is [a] means of communication. . . ." He had not, apparently, attended the International Radio and Television Society luncheon on February 4, 1970, just a few months before, where his other star reporter, Chet Huntley, had defined news as "social and political criticism."

Another manifestation of confusion lies in insufficient education. A good many partisan ideas are being beamed over the airwaves by men who suppose that they are repeating scientifically established truths. Thus reporters announce—as if it is fact—that "poverty causes crime" and are, apparently, quite unaware that they are proselytizing for an unproved theory.

On August 23, 1969, a review appeared in a sophisticated New York magazine, *The New Yorker*, on two sociological books: *On Understanding Poverty*, edited by Daniel P. Moynihan and *On Fighting Poverty*, edited by James L. Sundquist. Both are anthologies—the products of a year-long sociology seminar sponsored by The American Academy of Arts and Sciences. Wrote the astonished reviewer chosen by *The New Yorker* for this assignment: "These two volumes . . . teach us that we are only beginning to find out how little we know about poverty. *In the first vol-*

ume, we learn that all our concepts of poverty are merely theories, and that none commands the assent of every sociologist." (Italics mine)

It is certain that it would come as an equal shock to many network reporters to discover that their overworked bromide, "Poverty causes crime," is a hypothesis, not a truth—and a dubious one at that, since a causal principle which doesn't operate in most cases isn't much of a causal principle. Similarly, the notion that "society is guilty" of people's crimes is a hypothesis, not a truth. It is challenged by every philosophical, theological, moral, psychological and legal school which advocates volition, free will and moral responsibility. But reporters spew it over the airwaves as though it were a test-tube fact.

The arch value of these two theories is *political.* If "poverty causes crime" and if "society is guilty" of a man's crime, then, of course, we must tax "society" and make it pay for his regeneration, etc., etc. All of which furthers the redistribution of wealth much favored by certain political groups.

Men who repeat such pop-sociological bromides as factual truths may well be extremely confused by a charge that the are injecting politically loaded opinion into the coverage of social problems. Their actual sin is not bias so much as it is that they are ill-educated and intellectually pretentious. They have not read the books they are pretending to have read. Some, indeed, are not even aware of the existence of these books. They belong to the group defined by George W. Ball as "the illiterate intellectuals." Men of this type are slanting their stories—but they literally do not know that they are doing so.

In addition to the confused and the ignorant, there are those who are quite simply party liners. Many of these are guilty of little more than the pathetic crime of being parrots—of rushing to cover stories the way they have seen others cover them, of rushing to interview certain people because others have interviewed them, of expressing certain opinions because others have expressed them.

There are enough of these second-hand brains at the networks to have caused CBS' Bill Leonard to list this for *TV Guide,* September 27, 1969, as one of his chief problems as a news executive: "Most reporting is lousy. It is lousy because people are lazy . . . because they approach things in rote fashion."

These are doubtless the kind of men referred to by Whitney Young when he said that "many leaders are followed by 7 Negroes and 70 screaming reporters." The first two or three men who build up a unknown character as "leader" and who give him nationwide significance may be quite clearheaded about what they are doing—but how many of the others in the screaming pack genuinely know what they are doing is unknown.

Indeed, it is ABC commentator Howard K. Smith's conviction that most of the party-line journalism at the networks is of this mindless, imitative sort—the incestuous parroting of an "in" group. In *TV Guide*, February 28, 1970, he denounces network "conformism." Liberal newsmen, he says, have a set of automatic reactions: "They react the way political cartoonists do—with oversimplification. Oversimplify. Be sure to please your fellows, because that's what's 'good.' They're conventional, they're conformists. They're pleasing Walter Lippman, they're pleasing the *Washington Post*, they're pleasing the editors of the *New York Times*, and they're pleasing one another."

And whom are these overlords pleasing? According to Theodore H. White, author of *The Making of the President, 1968*: "The moral heights of New York are held by journals like *The Village Voice* and *The New York Review of Books*. They are so pure, and shriek with such passion that, in fashionable New York, they are the pulpit-voice of The Church of Good Liberals." (*Newsweek*, September 8, 1969)

> The picture of ignorance, confusion and parroting is further complicated by the existence of men of varying degrees of genuine insight into their own and each other's bias. This insight covers a remarkable range of issues and one cannot arrive at a solid assessment of network awareness without knowing what they are.
>
> Here is a detailed survey of the kind of understanding newsmen have displayed in the past few years—*before* the indictment of network bias by Vice President Agnew.

Many understood that selectivity was the cause of bias.

On April 11, 1964, a group of prominent broadcast newsmen stated for publication in *TV Guide* that selectivity was the essence of their work; and that it was impossible to cover news or produce public affairs programming of any kind without injecting their point of view.[1]

It was in this context that David Brinkley, of NBC, said: "News is what *I* say it is. It's something worth knowing by my standards."

In addition:

John Secondari, of ABC, said: "It's absolutely impossible to write a broadcast or put together pictures without having a point of view."

Gerald Green, of NBC, said: "It's impossible not to have a point of view. Once you start selecting facts and choosing what and whom to put on the air, a point of view is implicit."

Don Hewitt, of CBS, said: "Of course . . . news documentaries do take a point of view . . . it has to be understood that personality has to come through."

---

[1] "Why Speech on Television Is Not Really Free," by Edith Efron.

And Quincy Howe, a former president of the Association of Radio-TV News Analysts, said: "All news presented on radio and TV editorializes. The newscaster editorializes in what he emphasizes and what he plays down, in what he omits and what he includes."

At this same time, many of the men on network staffs agreed that the point of view that prevailed could be defined as "moderate liberalism."

NBC's news chief at that period, William McAndrew, said: "The prevailing opinion of the network, I would say, is moderate. We have the political spectrum interpreted by moderates."

CBS' Don Hewitt said: "The networks are in the hands of groups which see the issues the same way—as moderate liberals."

Many were aware that the prevailing network bias was distorting American realities.

In 1968, after the nationwide protest over TV's alleged role in further-ing the race riots, several prominent network newsmen declared in *TV Guide*, July 20, 1968,[2] that network coverage was falsifying the picture of the nation:

Chet Huntley, of NBC, said: "Our attention has been turned to the cities. That's where the problems are. But it is distorted. It doesn't reflect the rest of the country. We're ignoring the rest of America."

NBC Producer Bob Rogers said: "The responsible man, the productive man, the man without a chip on his shoulder, is 'the forgotten man.' You hardly ever see him on TV . . . The imbalance in coverage is causing Americans to mistrust each other."

Howard K. Smith of ABC said: "TV news isn't telling people the way life is. We're giving the public a wholly negative picture on a medium so vivid that it damages morale with a bombardment of despair."

NBC Producer Lou Hazam said: "I know this [distortion] has hurt people. It has hurt and frightened *me*. I often wonder, myself, is *every-thing* I love dying?"

Many were aware that network reporters were using news stories as vehicles of personal expression.

In 1968, after the nationwide protest over network TV's reporting of the antiwar riot in Chicago at the Democratic convention, awareness grew among political reporters that they were interpreting political news through the selective filter of their own values. Many indeed went so far as to argue, after the election, that this was psychologically inevitable:

David Brinkley, speaking on NET (December 22, 1968), said: "If I were objective, or if you were objective, or if anyone was, we would have

[2] "The Program That Explored *Real* America," by Edith Efron.

to be put away somewhere in an institution because we'd be some sort of vegetable. Objectivity is impossible to a human being."

Frank Reynolds, of ABC, said: "I think your program has to reflect what your basic feelings are. I'll plead guilty to that."

Bill Moyers, one of ABC's commentators during the campaign period, said: "Of all the myths of journalism, objectivity is the greatest."

Many were aware that many Americans felt the networks were favoring the radicals.

In *TV Guide*, September 27, 1969, this recognition was voiced by men at all networks.[3]

CBS News Chief Bill Leonard said: "The right and the middle complain that we put on irresponsible people from the left."

ABC producer Steve Fleischman said: "People feel we've given too much play to the radicals."

NBC News President Reuven Frank said: "The general view of the public is that we have too many radicals in network news departments."

And NBC producer Shad Northshield avowed: "Bias is on everybody's mind. We've claimed we don't have it. And the viewers say: 'Yes, you do.' I was stunned by the public reaction to Chicago. We all were. I was stunned, astonished, *hurt*. It is the key thing that opened my eyes to the cleavage between newsmen and the majority."

Many felt there were legitimate grounds for the bias charges of the majority.

Again, in the same *TV Guide* article, newsmen conceded that network coverage had been improperly focused on the protesting minorities, to the exclusion of the interest, values and views of the majority groups in the nation.

CBS' Phil Lewis said: "We're beginning to realize we've ignored the majority. America doesn't end at the Hudson!"

NBC's Shad Northshield said: "In TV news departments we appear to know a lot about the black minority. It's the silent majority we must explore. We haven't done it. We didn't know it was *there!*"

CBS newsman Joseph Benti said: "We spend so much time on angry blacks, angry youth. But what about that vast forgotten army out there? How many hard-working law-abiding whites are mad as hell because *their* story isn't being told?"

CBS's Desmond Smith: "The left and SDS have been getting a great deal of play. Americans are getting to feel they're not getting the whole story."

[3] "The Silent Majority Comes Into Focus," by Edith Efron.

Some were aware that this bias was caused by uniform democratic-liberal thinking.

In the same *TV Guide* story, Fred Freed on NBC said:

> This generation of newsmen is a product of the New Deal. Those beliefs of the New Deal are the beliefs that news has grown on. This is true of the networks, of *Newsweek,* of *The New York Times,* of all media.
>
> Men of like mind are in the news. It is provincial.
>
> The blue and white collar people who are in revolt now do have cause for complaint against us. We've ignored their point of view. It's bad. It's bad to pretend that they don't exist.
>
> We did this because we tend to be upper-middle-class liberals. We think the poor are "better" than the middle class. We romanticize them. The best thing that happened to me was a month I spent working in the Detroit slums after the riots. I stopped romanticizing the poor.
>
> I've come to understand that it's really the same with all classes. You've got to sit down with the cop, with the little storekeeper, and get their views. They're human beings like everyone else. Their attitudes emerge logically from their interests and values. They should be covered that way.

And some men in management conceded that there were reporters who slanted their stories.

Again, in the same story, CBS's Bill Leonard declared that keeping bias out of reporters' stories was one of his most difficult problems as an executive of CBS News: "The worst problem of all is the reporter who doesn't ask the next question—the cheap, lousy reporter who will quote an attack but doesn't go to the other side because the answer might kill his story . . . and these producers who develop and edit a broadcast from the point of view of the way *they* want it to turn out—with their own prejudices showing. That happens quite often . . . if we could get rid of those people, we'd be a lot closer to our goal of objectivity."

It was two months after these statements were made that Vice President Agnew made his speech in Des Moines charging network bias.

What insights did reporters have *after* the Agnew indictment? Very few.

One week after Mr. Agnew's Des Moines speech, on November 20, 1969, a letter appeared in *The New York Times* from David Jayne. It said:

> As a reporter and later a producer for one of the three networks for more than eight years now, I believe Vice President Agnew's comments on television news are in the main accurate, fair and long-overdue.
>
> Television news is controlled by a few powerful men who do think alike on most major issues. This control is not manifested, as Mr. Agnew may have implied, in a conspiratorial concerted attempt to present or distort the news according to these men's bias.
>
> But the end product, what's seen and heard on the air, especially in live

programming, too often results from these biases. The reason, I suggest, is not conscious prejudice, but the common implicit assumptions influencing the major commentators and producers. As the Vice President said, they do live in the provincial and parochial confines of Washington and New York City. They do read the same newspapers, bound on one flank by the *Times* and on the other by the *Washington Post*, with perhaps some turning to *Newsweek* and the *New Republic*. Their constant interaction does reinforce their common viewpoint.

There is an establishment point of view shared by the television news elite.

Several days later on CBS (November 25, 1969), Howard K. Smith of ABC, while expressing concern over the appearance of intimidation, said:

> . . . let us admit what we knew before Mr. Agnew said it: there is a problem. The tradition, deeply ingrained, of American journalism is negative. We are attracted mostly to what goes wrong in a nation where we must be doing something that is right. The emigration figures of people trying to get out of this country are very few. The immigration figures of people trying to get in are high. They must know something we are not adequately reporting.
>
> I am in no degree mystified that the public is irritated by daily reports of little but trouble, nor that politicians may exploit that irritation. I know of no specific solution that can be quickly stated—just exercising self-discipline, try harder to be fair . . .

On January 10, 1970, Terry H. Lee, TV Division Head of Storer Broadcasting, which owns CBS outlets in Detroit, Cleveland and Atlanta, as well as ABC affiliate in Milwaukee and NBC affiliate in Toledo, charged that editorial opinion was infiltrating the network newscasts that the networks were offering to the public. This station-group threatened to flash a disclaimer on the screen ("The views being expressed here are not necessarily those of the management of this station.") when network newsmen voiced what these stations felt to be editorial opinion in newscasts.

There may have been other such statements. If so, I have been unable to find them despite intensive research.

To the best of my knowledge, nothing else was publicly conceded in a major forum of opinion by anyone associated with the networks until February 28, 1970—five months after the Agnew speech. On that date, an article appeared in *TV Guide* based entirely on an interview with ABC commentator Howard K. Smith.[4] It is the most extensive analysis of network bias ever made by a network newsman. Here is a summary of Mr. Smith's major points:

Network bias, said Mr. Smith, is massive. The bias, he said, begins with the political composition of the staff, which is virtually all liberal.

4 "There *Is* a Network News Bias," by Edith Efron.

Liberals, by definition, have "a strong leftward bias": "Our tradition since FDR, has been leftward."

According to Mr. Smith, a series of positive and negative patterns of selectivity are determining much of the coverage. Here are the illustrations he cited of this negative selectivity:

"*Race:* During the Johnson Administration, six million people were raised above the poverty level . . . And there is a substantial and successful Negro middle class. But the newsmen are not interested in the Negro who succeeds—they're interested in the one who fails and makes a loud noise. They have ignored the developments in the South. The South has an increasing number of integrated schools. A large part of the South has *accepted* integration. We've had a President's Cabinet with a Negro in it, a Supreme Court with a Negro on it—but more important, we have 500 Negroes elected to local offices in the deep South! This is a tremendous achievement. But that achievement isn't what we see on the screen.

"*Conservatives:* If Agnew says something, it's bad, regardless of what he says. If Ronald Reagan says something, it's bad, regardless of what he says. Well, I'm unwilling to condemn an idea because a particular man said it. Most of my colleagues do just that.

"*The Middle Class:* Newsmen are *proud* of the fact that the middle class is antagonistic to them. They're proud of being out of contact with the middle class. Joseph Kraft did a column in which he said: Let's face it, we reporters have very little to do with middle America. They're not our kind of people . . . Well, I resent that. I'm *from* middle America!

"*The Vietnam War:* The networks have never given a complete picture of the war. For example: that terrible siege of Khe Sanh went on for five weeks before newsmen revealed that the South Vietnamese were fighting at our sides, and that they had higher casualties. And the Viet Cong's casualties were 100 times ours. But we never told *that.* We just showed pictures day after day of Americans getting the hell kicked out of them. That was enough to break America apart. That's also what it did.

"*The Presidency:* The negative attitude which destroyed Lyndon Johnson is now waiting to be applied to Richard Nixon. Johnson was actually politically assassinated. And some are trying to assassinate Nixon politically. They hate Richard Nixon irrationally."

Here are illustrations Mr. Smith cited of positive selectivity:

"*Russia:* Some have gone overboard in a wish to believe that our opponent has exclusively peaceful aims, and that there is no need for armaments and national security. The danger of Russian aggression is unreal to many of them, although some have begun to rethink since the invasion of Czechoslovakia. But there is a kind of basic bias in the left-wing soul that gives the Russians the benefit of the doubt.

"*Ho Chi Minh:* Many have described Ho Chi Minh as a nationalist leader comparable to George Washington. But his advent to power in Hanoi, in 1954, was marked by the murder of 50,000 of his people. His consistent method was terror. He was not his country's George Washington—he was more his country's Hitler or Stalin . . . I heard an eminent TV commentator say: 'It's an awful thing when you can trust Ho Chi Minh more than you can trust your President.' At the time he said that, Ho Chi Minh was lying! He was presiding over atrocities! And yet an American TV commentator could say that!

"The Viet Cong: The Viet Cong massacred 3000 Vietnamese at Hue alone—a massacre that dwarfs all allegations about My Lai. This was never reported on.

"Doves: Mr. Fulbright maneuvered the Gulf of Tonkin Resolution through—with a clause stating that Congress may revoke it. Ever since, he's been saying: 'This is a terribly immoral thing.' I asked him: 'If it's that bad, aren't *you* morally obligated to revoke it?' He runs away! And yet Mr. Fulbright—who incidentally has voted against *every* civil-rights act—is not criticized for his want of character. He is beloved by reporters, by everyone of my group, which is left-of-center. It's one of the mysteries of my time!

"Black Militants: A few Negroes—scavengers on the edge of society—have discovered they're riding a good thing with violence and talk of violence. They can get on TV and become nationally famous.

"The New Left: The New Left challenges America. They're rewriting the history of the Cold War. Some carry around the Viet Cong flag. Some shout for Mao—people who'd be assassinated in China! They've become *irrational!* But they're not portrayed as irrational. Reporters describe them as 'our children.' Well, they're not *my* children. *My* children don't throw bags of excrement at policemen . . . If right-wing students had done what left-wing students have done, everyone, including the reporters, would have called in the police and beaten their heads in. But we have a left-wing bias now, that has 30 years of momentum behind it."

The "emphasis" in network coverage, said Mr. Smith, is "anti-American." It tends to omit the good about America and focus on the *bad.* And it is also biased in *favor* of attackers-of-America by tending to *omit* the bad about them and focusing on the good. This, Mr. Smith finally said, is a reflection of the New Left line. "The New Left," he concluded, "has acquired a grave power over the liberal mind."

This is the interview to which I referred in Chapter V. It is generally confirmed by the findings of this study. It provoked an avalanche of mail from American citizens thanking Mr. Smith for having the "courage" to tell the truth.

After the Agnew speech, there is only one more concession from a network newsman that I am able to find, and it was made shortly after Mr. Smith's analysis.

On March 4, 1970, Walter Cronkite of CBS, interviewed on WTOP-TV in Washington, D.C., conceded what he had never conceded before: that the networks had been wrong in Chicago, two years earlier. Reported *Variety:*

> Cronkite said that the one area of criticism of network coverage of the 1968 Chicago Democratic Convention that he thinks is valid was the fact that "we hadn't shown provocation in the streets of Chicago."

In 1968 this would have been major news. By 1970 it was minutiae.

After the Vice President's indictment of network bias, only Howard K. Smith, of all the major figures on the air, had the moral capacity to concede the validity of the Vice President's general criticisms—criticisms known to be true by many of his colleagues because they had made these criticisms themselves.

For this, Clarence Streit, editor of *Freedom & Union,* hailed him in an extraordinary editorial entitled "Personal Tribute to a Brave Man" (May 1970). Mr. Streit, a former *New York Times* correspondent, writes: "Only a veteran newsman can appreciate fully the courage this took . . . I would rate it very high and rare . . . When the emotions of one's clan have reached the sizzling point, non-conformity takes special courage. Howard Smith's on this still echoing occasion was the more outstanding because it was so lonely . . ." (Copyright, *Freedom & Union,* 1970.)

Why did it take such "courage" for Howard Smith in a free country with the majority of the people, as well as the government, on his side to speak his mind? And why was he alone? Is Mr. Smith really the only man in the networks who perceived a bias so gross it was evident to 57% of the country? And if he is not—as he is not—why are the others silent?

The answer, as Mr. Streit names it, is that "clan" emotions have reached a "sizzling" point. It is a delicate way to describe psychological intimidation.

Psychological intimidation by blindly conformist thinkers is nothing but authoritarianism. Authoritarianism in the "liberal intellectual" community has become fierce in recent years—and the headquarters of ferocity is the communications world.

In *The Making of the President, 1968,* Theodore White describes "a new avant-garde" which "dominates the heights of national communication" and which "has come to despise its own country and its traditions." In a letter to Stewart Alsop, which Alsop reports on in *Newsweek* on September 8, 1969, Mr. White expands upon this thesis. He says: "In the

new intolerance, the United States government is the master of all evil,
the chief world agent of repression; the 'establishment' is as corrupt as the
Romanov dynasties; and the spokesmen of the new intolerance are in-
fected with a morality so stark that any deviation from their morality is
heresy, any difference of opinion villainy."

Mr. Alsop quoted this and said: "Mr. White's punishment was swift
and merciless—his book which received every enthusiastic reviews in
other cities was savagely attacked by almost every New York reviewer. . . .
White, a passionate and life-long liberal, was described as 'anti-peace,'
'anti-intellectual,' 'against students,' and 'against blacks'—a choice collection of demonstrable untruths."

We have in the past few years seen a series of other "swift and merciless
punishments" of the same kind. Such men as Dean Rusk, Walt Whitman
Rostow, Sidney Hook, S. I. Hayakawa, et al., have been virtually excom-
municated from the "liberal intellectual" world for supporting the war
and condemning violent radicals. And reports are now coming from the
universities of the "reign of terror" by leftists on the faculty against those
who disagree with them. John Roche, Brandeis professor of history and
former National ADA chairman, writing in *The New York Times
Magazine* on October 18, 1970, compares liberal academics these days to
"Holy Rollers" and to an "Anabaptist Sect"; he reports on "intimidation"
in the intellectual community; and he compares faculty meetings to
"lynch mobs."

This is why certain men are silent in the networks. They have seen
what happens to liberals who deviate significantly from the entrenched
line. They heard the invective that hit Chet Huntley and Howard K.
Smith for supporting the war in Vietnam. They saw the professional
punishment meted out. According to *New York Times* TV critic Jack
Gould, "Mr. Smith was practically in TV's coventry for his commentary
. . ." (March 10, 1970). They saw both men repudiated by colleagues who
had been close friends for 20 years. And when Howard Smith refused to
genuflect before pathological black extremists, they heard the newsman
who had been foremost in TV's battle for civil rights described by a
prominent CBS Murrow-legatee as a "Southerner who had reverted to
type." Finally, after his bias analysis had been published, they saw Mr.
Smith subjected to abuse by ABC and CBS men who sneered at him in
print in *Newsweek,* March 9, 1970, as "Howard K. Agnew," who attacked
him for "using a meat ax, Agnew style," for being on the side of the "far
right," etc.

They also saw Mr. Smith's fellow commentator, Frank Reynolds, who
was responsible for the most virulent personal attacks on candidate Nixon
that were aired during the campaign period, win an Emmy . . .

This meting out of liberal "justice" could have been predicted. Mr.

Smith, who, indeed, was filled with dread before the publication of his bias analysis, in anticipation of attack by his colleagues, predicted his own destiny to me. Any newsman at the networks who thinks as Mr. Smith does can predict it as easily. Those who know that this authoritarian strain has infiltrated into the networks are silent in order not to suffer such attacks.

And here—although there may be other types of reactions at the networks—I can stop using types of awareness because the variety given is sufficient.

If one reviews all these reactions—gibberish, confusion, inadequate education, varied levels of understanding to full comprehension (whether publicly expressed or not)—one will see that no single generalization will do to describe the state of awareness of the networks on the subject of their biased newscasts. Some men do know what is happening in network news coverage and approve of it. Some know and disapprove of it. Some don't know. Some "sort of" know. Some don't want to know. Some are afraid to know.

It is perfectly clear, however, that whatever the diversity of understanding, whatever the internal conflicts and fears, whatever the genuine confusion, one other element exists: active dishonesty.

On the top official level of the networks, the failure in honesty is gross —particularly in response to Vice President Agnew's bias charges.

At that time the heads of the three networks flatly denied the validity of these charges in statements redolent with professional exaltation and righteous indignation. And the single most striking thing about these statements is that all three of the networks engaged in blatant evasion of the bias admissions made by a group of their most prominent men *just two months before.*

If genuine confusion were their only state, and if honesty were their goal, every single network president and network news president would have conceded publicly that virtually all of Mr. Agnew's charges had already been proffered, in principle or concretely, by some of their own most trusted staff; that, as NBC's Shad Northshield had put it: "Bias is on everybody's mind"; and that the networks were struggling with these very issues behind the scenes.

But not one of the network officials said anything of the sort. They issued flat and pompous assertions of their impeccable fairness; they attacked Mr. Agnew as "repressive" and as embodying a "McCarthyist" trend: They pretended that their own reporters had not admitted what they had admitted in a publication read by 30,000,000 people.

• • •

The ultimate and most unpleasant question that one must answer is this:

Despite even extreme confusion over an admittedly complex issue, can *any* network newsman be speaking candidly when he claims to be unaware of liberal bias at the networks?

I think not.

The reason for which I say this is primitively simple: There isn't a man on the network staffs who is not aware that the overwhelming majority, if not 100%, of the network reporters are liberals. And it is precisely with the *staff*—the individuals whose judgments will culminate in news stories—that the selective processes start. *The liberal composition of network staffs renders it impossible for network news departments to be anything but liberal news agencies—with the full regalia of characteristic liberal biases.*

This is so painfully obvious a fact—that it is obvious to most network newsmen, for all their talk of "professionalism."

It is so painfully obvious a fact that when Vice President Agnew charged network newsmen with belonging to a "provincial" ideological world quite alien to the rest of America and with talking only to each other, the network response verged on idiocy.

On CBS' "60 Minutes" a remarkable performance was delivered by Walter Cronkite in which he indignantly listed the American birthplaces of the major newsmen; and network men granted interviews to *Time* and *Newsweek* in which they indignantly explained that they had not spoken to each other for months or years. But the newsmen had not been charged with having been born in Lodz or Omsk or with being in constant telephonic communication. They had been charged with *thinking* alike.

The magnitude of this evasion reveals the utter vulnerability of the networks on this issue. They could not even afford to admit that they *understood* the charge.

Jeffrey Hart in *National Review* (December 30, 1969) commented at the time: ". . . none of the media spokesmen hazarded anything resembling rebuttal. None stepped forward to say something like: 'Why, the Vice President is simply mistaken; we do present various points of view; although Mr. Brinkley, for example, is a liberal Democrat, Mr. Vanocur is an admirer of Governor Reagan; and if admittedly Charles Collingwood is pretty liberal, we also have Marvin Kalb who adores Nixon. Our staff is not only able, it is various.' But, of course, no such reply was possible."

It was not possible.[5] And it is not irrelevant that, in all three networks,

_____

[5] Network defenders did point out that ABC's Howard K. Smith and NBC's Chet Huntley supported the war, in contrast to their colleagues. This "defense" subsided rapidly, however, when this proved to be the sole exception anyone could dredge

a series of smokescreen-myths exist, in institutionalized form, on this very subject. No one who has ever dealt with network newsmen has failed to encounter this implacable mythology. And to understand the ultimate weapon of the news departments on the bias issue—ironclad evasion—one must know these myths.

There are three of these myths—all interlocking. Together they constitute the means by which a group of liberals can engage in liberal selective and exclusionary practices, and pretend to others and to themselves that this is not what is happening.

The first is *"The Myth of the Nonexistent Liberal."*

This myth is recited at the slightest provocation in an attempt to conceal the all-liberal composition of network staffs. It consists of saying, with a straight face, that the speaker does not know what a liberal is, does not know how to identify a liberal, and does not know whether he himself is a liberal. (The speakers, however, have no comparable difficulty in identifying liberals or conservatives on the air.)

Thus, without cracking a smile, ABC News Vice President Elmer Lower told his audience at the Columbia School of Law how he had no idea whatever of the political composition of his own staff. He said: "We don't buy the argument that most of the people who work for us are necessarily liberal. . . . While a man may take the liberal side on one issue, he may take a more conservative side on another issue."

Similarly, Chet Huntley, in his farewell article in *TV Guide*, August 1, 1970, said: "I do not know whether I am a liberal or a conservative."

Similarly, Wally Westfeldt, producer of the Huntley-Brinkley show, denied to *Newsweek*, right after the Agnew speech, that network newsmen were "liberals" while simultaneously expressing uncertainty about what a "liberal" was. He told *Newsweek* on November 24, 1969: "If being a liberal means that I am trying to find where society has gone wrong and show where it has gone wrong, and find where it is functioning, and show where it is functioning, then, yes, I'm a liberal."

Similarly, Walter Cronkite of CBS, according to *Variety*, November 4, 1970, revealed perplexity over the nature of liberalism. Although he conceded that he was a "true liberal," he defined this position as having no content at all: A liberal, said Mr. Cronkite, was one who "is not bound by doctrines or committed to a point of view in advance."

Similarly, on January 16, 1970, Eric Sevareid held forth in remarkable confusion over the meaning of liberalism with *TV Guide* reporter Neil Hickey. The exchange illustrates the evasive mechanism so brilliantly I reproduce it here:

up to the rule of network conformity on major issues. As the arch-exception to the rule, it had been repeatedly covered as "news" by the press.

HICKEY: There is a conviction around the country that newsmen in general both in TV and in print tend to be liberal and therefore are more friendly to the notion of dissent and change.

SEVAREID: Yes, Agnew feels that obviously; Frank Shakespeare has made whole speeches about it. I'm not quite so persuaded . . .

HICKEY: But whether we like it or not, most TV newsmen tend to be liberal, don't they?

SEVAREID: I don't know. I've never seen a head count of this kind [in the country]. How do you divide up these ideologies? . . .

HICKEY: It's the network people that Agnew and Nixon are complaining about. Isn't it an observable fact that most of them are liberal?

SEVAREID: Well, you're using that word carelessly, it seems to me. I don't know what that means, the word liberal, except a kind of open-mindedness, a basic humanitarian view of life and concern for people. It does not mean a whole set of positions about these bills in Congress or a dogmatic view in which you lump all this kind of action. That isn't what it is to me . . .

HICKEY: Isn't there, though, a kind of unspoken unanimity among what Agnew thinks of as the Eastern Establishment intellectual journalists that the Yippies and the hippies and the protesters are expressing something of real value in their dissent, that they're closer to the truth than some others?

SEVAREID: Oh, I'm not entirely persuaded of this. You're trying very hard to get me to say, yes, this whole thing is overly balanced with people of a particular political persuasion. But I don't know, I have great doubts about this . . .

HICKEY: But that's what a lot of people say; they think they detect a large portion of bias.

SEVAREID: A lot of people say a lot of things . . .

HICKEY: But intellectuals, wherever you find them, do tend to be liberal.

SEVAREID: Well, again, I don't know what you mean by this. They tend to be humanitarian in basic instincts and are concerned for oppressed people. They don't like injustices. Now why is that to be a liberal? And is a conservative the other way? I don't know . . .

Just a few weeks before on November 21, 1969, *Time* Magazine had said this of Mr. Sevareid: "Thoughtful, deliberate Eric Sevareid probably comes closest to the liberal intellectualism that is anathema to Agnew."

And three days later, *Newsweek* had published an off-the-record interview with an unidentified CBS newsman. Wrote *Newsweek:* "Like others who invoked the shade of Joseph McCarthy, a veteran CBS Washington commentator admitted deep alarm. 'My feeling,' he said, 'is that the White House is out to get all of us, all the liberals in the media. They've taken on television first because we are the most easily intimidated and because the right wing hates us most. We're in for some dangerous times.'"

CBS has only one "commentator" and he is stationed in Washington. His name is Eric Sevareid. Off the record Mr. Sevareid had no difficulty in establishing he is a liberal.

This ritual denial of one's liberalism is not an accident. It is seen as a necessity by network newsmen who are well aware that to state otherwise leaves the networks open to a charge that they are liberal agencies—a charge which is equivalent to saying: Only liberal selective processes are operating.

The second and supportive myth is: *"The Myth of the Nonpartisan Middle."*

The purpose of this myth is to deny the existence and identity of liberal opinion when it is actually on the air. It does so by a primitive means:

The networks *rename* liberal opinion. It is called "middle" opinion or "center" opinion or "moderate" opinion.

Thus, former NBC news chief William McAndrew said (*TV Guide,* April 11, 1964): "The prevailing opinion of this network, I'd say, is moderate. We have the political spectrum interpreted by moderates."

Thus, Mr. McAndrew's then-assistant Julian Goodman, who is today president of NBC, says to his audience of broadcasters on June 23, 1970, ". . . television operates at the *center* of American life. As a result, it is always under pressure from the left and right." (Italics mine)

Thus, NBC's stellar newsman, John Chancellor, was quoted in *Broadcasting* Magazine, November 16, 1970, as declaring that most newsmen "are members of the *extreme center."* (italics mine)

The implication is thus smuggled in that by giving their position a nonideological label, it ceases to be a political position—that being in the "middle" of left and right is equivalent to being *nonpartisan.*

The networks have been so successful in gaining the acceptance of this spurious equation that it is now widely accepted by the nonreflective.

The equation of "middle" opinion with "nonpartisan" opinion is, of course, an absurdity.

• • •

chapter 12   Rough
Justice
on a
Saigon Street

GEORGE A. BAILEY
and
LAWRENCE W. LICHTY

For American television news viewers in January 1968 the Vietnam war
seemed concentrated in the area just south of the DMZ. Anchormen reported the fighting with maps pinpointing the areas of heaviest action.
Military officers and correspondents frequently predicted an attack in
force at Khe Sanh during the coming Tet holiday. In an interview with
NBC's Howard Tuckner broadcast on January 22, General Westmoreland
predicted a major communist offensive in the area just south of the DMZ
and said that a spectacular victory there might be a political and psychological victory for the North Vietnamese.

Viewers' attention was also directed to other areas of Asia. In early
January American troops crossed into Cambodia "in the interest of
protecting the command." Welles Hangen in a film report from Laos on
NBC-TV said that Washington would not admit it but that too was an
American war.

On Tuesday, January 23, the evening news programs gave a number of reports on the capture of the *U.S.S. Pueblo*. On ABC-TV, John Scali said that "hawks and doves alike" agreed that the *Pueblo* capture was linked with the war in Vietnam. Two days later President Johnson called up the reserves and the American fleet showed force in the Sea of Japan.

The Viet Cong had announced a lunar New Year or Tet truce. But on January 29 and for the next few days the VC and NVA attacked nearly every important South Vietnamese town and held some for days. There was heavy fighting for several weeks in Saigon and Hue.

First film reports of the attack, which came a day early at Danang may be because of a mistake by VC and NVA troops in that area, were seen on the *CBS Evening News* January 30. By satellite Jeff Gralnick and George Syvertsen showed the aftermath of sapper attacks and the beginning of ground fighting around the city.

On Wednesday, January 31, the *Huntley-Brinkley Report* switched via satellite to Jack Perkins live in Tokyo. Perkins announced that he would show unedited film of fighting in and around the U.S. Embassy. The film had just been developed and Perkins narrated the story partly from information he was receiving at that time talking by telephone with Executive Producer Robert Northshield in New York. In other reports the networks covered the war in the cities along with reaction at home.

On Thursday, February 1, David Brinkley introduced John Chancellor who narrated seven still photographs from the wire service. Part of his narration follows:

> There was awful savagery. Here the Viet Cong killed a South Vietnamese colonel and murdered his wife and six children. And this South Vietnamese officer came home during a lull in the fighting to find the bodies of his murdered children. There was awful retribution. Here the infamous chief of the South Vietnamese National Police, General Loan, executed a captured Viet Cong officer. Rough justice on a Saigon street as the charmed life of the city of Saigon comes to a bloody end.

(The last picture was the now-famous photograph by Eddie Adams of the Associated Press. That picture won many awards including the Pulitzer Prize for Spot News Photography.)

Broadcasting those stills, the Huntley-Brinkley newsmen in New York did not yet know that an NBC film crew in Saigon had color motion pictures of the Loan execution and those pictures could be available for the next day's program. That next day, February 2, 1968, would be the most sensational day of broadcast coverage in that sensational week of the Tet Offensive, and to many observers the turning point in American opinion and policy toward the Vietnam war.

REPORTING THE LOAN STORY

By Thursday morning, Saigon time, the fighting was fierce all over the city. Particularly hard hit was Cholon, the Chinese quarter of Saigon where the Viet Cong had set up a headquarters in the Buddhist An Quang Pagoda. An NBC news crew and AP photographer Eddie Adams decided to share a car into Cholon. (The AP and NBC bureaus were adjacent on the fourth floor of the Eden building.)

The NBC correspondent was Howard Tuckner, the cameramen were two Vietnamese brothers, Vo Huynh and Vo Suu, and the sound man was Le Phuc Dinh. Huynh took an Arriflex to shoot silent film. Suu carried an Auricon sound-on-film camera.

The Tuckner crew and Adams were standing in a street near the Pagoda before noon. At the far end of the block they saw several South Vietnamese Marines with a prisoner in civilian clothes. The Marines walked up toward the newsmen to present the prisoner to Brigadier General Nguyen Ngoc Loan who had taken charge of the Pagoda action. The cameramen began filming, one Vo brother on each side of the street. Huynh shot a closeup of a pistol being carried by an ARVN Marine which had been taken from the prisoner who appeared to have been beaten. Tuckner later described what happened:

> He [the captive] was not scared; he was proud. I will never forget that look when he walked up the street. General Loan took one look at him and knew he was going to get no information out of him. Loan had been through this with many prisoners. There was not one word. Loan did not try to talk to him nor to scare him. He did not wave his gun at his face or his head. He did not put the gun to his temple. He just blew his brains out.

During that time Tuckner kept whispering into Suu's ear, "Keep rolling, keep rolling." Eddie Adams was snapping many photographs. Later Adams wrote that as Loan's hand came up so did his camera and he just snapped by instinct. The prisoner dropped to the street with blood spurting out of his head. An ARVN Marine placed a small red Viet Cong propaganda leaflet over the corpse's face. Tuckner and Adams were the only Westerners in sight. Tuckner feared that their film would be confiscated or worse. He signaled Suu to quickly change film magazines and hide the exposed footage. Tuckner stood silent as Loan walked up to him and said:

> Many Americans have been killed these last few days and many of my best Vietnamese friends. Now do you understand? Buddha will understand.

The NBC crew walked away and continued shooting scenes around the Pagoda. The corpse was lifted off the pavement and thrown on a flatbed truck. The South Vietnamese forces cleared the Pagoda of Viet Cong and their hostages as the Tuckner crew filmed the action. Later on Tuckner took time to write a "stand-upper" for the execution story, and his crew filmed him as he read the stand-up summary to the camera. Tuckner's summary was written to be shown after the execution film. In that stand-upper he related what Loan had said.

In the afternoon, Thursday February 1, Tuckner and the crew returned to NBC's Saigon bureau. Ron Steinman, the bureau chief, who had himself just returned from a briefing given for newsmen—escorted in a special armed convoy—by Ambassador Bunker, debriefed each crew member individually. Vo Suu was sure that he had recorded the shooting on the film, Tuckner was not convinced. Steinman also talked with Eddie Adams. Now it seemed that the film report would best end with the execution and the "stand-upper" would be anticlimactic. Tuckner wrote a simple substitute narration—with several variations to provide for the possibility that not all the film was good. This narration was recorded on audio tape at the bureau. In this script the story of the pagoda fighting is played first, before the execution, a reordering of actual events. Cameraman Suu wrote out captions for the film describing the material shot by shot and various technical matters for developing and editing. Meanwhile in the next office under the direction of Horst Faas, AP developed, printed, and transmitted the Adams photo to New York. At 8:16 A.M. Thursday morning New York time it was sent out to newspapers around the country—about 11 hours after the shooting. The NBC film was still in Saigon, undeveloped.

During this period of the war film was ordinarily sent by plane to New York for developing and editing but alternatively could be received in San Francisco, Los Angeles or less frequently Seattle or Chicago for editing and subsequent transmission via land lines if this would make a deadline for one of the evening or morning network programs. For faster transmission, the film could be sent to Tokyo, developed and edited there, and sent via Pacific satellite to New York for broadcast live or video taped. Each network had an arrangement with a Japanese broadcasting company to use Tokyo studios to originate the live and film transmissions.

Thursday the Tan Son Nhut airport was closed to commercial planes. The next flight out, a medevac taking wounded men to Japan or the U.S., would be Friday. During Tet, the military provided special cars or jeeps to carry newsfilm to the airport. NBC newsmen had prepared six film stories for shipment. The undeveloped film and audio tape was in cans with scripts and additional instructions. The material was placed in the standard red burlap bags marked "NBC" in big white and black letters. By one o'clock Friday afternoon in Saigon—about 28 hours after the shooting—the Loan film was still at the bureau.

Cable connections between Saigon and Tokyo were always poor. During Tet they were worse. NBC usually had fairly good telex connections between Saigon and New York. Steinman sent a telex message to New York advising the availability of the six film stories. New York would relay the information to Tokyo. Steinman did not want to overemphasize the shock nature of the film convinced that if it was as Suu insisted the impact would be obvious. Further, he feared that the telex might be monitored and there was still a chance that the film might be confiscated. The following is part of his telex to NBC New York sent at 0537 GMT—1:37 P.M. Friday afternoon in Saigon; 12:37 A.M. Friday morning in New York:

THE FOLLOWING IS THE SHIPPING ADVISORY. FILM HAS NOT YET BEEN SHIPPED. WHEN SHIPPED WE WILL CONFIRM FASTEST AND BEST WAY POSSIBLE. HOPEFULLY THE TELEX WILL STILL BE WORKING. SHIPPED IN THREE SEPARATE BAGS ARE FILM NUMBERS 456, 457, 458, 459, 460, AND 461.
FILM NUMBER 456 IS TUCKNERS PAGODA FIGHTING. GOVERNMENT TROOPS WENT INTO THE AN QUANG PAGODA, SEAT OF BUDDHIST MILITANCE AND TRIED TO CLEAN OUT THE VIET CONG WHO HAD TAKEN IT OVER. THIS STORY IS COMPETITIVE. CBS AND ABC WERE THERE BUT WE ARE THE ONLY ONES WHO HAVE FILM ON THE EXECUTION. TUCKNER HAS WRITTEN PRODUCTION NOTES AND SCRIPT TO GO WITH SUU AND HUYNHS 720 SOF 360 SIL NORMAL. DINH WAS SOUNDMAN. NARRATION ON FULL COAT AND AUDIO TAPE. ONE WILDTAPE. CLOSER ON FILMROLL ONE AND TWO BUT READ TUCKNERS DETAILED NOTE FOR EXACT CLOSER WE PREFER AND THINK SHOULD BE USED. THIS IS IMPORTANT BECAUSE WE ARE DEALING WITH A DELICATE PROBLEM. . . . VIETCONG OPEN UP ON MARINES. THEN THE LOAN SEGMENT. THIS IS ON SUUS SOUNDROLL AND HE THINKS HE GOT MOST OF IT. HIS CAPTIONS IN BRIEF READ AS FOLLOW: A VC OFFICER WAS CAPTURED. THE TROOPS BEAT HIM, THEY BRING HIM TO LOAN WHO IS HEAD OF SOUTH VIETNAMESE NATIONAL POLICE. LOAN PULLS OUT HIS PISTOL, FIRES AT THE HEAD OF THE VC, THE VC FALLS, ZOOM ON HIS HEAD, BLOOD SPRAYING OUT. IF HE HAS IT ALL ITS STARTLING STUFF. IF HE HAS PART OF IT ITS STILL MORE THAN ANYONE ELSE HAS. TUCKNERS COPY COVERS IT IN STRAIGHT NARRATIVE WITH SOME ALTERNATIVE COPY JUST IN CASE SOME OF THE SHOTS MAY BE DIFFERENT OR NOT ALL THERE. I SUGGEST YOU DEVELOP ALL OF THE FOOTAGE.

Just over two hours later New York sent Steinman's message on to the Tokyo bureau. The five other stories were each described as was the Loan story. That is, for each piece Steinman gave technical data, crew names, synopsis, suggestions for editing, and whether the other networks had

similar film. A total of more than 4,000 feet of film was readied for shipment, a running time of nearly two hours. From all that, less than eight
minutes would finally be broadcast on that day's *Huntley-Brinkley Report.*

NBC correspondent Ron Nessen had filed two of the stories; one was
film of fighting at Hue where the enemy was holding much of the city,
and the other was film of a Da Nang napalm dump destroyed by rockets.
Wilson Hall had covered the heavy fighting in the streets of Cholon and
narrated a silent film story of aftermath in the provincial capital of Ban
Me Thout shot by soundman Arndt. The last film was unnarrated footage
of a news conference by General Westmoreland in which, according to
the *New York Times,* he said the enemy's main effort still was to be an
attack on the Marines at Khe Sanh.

At this time there was only one color film processing lab in Tokyo and
it was used by the three networks. The film was processed in the order
it arrived at the lab. Since the film from all three networks often arrived on the same flight it was a race to get through Japanese customs—
traditionally slow and very careful—and through the streets to the lab.
During Tet NBC hired a grand prix motorcycle racer to speed the NBC
film to the lab first.

EDITING AND BROADCAST

Robert Northshield, executive producer of the *Huntley-Brinkley Report* arrived at the New York office that Friday about 10:00 in the morning. The night before he had broadcast the Adams stills. That morning
he saw most of the major newspapers consensually validate his assessment of the stills. The *New York Times* printed the moment-of-death
picture on the front page and reprinted it with others on page 12. The
Washington Post printed it across five columns of the front page. The
Chicago Tribune printed three Adams photos, but on the third page. The
Los Angeles Times filled three front page columns. The *New York Daily
News* filled the bottom half of its front page. Several papers printed
another photo nearby the Loan shot. That photo showed an ARVN
officer carrying the body of one of his children murdered by the Viet
Cong. The *Huntley-Brinkley Report* had broadcast that also Thursday
evening.

Northshield read the overnight cables and learned that NBC had
color film of the Loan incident that might include the moment of the
execution.

Northshield placed a phone call to talk with those who could view the
film.

At the Tokyo bureau were Jack Reynolds, news manager and satellite producer, several part-time editors used regularly by the bureau, Ray Weiss, sent from New York to help coordinate the bureau, Fred Rheinstein, a director who helped with film editing from the West Coast, and correspondent David Burrington who had previously reported from Vietnam. Weiss, Rheinstein, Burrington and two extra film editors—from New York and Los Angeles—were sent to Tokyo for the *Pueblo*-Tet stories. Correspondent Jack Perkins, producer Bill Wordam, cameraman Grant Wolfkill and soundman Waku who returned from Korea with coverage of the *Pueblo* also took part in the discussion and direction of the film editing.

In the discussion Northshield said that the telex from Saigon mentioned a zoom to a close-up of the corpse's bloody head and that would probably be in bad taste for television. Wordam assured Northshield that the film was "quite remarkable," and there was enough time "for the director to cut away before the zoom at the end of the film." He referred to the video director of the program in New York. So the film was deliberately edited long so that a final decision could be made in New York.

Another member of the NBC staff working on the film later said he thought some of the closeup should have been shown, for Americans were getting a "too sanitized" picture of the war and they should have had "their noses rubbed in" the violence and gore.

Northshield authorized use of the satellite to transmit the film to the States. The bill would be about $3,000 for a ten minute minimum. After a late lunch Northshield called Tokyo again. The Loan film had been edited to 4:12 and was set for transport to the NHK studio along with two of the other Saigon-originated stories. Ron Nessen's Hue report and Wilson Hall's narration of Ban Me Thuot fighting and aftermath had been selected.

The *Huntley-Brinkley Report* was fed over the NBC network twice each day. The first show was live at 6:30 Eastern time. If it went well, then a video tape was fed at 7:00. Changes could be made for the second feed if necessary. Northshield recalled the Friday broadcasts:

The film came in over satellite between 6:20 and 6:30 PM before airtime and it was recorded routinely on tape. I saw the pictures then and heard what was said over the pictures. John Chancellor happened to be in the studio that day. He saw it with me. We were both stunned, because the way it came in the general took the gun, shot him in the head, the man fell down, and we held the picture while Loan reholstered the gun and walked through the frame. You still see the corpse from whom blood is now gushing. So it was too much for me. Now here the interesting point is that those men in Tokyo had been looking at the rawest, roughest film anyone has ever seen. They saw it differently than I did in an airconditioned control room in New York. It was too rough for me. So I said to Chancellor, 'I thought that was awful rough.' He could hardly speak. I said I was going to trim it off a little. So when it went on the air you saw less than what I have described. That is, as soon as the man hits the ground we went to black. It had already been established between me and the director that we would go to black after the film, which is unusual for our show. Usually we go right to the Huntley-Brinkley slide. This time we went to black for three seconds and then to the slide.

(The *Huntley-Brinkley Report* typically used a title slide (logo) between a film story and a commercial break.)

The program that day presented Chet Huntley with Vietnam news. He said that the Tet Offensive was now five days old and heaviest fighting was at Hue. He introduced the Nessen film from there. After that, Huntley read some copy about fighting in provincial cities and introduced the Hall film from Ban Me Thuot. After that report Huntley was framed in the lower left of the screen with a map of Saigon at his back. He read this introduction:

A pall lay over Saigon where American and South Vietnamese forces struggled to eliminate stubborn pockets of Viet Cong resistance. The Americans even battled the enemy near the Saigon home of General Westmoreland, the American commander. There was fighting in the Cholon section, where the city's Chinese live. But the conflict was sharpest at the An Quang Pagoda near the Saigon race track. Here via satellite is a report from NBC News correspondent Howard Tuckner on the battle for Saigon.

Tuckner's report as edited by the program's director in New York for the first feed ran 3:55. The last 17 seconds of the Tokyo-edited version were trimmed off, excluding the zoom to a closeup of the victim's head. The first 3:03 of the report was the clearing action at the Pagoda which had actually taken place after the execution. The Loan sequence itself ran only 52 seconds. The following is the narration Tuckner read over the first part of the film. Taped sounds of gunfire, shouting, and other battle sounds were included:

In this part of Saigon government troops were ordered to get as much revenge as possible. The fighting was only one block from the An Quang Pagoda, a Buddhist church the Viet Cong had been using as their headquarters with the reported approval of the militant Buddhist monk Tri Quang. An hour earlier Viet Cong flags had flown from these rooftops. Now snipers were up there and government troops were trying to locate their positions. Crack South Vietnamese Marines considered all civilians potential enemies. No one was above suspicion. The Viet Cong were working their way to the An Quang Pagoda and now the government troops had to clear the area no matter how high the risk. The Viet Cong were now firing from the roof of the Pagoda. For half an hour it was like this. The Viet Cong fled through the back of the Buddhist church but many others were there. Some of these are undoubtably Viet Cong sympathizers; Some are undoubtably religious Buddhists who felt the temple was the safest place to be in times like these in Saigon. The bullets had wounded at least twenty of them. The government Marines knew that the night before here the Viet Cong had held a meeting and that the Buddhists had cheered when they were told the Viet Cong were in the city to liberate Saigon.

The execution sequence followed directly. Tuckner recorded very little narration relative to that recorded above. In the first scene the prisoner was marched down the street toward NBC cameras while the ARVN Marines questioned the captive. Tuckner said, "Government troops had captured the commander of the Viet Cong commando unit." During a medium closeup of the prisoner Tuckner said, "He was roughed up badly but refused to talk." The camera tilted down to show a pistol carried by one of the Marines. Tuckner said, "A South Vietnamese officer held the pistol taken from the enemy officer." A camera angle from behind Loan, a wide angle view, showed the general drawing his own revolver and waving it to shoo away onlookers. Tuckner said, "The chief of South Vietnam's National Police Force, Brigadier General Nguyen Ngoc Loan was waiting for him." That was the last line of narration. Loan moved around to the side of the captive and shot him directly in the side of the head. The corpse dropped to the pavement while blood spurted out of the head. The time between the shot and the end of the film broadcast was six seconds.

If the film had been broadcast in its complete Tokyo-edited version, then the time allotted to showing the bleeding corpse dropping and on the pavement would have been 23 seconds.

The interval from the execution in Saigon to its broadcast on NBC was 46 hours.

Robert Northshield viewed the first feed of the *Huntley-Brinkley Report* that day and decided to trim another two seconds from the film for the second feed at 7:00.

The Adams photograph has been reprinted in many newspapers, magazines, books, posters, and broadcast on television all over the world. The award of the Pulitzer Prize in Spring 1969 stimulated another wave of reproductions of the Adams photograph. It is certainly one of the most widely circulated photographs in history.

Several people we have talked with—some with media experience and knowledge—confused the Adams photo and the NBC film. Some thought the still photo was a frame from the NBC film. In fact, we discovered in a frame-by-frame analysis of the Loan film that the precise instant of the shot is *not* on film. Just as Loan raised his arm to fire, someone stepped across the front of the NBC camera. The view was blocked for seven frames or about one quarter of a second. In motion, however, the film does appear to show the complete action of the shooting.

One reason the NBC film of Loan was not circulated as widely as the Adams photograph was, of course, the differential natures of the print and cinematographic media. The motion film could not be presented in books or magazines.

A CYBERNETIC GATEKEEPING MODEL

The production of the Loan story by NBC News provides an opportunity to apply various gatekeeping models to the process of network television journalism.

In early models—best described as linear—the news editor was the object of analysis. He made private, binary, irrevocable decisions allowing portions of the news content arriving at his desk further passage toward publication. Generally, he acted on one story at a time and usually only once. The journalistic process seemed hardly less complicated than a plumbing system. Many of these earlier studies seem to imply that all these decisions are of equal importance. Yet, most news decisions are routine involving few journalistic or organizational judgments. Case studies and experiments often ignored even the most popularized concepts of the organization man whose behavior is a function of his position in a bureaucracy. Later studies introduced intervening variables which influenced gatekeeper behavior and noted the effect of peer groups, reference groups, formal training, informal socialization and the like—concession that the journalist was a human being afterall with social and psychological determinants of his actions.

A cybernetic model, such as suggested by Robinson, takes the news organization as the object of analysis. The *Huntley-Brinkley Report* was the output of formal and informal organizational processes centered at NBC News, a complex communication-decision network populated by members of a trained and socialized subculture. Input included all the events within the surveillance of the organization's reporters, cameramen, bureau managers and assistants, news and film editors, and the rest.

Decisions by NBC personnel which may have appeared to be personal, individual acts were in fact governed by powerful norms. Being members of the journalistic subculture, NBC gatekeepers assessed the newsworthiness of the Loan story along traditional, identifiable standards. For example, on the exclusivity of the story, Northshield said, "We alone had the story . . . we were way ahead of the competition." This attention to the story as a scoop was reflected throughout the organization. Steinman had cabled, "CBS AND ABC WERE THERE BUT WE ARE THE ONLY ONES WHO HAVE FILM ON THE EXECUTION."

Another traditional standard of newsworthiness is a story's significance, often measured by the importance of persons involved. Northshield said:

> The one thing that matters on this program is the significance of the story. This was, in my view, a significant event. That the chief of the security police, at a time like this, in the view of certainly hundreds and eventually millions, chose to kill a man. I think the fact that this is significant is unarguable, without question.

Northshield's judgment conformed to traditional criteria.

The journalistic subculture crosses formal organizational boundaries to influence gatekeeping decisions. Consensual validation of the newsworthiness of the film was provided by the *New York Times* which ran the AP picture twice. Those editors functioned as a reference group for NBC gatekeepers.

Informal communication-decision networks operated within NBC to reduce the individuality of decision. As one example of peer influence, John Chancellor happened to view the film as it came into New York before airtime. Northshield and Chancellor had great mutual respect. They had worked together on the *Today Show* and on a Chicago newspaper years before. The two had a short conversation about the film before Northshield made his decision to edit it. While that decision was formally the executive producer's alone, the judgment of a highly respected peer worked to reduce the individuality of Northshield's action.

More formal communications-decision networks also influenced individuals in the organization. Involved in the production of this story were such matters as the organizational decision more than three years earlier to maintain a large Saigon bureau, the daily assignment made by the bureau chief, and the interaction of the reporter-cameramen-soundman—even before the event. The film editor might seem the classic gatekeeper, but this case does not support that simplistic interpretation. The Loan film story was edited by a group. The organization was the gatekeeper. The film was selected by the bureau chief and suggestions were passed on to Tokyo for editing and New York for use. This editing involved a number of persons at the Tokyo bureau in frequent communication with New York. There were the cameramen's, correspondents' and bureau chief's suggestions as well as decisions by producers, news editors, film editors, film cutters, sound editors, the executive producer and others. As the story moved in various stages from Saigon to Tokyo to New York chronology and power were both important, with the other factors noted. In the case of a television story—probably more than with newspapers—the range of choices on how to handle a story are limited as it passes along. NBC had film of the moment of death—ABC did not. CBS had no film of the incident or its aftermath—and did not show the still. In Tokyo there was more than ten times as much film as was used—some was not developed on the advice of the Saigon bureau chief. It was impossible to reshoot or obtain more film. When the story was transmitted to New York little time remained to change it before going on the air. It was possible to shorten the film, and shorten it still more for a second feed. The range of possibilities in New York were small—go or no go. Yet, this should not be perceived as a simple "gate." New York had participated in the decision making many times. The power of the executive producer is great. This complex matter cannot be fully discussed here, but reporters, editors, producers, others know which stories are most likely to be broadcast. Each "gatekeeper" has to estimate how the program's executive producer—and even his superiors—will receive the story.

Yet clearly it is most accurate to conceive of this position as powerful in the sense that it is a central communications junction. The executive producer acts as a monitoring-governing device, relatively inoperative so long as the components of the organization function properly. In most instances producers and other program staff handle most of the communication-decision making until they feel the need to consult or are consulted.

Production of the Loan film involved more people, more activity, and more communications than usual for an ordinary film story but for the most part the organization functioned "normally," as was the case in a crisis situation described by Robinson. There were additional personnel in Tokyo because of the *Pueblo* and Tet, there were more phone calls, and more discussion. The cybernetic model predicts that there will be more communication in times of crisis.

A cybernetic organization functions with consideration to its environment—in this case the audience. The one standard news judgment overtly applied throughout the production of the Loan story was that of taste. The film included full-color shots of spurting blood and a closeup of the dead man's face. NBC edited the film according to its estimate of the taste standards of the audience. Feedback on the audience's reaction would come only later. But the cybernetic organization functions with the help of memory—knowledge of past reactions from its audience. This conception of audience thus influences gatekeeping decisions.

What then of the possible influence of an individual journalist's political or moral value system on his decision making in the Loan case? Much has been written arguing that the professional journalist is one who controls his prejudices aiming at a goal of objectivity. Correspondent Tuckner recorded his narration to play with the film. That narration was sparse, not much more than an identification of the principals in the film and the setting. The narration ended before the execution was actually seen. Later, off the air, Tuckner freely revealed his strong personal point of view on General Loan.

> It was the responsibility of the network to broadcast that film. The film showed, at a time when all eyes were on Saigon, that although the United States went over there ostensibly to keep South Vietnam free from Communism and the Communists were accused of atrocities, that a leading figure of the Saigon government killed a man in the street without a trial.

No similar comment or interpretation had been offered by Tuckner or the anchormen on the program.

Earlier gatekeeping models were deficient primarily because of a narrowness of perspective. To take the individual as the gatekeeper is to deny the great body of knowledge about the social and organizational context of individual behavior.

chapter 13   Violence, Mass News, and Social Values

DAVID J. LeROY

It would seem to many concerned citizens that violence in the mass media is clearly deleterious, be it in entertainment programs or the news. But as Otto Larsen has attempted to show, violence is controversial, since media owners are engaged on the one hand to remove violence from the airwaves, and on the other to protect their investment.[1] Since empirical research findings are often ambiguous, each side can almost select at will studies supporting their point of view. When one or two individuals in a mass society are shown to have been influenced by news media stories concerning hijackings, bombings, and so on, it is insufficient to effect reform. In a society of over 200 million people, acts affecting a hundred are considered curiosities.

There have been very few studies of the effects of mass news on the public. Studies comparing American and Canadian news coverage of violence have demonstrated that indeed we have a society which appears

[1] See Otto N. Larsen (ed.), *Violence and the Mass Media* (New York: Harper & Row, Publishers, 1968).

inundated with violence, protest, and riots.[2] The question is, why do mass news agencies dwell on violence and other forms of "bad" news?

One value of the recent studies and commissions that have studied the mass media and various social issues is that they provide a clearer view of the salient issues. First, laboratory experiments and anecdotal evidence suggests that there is a positive link between displays of violence and individual behavior. Defenders of the media argue that those people who behave aggressively or violently are predisposed to do so and that all the media have done is trigger the act.[3]

It is this scale of values that disturb people. We don't stop making automobiles if a few are proven defective, and the same should hold true for mass news violence. Violence may trigger one or two deranged individuals, but the consequence of eliminating violence from the media would have a disastrous economic effect on the country. Also, censoring news depictions of violence would be clearly against the principles of the freedom of the press. The notion of the relative "good" of product or practice versus its deleterious effects permeates most mass society institutions.

The surgeon general's recent report on violence and television argues to broaden the definitions of violence and aggression to include a wider variety of acts and a concern for the victim of such crimes. Falling within this broader scope would be a concern with housing and racial bias in which "the system" is the aggressor. While most of us would agree with this argument, the mass news system is woefully prepared to enact it.

For example, Milton Eisenhower, chairman of the former National Commission on the Causes and Prevention of Violence, noted that only four percent of the violent acts committed in America are what is termed group violence. The remainder are individual acts of violence. But if one surveys the mass news media, most of its reported acts of violence are group-generated. Does this mean that the news media give us an unbalanced view of reality?

Yes, in the sense of portraying an accurate proportion of American violence, the media dwell on groups rather than individuals (unless the crime is bizarre and unusual). Journalists argue that group violence is

---

2 See Benjamin D. Singer, "Violence, Protest, and War in Television News: The U.S. and Canada Compared," *Public Opinion Quarterly* (Winter 1970–71). About "bad" news, the watershed is still the article by Paul F. Lazersfeld and Robert K. Merton, "Mass Communication, Popular Taste, and Organized Social Action," in Wilbur Schramm and Donald F. Roberts (eds.), *The Process and Effects of Mass Communication,* rev. ed. (Urbana: University of Illinois Press, 1971).

3 While Joseph T. Klapper is most closely associated with this point of view, the most recent and more coherent presentation of this viewpoint is in "Report to the Surgeon General, United States Public Health Service," Washington, D.C.: *Television and Growing Up: The Impact of Televised Violence,* Washington, D.C.: U.S. Government Printing Office, 1972.

more important, since it has the greater potential impact on society. But even if the media instituted coverage (like that of the Vietnam war) of a daily body count of citizens murdered, raped, and attacked, the balance would not redress the salient issue. That is not violence per se, but its social ramification in terms of cause and effects. Editors reporting violence have already assumed that the act has a potential impact on society. But should editors be responsible to see that violent acts are reported in proper perspective?

It would be nice to say, yes, perspective and balance are attainable in mass news, especially in the area of violence. But reporters and editors are not intellectual giants. They are as confused and bewildered as anyone when confronted with "senseless" violence. Further, the mores of mass news rarely allow the reporter time to dwell on one story to explore its implications. Also, violence is a culturally defined norm. When society agrees that murder is a crime, the reporter has little confusion about how to write the story. But when norms are in flux, poorly defined, or subject to conflicting interpretation, the reporter falls back into his objective writing style, just stating the facts (time of the incident, number of people, and progression of events). Recall the confusion of the news media in reporting the war in Vietnam, the emergence of racial and sexual rights, and the impact of pollution on the ecosystem. Further, the norms in flux are often abstract and difficult to write or photograph. How does one measure the impact of racial bigotry. Ghettos and slums are manifestations of the disease, not the cause.

Certainly, the mass news system should constantly examine their practices and attempt to evolve new approaches to reporting violence and aggression. If they are successful, the howls of indignation from politicians about focusing on "bad" news should increase. But if reporting is to improve, a coherent and large-scale reform is needed within the news bureaucracy. The intellectual paucity of the media reaches to the core of the reporter's role.

section D Conflict
in
Norms

This section is designed to present some of the essential conflicts about journalistic normative behavior. After much thought, we have chosen three articles and a lengthy case study of the *Selling of the Pentagon*. To scholars of the field, perhaps our choices will seem somewhat arbitrary, given the hundreds of choices possible.

We perceive the progression in the articles as follows. Neil Hickey's article presents a critic's view of the interface between news subjects and the media. The key issue is: How can mass news develop a system of intelligence that reports on significant developments in society? As it now stands, mass news is forever ambushed by crisis. We learn about student unrest when buildings are seized, or the legacy of racism when the ghettos erupt. Although crisis makes for exciting news, it is intellectually sterile, and as meaningful as watching a string of firecrackers explode each and every day at an appointed time.

Consider the drug problem and how it has been reported. Certain types of drugs are labelled "a threat to our society." In the Nixon administration, the villain was street stuff—marijuana, ups and downs, and heroin. With great fanfare the leaders of the mass media were called to the White House for a series of public relations extravaganzas, complete with trained dogs smelling suitcases for illegal drugs, much smiling and milling in the Rose Garden, and the inevitable speech by the president about our decaying moral fiber. Then followed the pledge by the industry, especially television, to aid the president in his campaign to "crack down hard on drugs." There was no talk of government interference with the First Amendment or news manipulation.

Drug addiction, like alcoholism and nicotine addiction, is a complex social issue. Evidence pours out of the various governmental agencies in piles of statistics, claims, and counterclaims about the most efficient assistance program for the addict.[1]

How is the reporter supposed to deal with this flood of data, especially when there are competing government agencies in the same field? What training has the reporter had in coping with trend statistics or the proper evaluative criteria for assistance programs? Often the answer is none. He has, at best, a few hours to the get the story and file it. Rigorous investigative reporting of data and assistance programs requires both specialized knowledge and time to pursue a topic in sufficient detail. It is not surprising then, that a great deal of sensationalized and erroneous information flows through the news system.

There are two disturbing results. First, Klapper and other social scientists tell us that the mass media have their greatest impact in areas where people have no information or preconceptions. Thus, lumping together all the various illegal (or soon to be illegal) drugs, hastens the diffusion of stereotypes about society's drug problems. Reason is overcome by rhetoric.

Second, erroneous information adds to the news media's credibility problems among minorities. If the government seeks to correct an abuse, but employs hysterical appeals and erroneous information, the failure of any assistance program is not hard to imagine.[2]

Hickey deals with a similar issue when he discusses the distrust of television by college activists. The crisis-oriented gestalt of television exacerbates many situations. Television and radio journalism may not have caused any riots, but by their very reporting of the incidents help define it for the participants both in scope, techniques, and rationalization.

In sifting through the ashes of a collapsed drug assistance program or campus disturbance, there is usually a shelf full of study commission reports detailing the causes and proposed solutions to the problem. Suggestions for the improvement of the media are given their usual chapter or two, but sit on the shelf, fading and yellowing with the rest of the report.

As a result, there may be a black reporter hired (as we see in Stein's

---

1 See Marion K. Sanders, " 'Tripping' On The Drug Scene," *Columbia Journalism Review* (Fall 1971) for a discussion of these issues.

2 The research to date suggests that the mass media have their most pronounced effect in areas where a person has no information about a topic. After attitudes and opinions are formed they are more difficult to change.

article), or an "in depth" review of the problem in Sunday's paper or during sixty minutes of prime time television. Then it is back to business as usual. There have been some procedural changes in camera techniques for reporting riots, and a little more intelligence displayed in reporting on minority groups, but the mass news media continue to practice *reactive* reporting rather than *anticipatory* investigation of social problems. There is evidence that from time to time the wire services have tried to develop articles in this direction only to have local papers not run the stories. Broadcast journalism seems particularly rigid in its formats and reporting repertoire. It is able to show but not explain. Ideas require time but a single person talking to the camera ("talking heads") is frowned upon in the show biz world of action, tempo and "keep it moving." And this is a paradox for broadcast journalism, since its very popularity can be attributed to its fast pace and the lack of effort required to listen and watch someone read you the headlines. Even more pathetic is the fact that when given the opportunity, the money, and the time to develop new and innovative news programming (such as the experiments in public television), the results are usually more of the same old stuff.

Thus, Stein's article about the black journalist serves a double function: (1) It defines the relationship between reporters, a paper, and coverage of minority affairs; and (2) It examines the more fundamental epistemological question of the inherent limitations of objectivity as a behavioral more.

The bureaucratic rationalizations for objectivity should be clear by now. The requisite demands of doing business have also reduced the reporter from an intelligent and functioning human to nothing more than a "recorder." The fragmented role of the reporter as defined by "objectivity" seems incapable of further evolution and maturation. We will return to this topic in a different form in LeRoy's discussion of professionalism.

This leads us to a consideration of the last two articles in this section. The problems surrounding the subpoena focus on a fundamental confusion of roles. The journalist as reporter is often forced to dig for material, establish contacts with a variety of people, and develop intelligence networks for tips, information, and needed materials. Does the government, be it Congress or the local police chief, have a right of access to the reporter's gathered information?

The answer, in the past, has often depended on the character of the reporter or news organization. Many city hall reporters enjoy escorting the police on raids or influencing behind the scenes city hall decisions. This type of reporter is not representative of the fourth estate; rather, he is a public relation adjunct for the government agencies he seeks to report.[3]

---

[3] There is a vast literature on this topic. For examples see: Walter Gieber, "News Is What Newspapermen Make It," in Lewis A. Dexter and David M. White (eds.), *People, Society, Mass Communications* (New York: The Free Press, 1964), or James McCartney, "Vested Interests of the Reporter," in Louis M. Lyons (ed.), *Reporting The News* (New York: Atheneum Publishers, 1968).

But, when Earl Caldwell decides to say no, or Frank Stanton argues that film outtakes are as inviolate as the reporter's notes, we have joined a controversy. In opposition to C. Wright Mills notion of the power elite, we have two "institutions" arguing about role behaviors. Does a reporter have allegiance to his craft and ethical integrity, or is he a mere extension of interlocking mass society institutions? It would be nice to say that the press has matured into a viable and intelligent adversary of the government, with us, the citizenry, the beneficiary of ongoing interchanges. The value of Smith's article dealing with the *Selling of the Pentagon* confrontation is that it points to a great deal of remaining confusion concerning the shape of the journalistic enterprise beneath the rhetoric of "principles" and "inherent constitutional rights."

chapter 14   The
Student Movement
in the U.S.
and Its Relation
to the Media

NEIL HICKEY

When I was first invited to come here, I began thinking about what I
might say that would keep you in utter thralldom for a half hour or so.
I was aware that Marshall University is the headquarters for some pretty
sophisticated broadcast theorists, so that made the problem doubly difficult. As it happened, I was engaged at that time in the research and writing of a series of articles on the subject of student activism and its relation
to the media. I had been travelling around to various universities, like
Ohio State, Harvard, Brandeis, Columbia, Berkeley, and others—chatting
with student leaders, faculty, and administrators, and also with television
people in the communities where those schools are located. I had also
sat down with the presidents of the three network news divisions, with
various of their correspondents, and with the network bureau chiefs in
Washington. I don't know how many interviews were conducted altogether—perhaps seventy-five. At that same time, the Scranton Commission was putting its report together. And a short time earlier Chancellor

Neil Hickey, "The Student Movement in the U.S. and its Relation to the Media,"
from a speech at Marshall University, December 8, 1971. Reprinted by permission of
the author.

Alexander Heard of Vanderbilt had submitted findings of the President's Advisory Commission on Campus Unrest.

A Gallup poll taken in June showed that campus violence was, mind you, the number one problem facing the country—ahead of war, race, pollution, inflation, crime, and everything else. That seemed to me an incredible statistic. Even more instructive was a Harris poll which indicated that Americans by a margin of five to one believed that the students at Kent State and not the National Guard were primarily responsible for the killings of four students—a sentiment since shared by an Ohio grand jury. Another Harris poll, and I'm not making this up, showed that many Americans placed militant students lower on the social scale than, "prostitutes, atheists, and homosexuals."

Well, this was obviously something that needed interpretation for the American public, and I promptly appointed myself to the task. What really clinched my desire to write something on this subject, though, was a quotation I came across from one of our leading social philosophers, Mrs. Martha Mitchell. She said: "The academic society is responsible for all our troubles in this country. These are the people that are destroying our country." Well, first of all, I want to say that you should all be ashamed of yourselves. But Mrs. Mitchell's own, rather exotic conclusion, combined with those polls I just mentioned, added up to the unmistakable fact that students in America—taken as a class—are not highly thought of by large segments of our population.

Now, that swiftly moves us to a very central question: How do large segments of the population make up their minds about such things? How do they arrive at such fervently held beliefs anyway? In brief, how is opinion made in this country in these years? And what is the effect of that opinion-making process on our society? Those obviously are questions truly worthy of our mettle as media philosophers. They even transcend the rather more ephemeral matter of campus unrest. Indeed the radical student movement is of value to us here principally as a metaphor. Or perhaps as an instance of how communications—particularly electronic communications—operates to affect the quality of all our lives.

If you will hold on to the edge of your chairs I will now interpolate here a brief parenthesis during which you will be exposed for the first time in you lives to what future generations are certain to call Hickey's Circular Theory of Social Dynamics. Grown men have been known to suffer vertigo at its blinding clarity and insightful brilliance. So I adjure you to concentrate hard for the next thirty seconds or so, after which you can relax again, and stop thinking. Stated in its proper Viconian terms, the law is simply: Public opinion in an electronic age is inexorably transmuted into public policy. Little do you know how pregnant, how gravid, is that statement.

Let's examine it. First of all, were we living in a Periclean age of pure democracy—with a smallish, manageable society—it would be a jolly good thing if public opinion were transmuted into public policy. But alas, our American society is unhomogenized, inchoate, disparate, diffuse. And electronics in the last twenty years—a pittance of time—has bound us up together again, retribalized us, given us a hotline to each other. As a result, we are able—right in our own living rooms—to observe the assassination of our presidents. And we are able to observe the hand-to-hand combat on American streets during our political conventions. And we are able to observe the skirmishes between our students and our Army.

And those pictures lead Americans to varying conclusions, as we know: One television viewer sees provocation by hippies; another sees police brutality; one grand juror (let us say) sees rock-throwing by students; another sees unprovoked point-blank rifle fire by National Guardsmen. And when asked by public opinion pollsters what they saw, Americans are quick to give them an earful. In the 1968 election year, $6 million was spent by candidates on opinion research alone. Candidates need that information so that they can tell the voters what they want to hear, so that they can get themselves elected.

Therefore, a schematic diagram of our history-making Circular Theory of Social Dynamics looks something like this: It begins with a news event, then goes to electronic medium, to viewer, to opinion researcher, to politician, to policy—which becomes a news event. It's a circular, perpetual motion mechanism, and standing at the power switch as its custodian, is an awkward, reluctant, slightly retarded adolescent behemoth called television.

The process itself has the inexorable rectitude of the first paragraph of *Finnegan's Wake*—a circular novel—which begins, as you remember, in the middle of a sentence, the first part of which is at the end of the book. The opening words are "riverrun, past Eve and Adam's, from swerve of shore to bend of bay, brings us by a commodius vicus of recirculation back to Howth Castle and Environs." Joyce remarked elsewhere that "History is a nightmare from which we are trying to awake." To which we might append that current American history is a trap from which we are trying to escape. And that trap is of our own making, a product of our ideas, our perceptions, our misimpressions, our miscalculations. We exist at a time which has an infinite capacity for the generation and perpetuation of misimpressions. That's why it's important that right-thinkers like you and me give some of our energies to television, the instrument which provides most Americans with most of their news.

Some old friends say to me: "Why are you involved with television? It's so trivial. It's nothing but the Beverly Hillbillies." And at times I think they're right, especially when I ponder that I haven't even finished reading *Finnegan's Wake* yet. In fact, I'm still working on that first paragraph. But then, I remember that television is perhaps the single most pervasive force in all our lives, that the medium is indeed the message, and that television's future as an educator and enricher is one of the genuinely bright prospects before us.

Very well, let's end that parenthesis and return to our students. I set out last summer to find out how the transmittal of information about American students has led Americans to such conclusions as (1) that students are of a lower order than prostitutes, atheists, and homosexuals; (2) that they are "primarily responsible" for getting themselves killed by National Guardsmen; and (3) that the Bill of Rights ought to be abridged to prevent student protest. A Harris poll indicated that 52 percent of Americans think students ought not to have the right to protest, peacefully or otherwise. Such polls as those, incidentally, led the Nixon Administration in last November's elections to key its whole campaign for the capture of the Senate to the so-called social issues of permissiveness, law and order, lack of respect for the country's institutions, and the Bolshevik tendencies of people with long hair. It permitted the Administration to breeze through the campaign without ever once mentioning the war or the recession.

The results of our researches into the student movement [were published in January-February of 1971] in a five-part series. I had hoped to do it in a shorter space, but the subject turned out to be an expansive one. Perhaps I can take you behind the scenes of that series for a moment. A few very well-defined patterns emerged from our interviewing. For example: Activist students, for a spectrum of reasons, almost universally dismiss television news as being unresponsive, obtuse, and largely irredeemable as an instrument of illuminating the root issues of student unrest. To them, television is "the pig press," the enemy, a cynical arm of the same unyielding establishment they claim to despise. It's also a financial dependent of the materialistic "consumer culture;" a cog in the great machine of interlocking power blocs which has set the country on a path of war, racism, environmental decay, and polarization. Many of them see it as a narcotic to soothe and lull the masses while it— purposely or unwittingly—distorts the facts about our health as a nation and the true meaning of student discontent.

To many television newsmen at local stations around the country— particularly those in the shadow of large universities who have been roughed up in the performance of their duties—the radical students are implacable elitists with a line of goods they're eager to force upon the American public by whatever terrorist means they can muster.

To many hard-working middle-class Americans who get most of their news from television—and that's about two-thirds of our adults—militant

students are an ungrateful subculture afflicted with a chronic and un-
reasoned dissatisfaction. Many Americans are fond of saying that if the
sensation-seeking television cameras would simply ignore students altogether, or simply clamp a tight lid on coverage of the "agitators" who
are fomenting trouble, then the whole problem would melt away quite
spontaneously.

College administrators told me that TV's presence on the campus
complicates enormously their task of cooling down a bad situation. Student leaders complain hotly that television has made no attempt at all
to ventilate the complex, prickly issues which lead up to a confrontation,
but is johnny-on-the-spot whenever a building is seized or a skirmish
breaks out. High network news officials in New York told me that they're
weary of student demands for airtime to talk about the underlying issues
of student unrest; and that activist students have no right to foist their
own, rather parochial concerns, on the mass television audiences.

These matters raise the question of "access" to the airwaves and how
to achieve it. At least one FCC commissioner has wondered to what extent the denial of civilized TV time to young activist groups has contributed to feelings of voicelessness and frustration which then later
erupt into violence.

So—to state it simply—no party to the controversy over campus unrest is pleased with the way television is handling the story, and many
are quite simply enraged by it. Some TV executives take this as proof
positive that they're doing a balanced job of reporting on campus unrest, since everybody hates them. And that is the most desperate kind of
wishful thinking.

Now, let me document this for you with some specifics. You will
either agree or disagree with the people whose opinions I'm about to
outline for you. That's secondary to the fact that these are indeed the
opinions—the fervently held opinions—of a few people whose lives have
been involved, in different ways, with the student movement in America.

First, let's listen to 21-year-old Leigh Steinberg, president of the student body at Berkeley. He's a nonradical who won an overwhelming
victory last spring as head of the moderate Nonviolent Action Party, and
he rejects violence as an instrument of reform. He told us, "Television
is using the University of California to sell commercials because people
enjoy watching students getting their heads beaten in. It completely ignores the positive, constructive aspects of the campus peace movement.
For example, we have nonviolent student groups working for constructive social change, but we can't beg, borrow, or steal TV time for *them*.
TV isn't interested in that. They'll be out for the confrontations,
though."

Steinberg went on to say that if television's main function is to entertain, then obviously TV will gravitate to what is exciting and what thrills its viewers and what wins ratings points for its news programs. But if television has any conscience at all, he said, it will start spending time doing serious background reporting on campus issues, and not show up only when the flames are in the sky. But Steinberg is not optimistic. He said, "I'm afraid, however, that television is merely an entertainment and advertising medium. The basic issues are not being elucidated by television. Since there's no coverage of the previolence issues, a demonstration is sprung on the viewers as a surprise and they think it's a sudden lark. They miss the step-by-step efforts to avoid a confrontation." I chose that quotation because it was typical of many others I heard.

That problem of television's alleged obtuseness about issue coverage as opposed to event coverage was perhaps the single most widely heard complaint in all our interviewing. Another student, a member of the Ad Hoc Committee for Student Rights at Ohio State, put it this way, "No station will devote sufficient time to unravelling all the issues, many of which are, admittedly, both complex and unpleasant. But the minute a bunch of students seize a building, the TV reporters come rushing onto the campus taking pictures and demanding to know why the building was seized. They should *know* why the building was seized. But they never do, and probably never will." The effect of that kind of reporting, obviously, is to create in viewers' minds the impression that a particular campus confrontation is the work of dilletantes, pranksters, or nonstudent professional agitators, who are using the university as a proscenium to dramatize their own extremism.

Another Berkeley student leader is Jim Nabors, who is a former president of the Afro-American Student Union and an organizer of last February's Third World Strike at Berkeley, during which he was arrested four times. Nabors complained to us that he doesn't quite recognize himself on the television news programs. He said, "They always manage to catch me supposedly stirring up trouble, saying that black people ought to arm themselves—and they ignore all the rest. There has been no attempt by TV to approach any of us to give the history, intent or future of the student movement. Perhaps that's because TV is strife-oriented. If Jerry Rubin ever stopped making inflammatory speeches and opened a quiet school in Appalachia, you'd never hear of him again on television."

That remark suggests one of the other principal complaints of practically all student activist leaders against television, namely the medium's allegedly insatiable desire for stereotypes—for good guys and bad guys, for black hats and white hats, for spokesmen who can be pigeon-holed, labelled, precisely defined, and thereby disposed of. I remember discussing this once with James Simon Kunen, author of *The Strawberry State-*

ment, and he recalled the time he was invited to go on the Merv Griffin show shortly after the book was published. The producers appeared to be looking for a certified bomb-throwing, preferably wild-eyed radical to pit against some students from the YAF for a discussion of campus upheaval. During a preinterview with one of Griffin's talent coordinators, Kunen explained that they shouldn't really expect from him any inflamed rhetoric in defense of campus mayhem and arson; that he was really a moderate and would be happy to discuss the whole subject rationally from that perspective. The talent coordinator looked at him perplexedly for a moment, and then after a long pause, said: "Perhaps we should get somebody else." In order to get onto the program where he could make a few quiet points, Kunen hastily assured the talent person that he could be as wild-eyed as the next radical.

Kunen feels that television was principally responsible for making Mark Rudd the leading character in the Columbia insurrection of 1968, even though Rudd was only one of a group of students who engineered it. But the TV reporters needed somebody to talk to, and by some process they chose him. As a result, the Columbia students, the administration, and the local television viewers all began to think of Rudd as the mastermind of the confrontation. And in the end—so did Rudd.

In Washington one day recently, I talked with David Ifshen, this year's president of the National Student Association and last year's president of the student body at Syracuse. He sees absolutely no "intelligent transmittal" of American student life to the public via television, but rather an accretion of myths which is gradually hardening the various components of the nation's population into hostile camps. He's convinced that—thanks to television—many Americans think of Charles Manson as a typical college student—although Manson is obviously not a college student and never has been. Ifshen feels that television has, wittingly or unwittingly—and I must always insert that qualification in such opinions—cast such black leaders as Stokely Carmichael as lunatics. But Carmichael once went to Syracuse University to give a speech, and in those surroundings—live and unedited—gave what Ifshen says was one of the most brilliant expositions of black perspectives he had ever heard. No such coherent presentation can filter through the chopped-up and stage-managed TV news and talk show, said the president of NSA.

Ifshen is not alone in thinking that—for such reasons—many student leaders are simply no longer eager for access to television at all; that TV exposure of the student movement has resulted only in the perpetuation of stereotypes, on the one hand, and, on the other, the misimpression that America's seven million students are on a constant rampage of arson, pillage, and plunder. Ifshen insists that the violence on American campuses is infinitesimal and immeasurable by comparison with the mayhem that occurs daily in any city of the world containing seven million people. And indeed, the Scranton Report pointed out that while 30 percent of American universities reported some strike activity during last spring's moratorium, only 5 percent experienced violence.

The subject of violence came up on another occasion when I was visiting Brandeis University last summer to meet with some volunteers who were manning what was then called the National Student Strike Center. They were in contact with hundreds of other schools all over the country, exchanging and processing information on the nationwide student strike which had taken place in the wake of Kent State and Cambodia.

About thirty of them took time out one afternoon to spend several hours with me. We sat in a huge circle in a student lounge, with myself occupying part of the periphery, and listening to their thoughts and experiences on how television has interpreted their actions and goals. To put it mildly, they were an angry group of students, charged up and ready for me. It was just my luck that nobody had ever asked them their opinions on this subject before. A few of them mistook me for the enemy and wanted to hold me personally responsible for all the depredations they claimed had been visited on them by television.

Nonetheless, they were enormously articulate, polite, helpful, and pleased that somebody was listening to them. One of them said, look, consider the hypocrisy: Television editorializes piously about student violence while searching the world for violent scenes with which to fill up their news programs—and for action stories to fill their adventure programs. He claimed that the central American myths—of which television is now the principal purveyor—is the story of the peaceable man, the good man—Gary Cooper, Jimmy Stewart—who hangs up his guns, marries him a school marm, and settles down to farming. And then a band of mean guys with black hats come to the valley and threaten the peace. So the hero reluctantly straps his guns back on again, and shoots the most terrible holes right through the entire band of outlaws.

And that, of course, is a parable about which some eager young anthropologist, out to make a name for himself, might write an article in the Journal of American Folklore. The title might be, "Some Notes Toward a Study of The Rectitude of Selective Violence in American Mythmaking." In fact, if there are any anthropologists in the audience, I give you that title—gladly.

But the most pervasive complaint among that group of students at the Strike Center was what seemed to them the systematic exclusion of radical perspectives from the airwaves. It's easier, they claimed, for a sex murderer to get a hearing on television than it is for anybody to the left of John Kenneth Galbraith. They were indignant about what they called the sordid treatment given the Black Panthers by the media, claiming that if the Panthers had gotten rational coverage from the outset instead of being stereotyped as implacable guerillas, then the irreconcilable hostility between them and white law enforcers might never have hardened. They've consistently been projected by the media as theater—said the students—and not to be taken seriously, in spite of such activities as their breakfast program for children and the patently reasonable and rational position documents of their leaders—Huey Newton, Bobby Seale, and Eldridge Cleaver.

Let me move on now to a few nonstudent opinions which I gleaned while synthesizing this rather picaresque exercise in journalism—one a faculty member, the other a university administrator. My chat with the faculty member took place in the White House because he was then occupied as a member of the President's Advisory Commission on Campus Unrest—Dr. John Searle, professor of philosophy at Berkeley, on leave.

His opinion of television news vis-a-vis the student movement was—to state it in the least profane terms—unequivocal. Let me quote him. "I watch television news not to find out what's happening, but what other people think is happening. Anytime you're personally involved in a news event, as I have been at Berkeley, and then you later see a report of that event on television, you're struck by the fact that somehow they just didn't get the story quite straight. And there's a structural reason for that. TV news departments are in the business of providing dramatic entertainment based on current events, not pictures of an independent reality."

So spake Dr. Searle. The administrator I want to mention here was Dr. Robben Fleming, president of the University of Michigan, with whom I spent one very enjoyable breakfast listening to stories of his encounters with television news—all of them quite funny, and delivered in Dr. Fleming's wry tones—compounded more of amused incredulity than of anger. I'll tell you just one of them.

During one particular period of campus strife in the state of Michigan, Fleming and Dr. Clifton Wharton, president of Michigan State University, were invited by a Detroit television station to have luncheon with the station's top executives for a heart to heart chat on campus problems and how TV could best handle them. Fleming and Wharton spent several hours earnestly explaining their chief complaint: Namely, that TV reporters are much too quick to come onto a campus in time of trouble and create instant scenarios with regard to the operative issues—scenarios which are marvelously suspenseful but which bear little relation to the facts. The two administrators then also suggested that it would make their own lives enormously easier if TV reporters would not always assume apocalypse in their interviewing of campus personalities, thereby creating self-fulfilling prophecies about pillage yet to come.

The TV station executives nodded gravely, and allowed that those were certainly reasonable criticisms.

As the luncheon ended, the TV executives wondered if Fleming and Wharton would agree to tape a brief interview for the evening news program. They said yes, and a reporter—who had not been present at the luncheon—was promptly summoned to conduct the interview. As the station's top brass stood by approvingly, Fleming recalls, that reporter proceeded to ask the most sensationalized, supercharged questions about impending doom on the campuses—precisely the kind of questions which he and Wharton had just spent two hours denouncing.

Well, let us merely posit that university people for varying reasons feel hostile toward television news—and I assure you that in many quarters of TV news the feeling is mutual. By all odds, one of the most important news executives in the country is Reuven Frank, president of NBC News. After years of covering student strife, he freely announces his conviction that the militants are snobbish elitists of "no significance" —malcontents with no real claim on his attentions.

Students are a news coverage problem the same as other pressure groups, he says, and no amount of nudging is going to induce him to give what he calls these world changers and altruists any more air time than audiences are interested in or will watch. Since student caterwauling bores him, he assumes it bores his audiences, and he claims to have no mandate to be a bore. To the charge that his network is not covering the underlying issues of campus unrest, Frank responds—rather disarmingly, I must say—"So what!" He claims a national audience can't possibly absorb all the issues causing campus troubles, but when the public order is breached, the public is entitled to know that, and, as he puts it, we cover it under the old-fashioned, dimwitted rules of journalism— namely that the reporter doesn't know what happened until he gets there.

Frank is the kind of news boss who is not fond of advices from outsiders about how he should deploy his staff or expend his airtime. He puts it this way: "Who's to say what's news? That's what I'm here for. The students can trust television to me. I don't want to elect anybody, I don't want to push any cause. I just want to cover the news. That's a simpleminded response, but that's it."

If that sounds a little imperious, please remember that the president of a network news operation can afford to be imperious—more so than, let us say, the more than 600 news directors at local stations around the country, many of whom exist in the shadow of huge universities. Those men are truly in the trenches—caught in a crossfire between various constituencies of their viewership, their own bosses at the management level who, incidentally, are businessmen not journalists, and their own sturdy but sometimes frayed sense of journalistic rectitude.

One of them is a young fellow at WBNS in Columbus named Tom Dorsey who has the job not only of covering the city, but also the 45,000 students of Ohio State University, which is just across the road from his office. Dorsey told me that although he and his staff try mightily to cover the student story—and there was a great deal of action on the OSU campus last spring—he is nowhere near doing an optimum job—partly because of a lack of money, partly because of viewer resistance to unpleasant news, partly because of the covert—and sometimes overt—hostility of students and administrators. The truth is, he says, we don't know what the truth is.

And so it goes. All the foregoing examples are a few random shards of cut glass in the mosaic which adds up to a picture of contentiousness among parties to the student movement and the television medium covering them. There are many more pieces to the mosaic than we have time to study here, and this wide-angle view of the terrain which I've been describing obviously raises more questions than it answers. It is for such people as yourselves in the academic community to provide properly designed studies which will both define the problem and point the way to solutions. But let's rush in fearlessly anyway, shall we, and skewer a few conclusions by way of tying up the loose ends of this. First of all, there are those in the broadcast business who will tell you that it's a tacky exercise these days to say anything negative about television networks in this their hour of agony—inflation has hit them hard, cigarette advertising is deserting them, the new prime time rule has them in a tizzy, and arrayed outside the walls in battle dress are the barbarians of cable television, cassettes, and home video recording—waiting for the right moment to lay the seige, take over the castle and make paté out of the goose that laid the golden egg.

Yes, the vibrations are bad. I know. My office in New York is sandwiched in between the three networks: NBC, whose headquarters is called 30 Rock, there at 30 Rockefeller Plaza; CBS, whose building is called Black Rock; and ABC, known in the trade as Pop Rock, in deference to its attentions to youthful audiences. Across the street, by the way, is the New York Hilton Hotel where many broadcast executives stay. It's called—inevitably—Bedrock.

But the vibrations indicate that many network executives, if they really had the choice, would be secretly pleased to dispose of their news operations—which only lose them huge sums of money and embroil them in controversy and distract viewers from the commercials. But they're locked in. In their search for mass audiences, they've also created mass news audiences. Two-thirds of Americans get most of their news from television and consider it the most credible medium. There's no going back from that. Whether television likes it or not, it is now an irreplaceable bit of the machinery which determines the present life and the future of our society. And that's why it's worth thinking about and writing about.

The new thing under our sun, born in the life of each of us, is television journalism. Many years ago, Walter Lippmann remarked that it is the function of journalism to present a picture of the world upon which men can act. More recently, David Brinkley said that, "If most people in this country are getting most of their news from television, they are getting damned little news."

I think those two statements should be embroidered on the same sampler and framed. Because in the tension between them is the dilemma of information processing which is an aspect of the electronic age. Our principal mass medium, upon which most people depend for information to make up their minds, is capable of only the most delimited explication of the events, issues and people of our time. It necessarily settles for stereotypes and simplifications. And in this one metaphor which we have been employing tonight, namely the student movement, there are observable and unfortunate by-products of that compromise.

But, through no one's fault, for there is no conspiracy here, similar grotesqueries grow out of our perceptions of all the other societal problems we face: the war, race, crime, environmental pollution, overpopulation, military spending, women's rights, inflation, poverty, nutrition, drug use, housing, unemployment, consumer fraud, illiteracy, invasions of privacy, Congressional ethics, penal reform, urban renewal, arms control. We see them all through a glass darkly and we vote our perceptions. Our political leaders too often give us the legislation we want instead of the legislation we need. They follow public opinion rather than lead it. And they thus complete the circle, in our now famous Circular Theory of Social Dynamics, the final result of which is a society which is misshapen and inefficient at best, and, at its worst, in some danger of breaking down.

Arthur Schlesinger noted recently that we are hurrying into the fantastic new epoch of the electronic age which has been foreshadowed by television and the computer, and that one need not be a McLuhanite to observe that history is profoundly affected by changes in the means of communication. He added, and I'd like to quote this, that "the electronic age will have penetrating effects not just on the structure and processes of society but on the very reflexes of individual perception. Already television," he said, "by its collectiveness and simultaneity, has fostered an intense desire for political self-expression and visibility, as it has spread the habit of instant reaction and stimulated the hope of instant results."

But it is now apparent that television as it is now constituted in this country is not the optimum conduit for the exchange of information about ourselves. Students, and all other activists, have been slow to understand that the franchised entrepreneurs of American TV stations and networks are neither ideologues nor social philosophers, but businessmen whose first concern is, and perhaps ought to be, maintaining the commercial viability of their businesses. To one university administrator we talked to, however, that practice constitutes a disabling myopia when it thwarts the public interest instead of serving it. He said, "It's like fiddling while the American society—which produces these huge profits for broadcasters in the first place—burns." His gloomy diagnosis is supported by the fact that the serious prime time television documentary is almost a thing of the past—like Mr. Peepers and Pinky Lee.

It may turn out that public television—if it survives its rather anemic, poverty-stricken infancy—will be the logical alternative as the voluntary forum for extended, serious national dialogue. That would ease the consciences of commercial broadcasters, and allow them to pursue their chosen, natural roles as businessmen in the entertainment and advertising fields.

But a score of years of television's trying to sell to young people toys and breakfast foods, as well as cigarettes and cars, has produced in a disproportionately large segment of the nation's youth a pervasive hostility toward the medium. The Scranton Report noted, rather sadly, that a nation that has lost the allegiance of part of its youth is a nation that has lost part of its future. We might say that: A medium that has lost the allegiance of part of its youth is a medium that has lost part of its future. And that is a dilemma which the managers of American television must ponder in some dark night of their soul.

chapter 15 # The Black Reporter and His Problems

M. L. STEIN

Black reporters on daily newspapers are deeply frustrated as the result of a conflict between their conception of their role and the traditional journalistic values to which they are expected to conform. They also are disturbed over what they consider tokenism and bias *inside* the newsroom as well as in hiring practices. After talking to several black journalists and white editors, I am convinced that some kind of understanding by the two groups is necessary to prevent a bad situation from becoming worse.

This is not to suggest that blacks are being employed in large numbers for news jobs. The opposite is true. Dr. Edward J. Trayes, associate professor of communications at Temple University, found in a recent survey that black participation on daily newspaper staffs was at an "extremely low level and quite disproportionate to the growing Negro population throughout America." His findings revealed that of 7,152 news executives, deskmen, reporters, and photographers on 196 dailies of more than 10,000 circulation, 111, or 1.55 per cent, were black. Only five executives (assistant city editor through editor) were Negro. Of the 3,691 reporters represented in the study, eighty-three, or 2.25 per cent, were black. Out of the total number of news personnel, Professor Trayes concluded that only about one in sixty-five was black.

The ratio of blacks to whites in broadcast journalism is even lower. The three major television networks have only five black newscasters among them, and only a handful are reporting for local outlets.

Still, particularly on newspapers, a breakthrough has been achieved in the past four years. For example, as a newsman in San Francisco from 1951 to 1961, I cannot recall a single black reporter or photographer on the city's four dailies during that period, a situation that also existed in many other communities. Currently, the San Francisco *Examiner* has its own training program for black reporters, a sprinkling of whom are working for the city's news media. But the breakthrough has created its own problem for some black newsmen and women. They say they were hired during a time of racial rioting and are being largely ignored by editors now that the strife has waned.

"Many black reporters throughout the country are undergoing a severe crisis because they were brought in during a crisis period," said Charlayne Hunter, a black reporter for *The New York Times*. "They were assigned to get into the ghetto areas during the trouble, and now that riots have spent themselves the need to utilize them is not as great. Some are just sitting around newspaper city rooms."

Miss Hunter's charge was endorsed by other black newsmen in New York City, Washington, and Chicago. They complained that they were not developing as newsmen because of the lack of good writing assignments. Many resented doing leg work for stories that are written by white reporters.

There are, of course, outstanding exceptions. Miss Hunter and Thomas A. Johnson, of the *Times*; William Raspberry, of the Washington *Post*; L. F. Palmer, Jr., and Betty Washington, of the Chicago *Daily News*, and a few other black journalists are covering major stories or writing columns. Miss Hunter, who runs a recently created Harlem news bureau for the *Times*, said young black reporters feel they are not being given a chance to test their capabilities. "They get little direction or guidance from the desk," she added. "These reporters are saying, 'You can't treat us special and then not special.'"

The problem is recognized by some newspapers. Henry Stasiuk, managing editor of the Newark (New Jersey) *Star-Ledger*, said that under a new policy "all city-side reporters are on general assignment and no one covers a black beat." He further explained, "If we feel that a particular story can be best covered by a black reporter, we send one, but generally everyone here writes stories and legs them."

Thomas Boardman, editor of the Cleveland *Press,* said the four black journeymen reporters on his staff are assigned "general duties" and that one is an assistant editor. He noted that the *Press* also has a training program for young blacks recruited from inner-city high schools.

The issue is not always solved by keeping the black reporter busy covering general news. Some black newsmen object to being assigned a "black beat," but others strongly feel that they are best qualified by their black experience to report news with a racial background, an opinion that is not universally accepted by white editors.

L. F. Palmer, Jr., of the Chicago *Daily News,* who is on general assignment and writes a syndicated column expressing a black point of view, believes that the Negro reporter is usually better qualified to report on the black community. "Some blacks," he said, "are more sensitive to the whole black and white conflict than others. My own feeling is that this conflict is the biggest running story of the day, and it's not being adequately or honestly covered. I believe that the black perspective must be presented and only blacks can present it. I simply don't believe that a white reporter can understand all the nuances, all the meanings, behind some stories."

Other black newsmen supported Palmer's view. Richard Prince, of the Washington *Post,* observed: "There's no question that in some situations a black reporter is able to make a better judgment on a story. Besides, many black community leaders specifically ask newspapers to send blacks to cover events in those areas." As an example, Prince cited the memorial service in Washington for Ralph Featherstone, a black militant killed in a bomb explosion. According to Prince, only black reporters were allowed inside the hall where the service was held. "It's just not a black and white issue," he added. "It's also a matter of good journalism practice. The reporter best qualified should cover the story."

Betty Washington, of the Chicago *Daily News,* said, "I prefer to think of myself as a reporter rather than as a black reporter, but I don't run away from stories about blacks. If something happens concerning the Black Panthers, for example, I want to be there. I think in touchy situations like that the black reporter can, in fact, do a better job of coverage than a white reporter."

The notion that only blacks be assigned to black-related news is difficult to accept for a generation of editors raised on the theory that any journeyman reporter should be able to handle any kind of story. Many white editors with black staff members are continuing to assign whites to black-oriented stories despite the resentment of some black reporters. One such boss, Harry M. Rosenfeld, Washington *Post* metropolitan editor, said he felt "uncomfortable" with the demand that only blacks cover the black community.

"I think I understand one of the reasons for this insistence," Rosenfeld continued. "It's a means of encouraging the use of more blacks on daily newspapers, and I'm entirely in agreement with this desire. The big-city papers should be more representative of their communities. But I also believe that a newspaper should tell about the *whole* community. I would be unhappy if I could only assign a black to cover a black story just as I would be unhappy if I had to assign a Jew to a Jewish story or an Italian to an Italian story."

Rosenfeld, whose metropolitan staff includes eight black reporters, pointed out, however, that he and other deskmen make "pragmatic exceptions" to the general assignment rule. "If," he explained, "an editor feels that a black reporter could best cover a particular situation, he will be assigned to it."

A similar policy appears to be in force at the Chicago *Daily News.* Editor Roy M. Fisher said, "We consider that all of our reporters are available to any assignment regardless of race. They do, however, have special advantages in reporting the blacks' side of racial controversy and tend to specialize in the racial and social problems of the inner city."

The *New York Times,* which has thirteen black reporters and photographers, deploys them on any kind of story, but editors prefer to use them for racial matters "when it appears necessary," according to Managing Editor A. M. Rosenthal. He added that no reporter is restricted in what he can cover and that it is not uncommon for white reporters to cover black stories and blacks to get general news assignments.

Being assigned to a "black beat" is not always an ideal situation for a black reporter. Some encounter hostility from community blacks who have hurled such epithets at the newsmen as "Uncle Tom," "spy," and "sellout." Then, too, black news sources have been used to dealing with Negro weekly papers and are uneasy and hesitant under the demands of more professional reporters with daily deadlines. A black reporter who frequently covers the ghetto for a New York daily said: "Some black organizations don't even know how to set up a press conference, and they're suspicious of me when I try to help them with it."

The question of assignments inevitably leads to the issue of objectivity, that journalistic byword so buffeted about these days. A number of black journalists feel that objectivity—or even the new term, fairness—is for them an unworkable, if not insulting, concept. One of their most severe conflicts arises from their efforts to be fair and objective, while having little or no faith in the idea. Arguments between white editors and black reporters over objectivity have erupted in more than one newsroom.

Robert A. DeLeon, a black man who, until recently, reported for the

Atlanta *Constitution* and *Newsday* recalled his newspaper days with a bitterness echoed by many of his colleagues. "Once involved in the black community," he said, "I found it increasingly difficult to remain in the position of objective observer and soon learned that such attempts were futile. I realized that my biases and subjectivity entered into the picture even before I began reporting a story. Because white papers—and the media in general—traditionally have neglected and, in fact, ignored the black community, editors provided little guidance in the selection of stories in the black community, and the whole process of selection became a personal matter. I had to dismiss the notion of objectivity. In choosing stories I constantly found that I was seeking *good things* that were being done in the black community. I guess I was trying to prove to whites that blacks were human and wanted, basically, to share in the same things as everyone else. For this bias I have never apologized, because white journalists have been doing it all along as it relates to the day-to-day happenings in the white community."

Betty Washington said she strives for fairness in any story she covers "even when I'm emotionally upset about something like a police-Panther shootout. However," she admitted, "my story is bound to be biased to a certain extent. I don't care, because I know how some other stories are written in the paper. Actually, I don't believe that anyone is objective. Newspapers certainly are not objective."

Miss Washington's colleague, L. F. Palmer, agreed, terming objectivity a myth. "I believe in advocacy journalism, particularly for blacks," he asserted. "At the same time, I feel that a reader is in a better position to evaluate a story if the biases of the writer are not hidden. It's when they're concealed that the reader gets taken. If a reader knows that I'm a pro-black writer, which I am, he can more competently deal with what I'm saying."

Nevertheless, many white editors continue to insist on objectivity, except in columns. Thomas Boardman, of the Cleveland *Press*, expressed a common city-room attitude when he stated: "We expect the same objectivity from black reporters as anyone else."

Grievances of black newsmen have led them into forming their own organizations as a means of expression. The first National Conference of Black Newsmedia Workers was held last summer at Lincoln University in Jefferson City, Missouri. Rush Greenlee, a black San Francisco journalist, said the meeting was called because "there is a hunger among black journalists to know who they are, to clarify the role they have been playing and the one they might play in the black liberation struggle."

The dispute will likely simmer for years unless there is some dramatic shift by the newspapers. A growing number of young blacks in journalism schools and elsewhere are even more militant than those now in the media. At a journalism workshop for minority students at New York University last summer, several black youngsters ridiculed the principle of objectivity. Betty Washington said she has talked to inner-city black pupils who want to go into journalism, but seek to do their own kind of writing. "Some of them said that if things don't go their way they'll throw bolts into the presses," she reported.

Whether these young people will be hired at all is another major area of conflict in the minds of black newsmen on Establishment newspapers. They blame editors for the scarcity of black staffers, charging that they are not recruiting hard enough because they're not sincere about wanting more blacks. Black reporters scoffed at the frequently voiced excuse by editors that not enough "qualified" blacks are available. Many believe that the term "qualified" is itself a convenient dodge to limit black employment on newspapers. Bristling at the mention of the word, a black Washington newsman snapped: "I always hear the term 'qualified' applied to black applicants in the media. Are all white applicants qualified? I doubt it, yet I never hear of editors sending out requests for *qualified* white beginners."

Metropolitan daily editors deny the accusation and claim they are honestly seeking more blacks for their editorial departments but can't find them. One reason for this, they say, is that the journalism schools and departments are not turning out enough black majors. True enough. Professor Trayes found that, although the proportion of Negro journalism majors has jumped 50 per cent in the past year, the total number is still very low. Of the 7,440 juniors and seniors majoring in news-editorial or photo-journalism sequences at 103 schools, 237, or 3.19 per cent, are black.

L. F. Palmer conceded that journalism schools should be producing more black graduates, but he contended that the newspapers are nevertheless dragging their feet on hiring them. "Take Chicago," Palmer said. "Officials at the four metropolitan daily newspapers report that they employ eight hundred and eleven editorial employees at and above the reporter/photographer rank. Of this number, seventeen are black. This is just two per cent in a city expected to be fifty per cent black by 1980."

For the answer to the problem, one must go deeper than journalism school enrollment or debating arguments. Black enrollment in journalism schools is low because for years journalism was a career virtually closed to blacks. But even now that the opportunities have opened up in the field, the ratio of black journalism majors is still far below what it should be. One reason is that few black youngsters in secondary schools are getting encouragement to study journalism or work in the field. If journalism schools are to increase their black enrollment, a pipeline must be laid to the high schools. This is the responsibility of journalism schools, the news media, black journalists, black community leaders, and high school teachers, counselors, and administrators. More programs are needed, such as the one recently initiated by the Association for Education in Journalism, establishing media internships for black students. The American Newspaper Publishers Association Foundation offers cash scholarships to black journalism students, and other organizations are engaged in similar efforts.

"Most black high school kids have never seen a reporter," said Ernest Johnston, Jr., black reported for the New York *Post*. "Black journalists should be brought into the classroom. Just their being there will give students a better insight into journalism. There should also be more and better school papers to stimulate the interest of youngsters and develop their skills."

In any case, some black journalists fear that if and when the black students are hired on newspapers they will have a tougher time surviving their probationary period and getting promoted than starting white reporters. Said one black reporter: "The editors don't expect us to be as good. One editor, in fact, told me that he didn't expect too much from me. This is a hell of a way to get into a new job. I've talked this over with other black reporters, and most of them feel that they have to be in training longer than whites. And even then they stand a good chance of being fired."

White editors said *their* big problem is keeping the black reporters they've hired. In recent months, *Newsday*, the *New York Times*, the *Long Island Press*, and the Cleveland *Press*, among other newspapers, have lost black newsmen to public relations or broadcasting. The lure usually has been the same as that for white reporters who took the same route—more money.

chapter 16 Journalism: Liberal or Conservative?

DAVID J. LeROY

In the last few years a number of polemic books and quite a few politicians have accused reporters and the "press" of being biased toward the liberal point of view. So, are the reporters liberal and the owners conservative? This is one of those chicken and the egg questions: Do liberals become reporters, or do reporters become liberals? A variety of people from all political areas have suggested that people who become reporters tend to share the same background and personality traits. There is little evidence to support this notion but it is enticing. Unfortunately it also obscures the crucial issue that the press is more a conservative force in American politics than a liberal one. If journalism is biased toward the liberal side, it is an accidental liberalism.

Let us look at some reporting norms responsible for this accidental liberalism. First, reports tend to focus on politicians as individuals; something is said, is picked up and stressed in the story (the angle), and the headline writer takes over. Since politicians are frequently redundant, the reporter is reduced to "finding something new"—usually some slip of the tongue. Frequently this type of reporting focuses on conservative politicians because the liberals are allied with a second reporting norm that functions somewhat differently.

This second reporting norm, which gives the appearance of liberalism, is the idea of reporting the deviant or the things wrong with society. The journalist's continued emphasis upon what is missing or wrong infuriates businessmen and some politicians, since they would rather emphasize their accomplishments (for example, making a profit from a bad investment or getting a bill passed without serious compromise). However, the mass news emphasis on social problems and unfulfilled needs is congruent with the typical legislative strategy of American liberals who employ unfulfilled needs and social problems as reasons for enacting legislation. In a sense then, reporting norms and liberal tactics join in a convenient marriage with, unfortunately perhaps, one serious difference. Mass news merely reports the story one day and then moves on to something else. There is little sustained coverage of a social problem and the fate of its proposed remedy. Mass news merely reports and rarely advocates. Further, the politician, regardless of his motives, can exploit the media by finding social problems and announcing with great fanfare the forthcoming legislation to correct the situation. Since promises rarely match performance, mass news only raises the hopes of the afflicted.

In this sense then, reporting norms differentially favor certain types of politicians. However, as many demonstrators and protesters discovered throughout the sixties, it is safe to assume that all reporters are sympathetic to liberal causes. Many protesters made the news simply because they were disruptive, not because the reporter was sympathetic with their cause.

But the next issue is, why is the press a more conservative or reinforcing element in society? In reporting politics, many reporters have become inadvertent reinforcers of the status quo through the norm of objective reporting. The following example shows how the very act of reporting imbues an event with order, rationality, and coherence.

David Paletz and his colleagues attended their local city council meetings for a number of months.[1] They took notes on the subject of the council's actions, and also on the emotion and counterplay of the meetings. They noted jokes, the sleeping councilmen, and the mayor's natty dress and manner.

They then compared their notes and impressions with published newspaper stories of the same meetings. Paletz argued that the newspaper accounts gave the appearance of coherence and rationality to the council meetings. The reporter mentioned none of the sidelights of the sleeping

[1] David L. Paletz, Peggy Reichert, and Barbara McIntyre, "How the Media Support Local Governmental Authority," *Public Opinion Quarterly*, 35:1 (Spring 1971), pp. 80–92.

councilmen, the jokes, the meandering, or the emotional discussions of some issues. Only the decisions made or avoided were noted.

What we have here is two views of reality. The newspaper, true to its perception of journalism, focused on the facts. Paletz argues that the newspaper presented a distorted view of the situation. The stories were not critical but passive in nature. They reinforced the system, in his view, by not presenting a fair and representative report of what occurred.

Most editors and reporters would dismiss this criticism by arguing that council meetings have always had sleeping councilmen and unfocused and emotional discussions. Reporters are concerned with the news, not gossip or inferences about councilmen. They do not have enough space for such prattle, and they also run the risk of being sued.

This is a perplexing issue. Certainly many of us would like to know if *our* councilmen sleep through the meetings; or whether one or two members seem to direct all of the council's decisions on certain issues (for example, land rezoning or liquor licenses). If the local newspaper will not tell us, who will?

Implicitly we have been nudging toward the notion that objective-reflective reporting—although the easiest and quickest way to report about highly visible events perhaps has faults which require some correction. But how is the reporter going to change if the news bureaucracy is oriented toward and skilled in only one type of reporting?

Let us suggest that mass news bureaucracy is a legitimate controversial issue. It will not change, however, unless the news public demands change. Reporters, also, should legislate for some control over their essential task —reporting, analyzing, and advocating particular points of view.

chapter 17   # Subpoenas:
Should Reporters
Be Forced
to Tell
What They Know?

MARCUS COHN

Newspaper publishers, editors, and reporters are understandably schizophrenic about recent constitutional law developments. They loved the
Supreme Court when it expanded the parameters of the First Amendment
—and almost eliminated libel suits—in *New York Times* v. *Sullivan* and
a number of cases that followed. They grumbled when the Court held
that their conduct (along with that of television cameramen) had made it
impossible for Dr. Sam Sheppard to receive the kind of trial guaranteed
to him by the Constitution and commented that "unfair and prejudicial
news" coverage of criminal trials had "become increasingly prevalent."

But broadcasters and their reporters haven't even had the pleasure
of ambivalence. They were downright distraught when, in the *Billie Sol
Estes* case, the Court held that television cameras in the courtroom violated a defendant's Sixth Amendment rights to have a fair trial and then

last year held in the *Red Lion* case, which sustained the FCC's Fairness Doctrine, that the First Amendment right was that "of the viewers and listeners, [and] not the right of the broadcasters."

At the very time that these developments in constitutional law—one protecting and one spanking the media—were taking place, newspapers and television stations were becoming more and more caught up in society's current convulsively volatile social problems. Their aggressive involvement was accentuated by the fact that a new breed of reporters— young, bright, sensitive, and personally involved in social issues—had entrées and relationships with the social activists of our time, which the old establishment did not seem to have.

Today's big social issue stories do not deal with the graft and corruption of government officials, but with social movements involving large numbers of people who, in their collectivity and joint action, cause news to occur: the 1968 Democratic Convention in Chicago, the several recent mass rallies in Washington, the Woodstocks, and the frequent political and social protest marches around the country. The very nature of what the participants do in those events lends itself to pictorial reporting. Indeed, what any one of them *says* becomes comparatively unimportant. What they *do* becomes the important event and, thus, the television camera becomes a more meaningful messenger of the news than do the notebook and pencil.

Every lawyer knows that, given a choice of oral testimony, on the one hand, or photographic evidence, on the other, the latter is always more persuasive to a jury. Consequently, it was quite logical, as more and more television cameramen showed up at the scenes of social protest, for prosecuting attorneys later to want to secure and present to grand juries the photographs and the motion pictures that they had made of the alleged crime. These films had two functions. In the first place, they were able vividly to portray the *act* itself and, secondly, they could positively identify the person involved in the act. The work product of the television reporter became, in a real sense, the best evidence of what had occurred and certainly far better than the notes of the newspaper reporter or the oral testimony of one of the participants in the event.

And if the number and frequency of "political crimes" increases, it will only be natural for the prosecutor to want to see and be even more dependent upon the films shot by television cameramen.

Although during the past seventy-four years, seventeen state legislatures have dealt with and attempted to resolve by various types of legislation the limits to which a state grand jury could subpoena newspaper reporters (and in a few instances broadcasting reporters), federal grand juries have had no comparable legislative guidance. Moreover, the Supreme Court has never had the occasion either to discuss or decide the issue.

Most of the recent prosecutions for activities arising from the social stresses of our time have been in federal courts. Thus, who appears and what notes, photographs, tapes, and films he is required to bring with him are questions decided by the United States Attorney.

The prosecutor normally has very little difficulty in securing that portion of television tapes which were actually telecast or that portion of the news reporter's story which was published. The problem arises when he desires to have the television "out-take" (the portion of the film which was not televised, generally constituting the bulk of what was actually recorded) and the notes or tapes of the newspaper reporter.

Until recently, reporters in most cases were able to negotiate successfully with the prosecutor and narrow the scope of the subpoena.

However, during the past several years, the attitude of prosecuting attorneys has toughened. They have taken to subpoenaing reporters more often; the desired testimony has dealt with information given in confidence and never published or exhibited; and the information has come from reporters' peers who have been protesting against the establishments. Reporters were being asked to betray friends. They began to resist these command performances and to raise a number of questions.

If, indeed, it is true that the First Amendment protects reporters not only against direct interference by the government, but also—to use the Supreme Court's words in the *Dombrowski* case—any act which would have a "chilling effect" upon the opportunity to gather and publish news, then *any* subpoena which required the revelation of *any* information given in confidence was unconstitutional. To give it would not only drop the informer's temperature, but would freeze him into complete silence. Earl Caldwell, the reporter of the *New York Times* who has covered the Black Panther movement extensively, has refused even to appear before a grand jury, pursuant to a subpoena, even though a federal district judge has told him that he may have the advice of counsel throughout the proceedings and come back to the Court for protection in the event the jury's questions require him to reveal confidential sources of information. Caldwell replied that once he sets foot in the grand jury room, he has cracked the cement of confidentiality and his informants will no longer trust him. This, in turn, will make it impossible for him to exercise his First Amendment right to gather news.

When the subpoena proponents argue that total truth in the "market place" is as important in the judicial as it is in the political process, the media reply that society has historically recognized that individual liberties and rights sometimes take precedence over the jury's or the judge's right to know. A number of these barriers to the revelation of all the facts are constitutionally protected in the Fifth and other constitutional amendments. Moreover, society made a decision a long time ago to protect the communications between a lawyer and his client, a doctor and his patient, and the clergyman and his parishioner.*

If a reporter does not have this constitutional protection, then, in order to protect his own dignity and to be certain that confidential communications remain confidential, he will destroy all memoranda, photos, and films once his story has been written and his photograph or film exhibited. Because normally the television reporter shoots far more footage than he will ever use and stores most of the rest for future use and reference, the net result will be that broadcasters may be driven to destroy large libraries of current events and deprive society of historical documentation they would otherwise have.

And then, lastly, reporters point out that if it is common knowledge that their notes and their films are always subject to examination by a grand jury, they will be subject to harassment by their normal sources because, in the eyes of the disadvantaged, they have become spies for the police and the very notes, photographs, and films become symbols of oppression and, thus, should be destroyed.

The prosecutor's reply to these arguments is basically quite simple: I've got a job to do. I want to give the grand jury all the information available. As long as a reporter does not have the protection of a statute which gives him the right to refuse to testify, then he has an obligation to give the grand jury any information which may have a bearing on its investigation.

Putting aside the prosecuting attorney's desire to justify his pay check, there are basic and fundamental issues posed to society if newsmen may decide for themselves whether they should testify before a grand jury. If newsmen may successfully resist grand jury subpoenas on the ground of confidentiality, then what is to preclude them from invoking the same privilege when a *defendant* in a criminal case subpoenas them in order to establish his innocence under *his* guaranteed Sixth Amendment right to a fair trial? The civil libertarians who now cry for the protection of the reporter, because his confidants have been society's social critics, may find themselves denying justice to those very same social critics seeking the testimony of the reporter who stands on his constitutional rights.

Moreover, the Fifth Amendment explicitly recognizes the function and purpose of the grand jury. It was placed there for the protection of people who are suspected of crimes. Its existence has made it mandatory that indictments be issued by a legally constituted body whose members reside in the area where the crime occurred. The jury members hear and

---

* Of course, in these cases the "informant" (the client, patient or parishioner) is seeking personal help and guidance—he wants to save his own skin or soul—and, at least for the time being, is totally unconcerned with what relationship, if any, his problem has to any major social issue.

sift all the available evidence before issuing an indictment rather than, as in pre-Constitution days, a single magistrate issued the indictment merely because the prosecutor requested him to do it. Any interpretation of the First Amendment which would give reporters the right to decide whether they wish to testify before a grand jury weakens that system and could result in the indictment of innocent people.

On February 5, 1970, Attorney General Mitchell issued a two-and-a-half page double-spaced statement in which he announced that henceforth the Justice Department would be willing to negotiate the scope of subpoenas to the press prior to their issuance and be willing to discuss modifications afterward. It referred to the "press" eleven different times. Neither radio, television, nor broadcasting was mentioned once. It ended with the prayer that "this policy of caution, negotiation and attempted compromise will continue to prove as workable in the future as it has in the past." Putting aside the question of its past workability, obviously the Attorney General's prayer for the future went unanswered. Six months later (August 10) he delivered a twenty-six-page address on the same subject to the American Bar Association, in which he referred to all the media. In it he indicated a far greater concern over the issue, set forth a detailed series of guidelines for those responsible for the issuance of subpoenas, and adopted a procedure where subpoenaed reporters could appeal their cases directly to him.

In essence, the guidelines require the United States Attorney to attempt to obtain the desired information from non-press sources before subpoenaing the press. Failing this, the prosecutor is now required to confer ahead of time with the reporter whom he proposes to subpoena and attempt to negotiate a mutually satisfactory scope for the subpoena. If the negotiations fail, then the prosecutor must request the Attorney General's approval before issuing the subpoena.

The principles which will guide the Attorney General's decision on whether or not to issue the subpoena are: that there is reason to believe that a crime has been committed; that the information requested is "essential" to a successful investigation; that the government tried unsuccessfully to get the information from non-press sources; and that, "wherever possible," the subpoena should be directed at "material information regarding a reasonably limited subject matter." The subpoena should cover only a "reasonably limited time period" and should avoid the requirement of producing "a large volume" of unpublished material. "Normally," the subpoena should be limited to verification of published information and circumstances relating to its accuracy.

These vague and amorphous expressions of concern are extended even further in the penultimate standard. The Attorney General promises to exercise "great caution" in subpoenaing unpublished information where an "orthodox" First Amendment defense is raised or where a "serious claim" is made that the information was received on a confidential basis.

"Great," "orthodox," and "serious" allow for tremendous latitude of non-appealable interpretations. Indeed, they may vary dramatically from time to time, and the intensity of the "sensitivity" with which they are to be administered will, of course, depend upon *who* is the Attorney General.

The intensity with which broadcasters and their news reporters will assert First Amendment rights when subpoenaed by grand juries—despite the Mitchell statement—must be viewed in the context of the total present political climate. Vice President Agnew has repeatedly warned the federally licensed broadcasters that their behavior was less than desirable because they overexposed socially disruptive movements and personalities. FCC Chairman Burch has endorsed what the Vice President said. Although there is no hard evidence that broadcasters have been intimidated by what Mr. Agnew said, nevertheless, there can be little doubt that they will want to give thought to the question of whether they should compound the administration's antagonism toward them by now defying grand jury subpoenas.

The ominous character of the Vice President's scolding of the television industry takes on added significance in light of the fact that the Attorney General, in his recent twenty-six-page peace-making guidelines which established the criteria under which newspapermen might be subpoenaed before grand juries, specifically limited the guidelines to the "press." Indeed, in his speech he asked the question whether there shouldn't be "a distinction among different categories of media." He did not explain why radio and television might be treated any differently than the press, but obviously he also had been reading the Vice President's speeches. He knew of one distinction: Newspapers are not licensed by the federal government, whereas broadcasting stations are. Merely by raising the question, there is an intimation that broadcasters would be more intimidatable than newspapers.

In the spring of this year—just after the Attorney General issued his two-and-a-half-page statement on the subject—legislation was introduced in the House (Congressman Ottinger and twenty-one co-sponsors) and in the Senate (Senator McIntyre and nine co-sponsors) which would drastically limit the subpoenaing of reporters from *any* of the media. It refers specifically to radio and television. It would prohibit all such subpoenas (whether issued by a grand jury, a court, an agency or department of the federal government, or Congress itself) except under very limited and precisely defined circumstances: when the confidential *information* itself had been made public by the person who had the right to claim the privilege; where the disclosure of the *source* of an alleged slander or libel was needed by a defendant in order to assert a defense in a civil suit; and when the details of secret sessions, such as that of a grand jury, are published. The privilege would not apply to either the source or the information, when the inquiring body deals with a question involving a "threat of foreign aggression." However, in such a situation there must first be a determination by a federal district court that the exception is applicable.

There is a question whether Congress can constitutionally include broadcast reporters in such legislation. If *Red Lion* really means what it says and it is the public, rather than the broadcaster (a mere licensee of the federal government), who has First Amendment rights, then one of the constitutional issues which must ultimately arise is whether the broadcast reporter can claim any kind of First Amendment protection when he is subpoenaed by a grand jury—whether or not he is included in the proposed legislation.

Hearings on these pending bills may provide the very kind of study which is urgently needed. There has never been a national formalized discussion of the issue. The results of the hearings may also have the effect of stimulating the thirty-three states which have not, as yet, adopted any legislation on the matter to face up to the problems and to do something about it.

In his August 1970 ABA speech, the Attorney General made a point of saying that he would not oppose legislative guidelines. That is understandable. Legislation would take him and the administration off the hot seat.

chapter 18 # CBS Reports:
The Selling
Of
The Pentagon

F. LESLIE SMITH

At 10 PM, EST, on February 23, 1971, CBS broadcasted a television documentary titled "CBS Reports: The Selling of the Pentagon." This
documentary took a critical look at the massive public relations and
promotional activities of the Department of Defense.[1] It subsequently

F. Leslie Smith, "CBS Reports: The Selling of the Pentagon (A Case Study of a
Controversy)." Published here for the first time by permission of the author.
[1] According to "The Selling of the Pentagon," the military attempts to "sell" to
the American civilian population its ideas on foreign policy (especially in Southeast
Asia); the necessity of maintaining a large defense establishment; and the wisdom,
skill, and invincibility of the armed forces and their leaders. The Pentagon does
this selling with an estimated $190 million of taxpayers' money. The documentary
illustrated its criticisms with specific examples of the modes of military persuasion:
television programs produced by the Department of Defense, public demonstration
of weaponry and tactical skills, public lectures, control of press access to defense
information, expensive VIP orientational tours for influential civilians, etc. Actually,
according to two scholars, CBS seems to have "lifted" much of the information in
"Selling's" verbal narration from statements made previously by Senator J. William
Fulbright, particularly in his book, *The Pentagon Propaganda Machine*. See Jimmie
N. Rogers and Theodore Clevenger, Jr., "'The Selling of the Pentagon:' Was CBS
the Fulbright Propaganda Machine?", *Quarterly Journal of Speech* (November 1971).

ignited a public controversy which was to evolve and build for four and a half months, concluding with an historic refusal by the United States House of Representatives to back the contempt citation of one of its committees. The issue at stake, the forces involved, and the philosophical background against which they interacted in this controversy yielded a matrix of relationships which may portend changes in basic American institutions—the people, the government, and the press.

"Selling," as a public controversy went through three distinct phases. The first phase was six weeks long and began with Representative F. Edward Hebert's attack on the program soon after its first showing. In this phase, the program itself was being examined and identified as a possible candidate for full-fledged controversy. While there was discussion of the program pro and con, the controversy was still an infant and could live or die. The issuance of the April 7 subpoena by a Congressional subcommittee signaled the start of the two-week second phase. During this phase, the controversy developed and intensified but, had CBS decided to comply with the subpoena, it could still have died before reaching maturity. The controversy entered its final phase on April 20, when CBS first refused to comply with the subpoena. This was the confrontation phase, twelve weeks long, and this was where the action—and the muscle —was.

As mentioned above, Representative F. Edward Hebert, Chairman of the House Armed Services Committee got in the first word. Hebert had not actually seen the documentary, but he had read a *New York Times* review of it and felt he knew enough about it to call it "the most misleading and damaging attack on our people that I ever heard of." Such early statements did little to define the issues, but not long afterward two individuals who had appeared in "The Selling of the Pentagon" claimed that the words they actually uttered had been edited and twisted in meaning. Daniel J. Henkin, assistant secretary of defense for public affairs, said that the answers he had given Roger Mudd during a filmed interview had been rearranged so as to distort his intent. Marine Colonel John A. MacNeil claimed that filmed segments from a speech he had given in Peoria, Illinois, had been taken out of context so that he seemed to be commenting on U.S. foreign policy when actually he had been quoting the Prime Minister of Laos. These claims became the face issues, both *cause celebre* and *raison d'etre* for the fledgling controversy. Representative Hebert filed a complaint with the Federal Communications Commission (FCC) citing the Henkin and MacNeil charges. The FCC received a similar complaint from another Congressman, but this was not made public for a number of weeks. The other complaint was filed by Representative Harley O. Staggers, chairman of the House Committee on

Interstate and Foreign Commerce and of its Special Subcommittee on Investigations.

On March 31, Representative Staggers met privately with the Special Investigations Subcommittee and instructed its staff to prepare materials on "The Selling of the Pentagon." One week later, Staggers and the Subcommittee made public their interest, intensified the controversy, and forced it into its second phase. On April 7, the Subcommittee gave its staff authority to issue a subpoena to CBS for all materials that had gone into the production of "Selling," to include: the complete 16 mm sound film copy and written text of the documentary; all outtakes, workprints, sound tape recordings, written scripts, and transcripts, whether or not used in the completed documentary; and information about payment to any person who appeared in the program, as well as the names and addresses of individuals who were shown, except such persons as military officers and congressmen. Similar subpoenas had been issued to NBC and to Wolper Productions demanding parallel material from "Say Goodbye," a program that dealt with vanishing wildlife and which had been attacked by hunters as being falsified in spots. But the consensus among broadcasting industry sources seemed to be that the Wolper and NBC subpoenas were simply distractions constructed by the Subcommittee to mask its real target, CBS. In a statement to the press, CBS president Dr. Frank Stanton declared that CBS would furnish film and transcripts of the program as broadcast, but would not provide the outtakes, workprints, sound recordings, and other material required by the subpoena. Thus, the subpoena served also to identify the spokesmen for the opposing sides—Staggers, the Congressman, chairing his Subcommittee, and Stanton, the company president, directing the CBS strategy.

Exposure of the controversy through the public channels of communication had begun with Hebert's initial comment, and had continued through the first two phases. The print press publicized the controversy with articles and commentary. On March 23, CBS rebroadcast "The Selling of the Pentagon," following it with twenty minutes of pro and con statements from various persons; then on April 18 the network had aired its "Perspective: The Selling of the Pentagon," featuring comments by both critics and supporters of the Pentagon. The stage was now set for the next move.

CBS made it through its deputy general counsel, John D. Appel, on the afternoon of April 20 in room 2322 of the Rayburn House Office Building. The occasion was an executive session meeting of the Special Subcommittee on Investigations for the first of three hearings on "Subpoenaed Material Re Certain News Documentary Programs." After NBC and Wolper had complied with their subpoenas, handing in all material pertinent to the production of "Say Goodbye," Appel read into the record a letter from his boss, Robert V. Evans, CBS vice president and general counsel. In the letter, Evans notified the Subcommittee that CBS could not "conceive of any legitimate legislative purpose to which the materials could be relevant," and therefore was submitting *voluntarily* film and script of the complete "The Selling of the Pentagon," but none of the other material directed by the subpoena. At the conclusion of the hearing Daniel J. Manelli, the Subcommittee's acting general counsel, said that should CBS persist in its noncompliance with the subpoena, the Subcommittee would have no choice but to force the network to yield the material through a contempt-of-Congress citation. CBS had accepted the challenge, the Subcommittee was committed, and the confrontation was on.

There is some reason to suspect that the Subcommittee was not as sure of its own legal case as it might have wished. A contempt-of-Congress citation (which required a majority vote of the House) would have called for the prosecution of the cited party in a Federal Court. If the Court were to decide against the Government and the Supreme Court were to uphold the decision, the result would have been to proscribe the limits of Congressional inquiry. The Subcommittee certainly did not wish to risk this, so when CBS so confidently refused to comply with the subpoena, the Subcommittee asked the network to submit a memorandum within ten days outlining the legal bases for its refusal. This memorandum would allow the Subcommittee to determine the strength of the CBS case. Further, the Subcommittee had already acquired what it needed to determine how CBS had edited some of the original material on the "Selling of the Pentagon." Thanks to Henkin and Representative Hebert, it possessed transcripts of the complete Henkin/Mudd interview and the MacNeil speech and a videotape made by Pentagon technicians of the actual Henkin/Mudd interview. Further, much of the documentary consisted of Department of Defense footage, readily available to the Subcommittee. This led to some fear in the full Commerce Committee and among other members of the House that this was not a good test case, there being no "compelling need" to obtain the outtakes since "alternative means" existed to obtain the desired information—how CBS had edited the documentary.

Some further developments could not have strengthened the Subcommittee's confidence in its case. First, the FCC notified Staggers that it had decided *not* to investigate the complaints concerning "The Selling of the Pentagon." The Commission told the chairman that it had reached this decision "not because the issues involved are unsubstantial. Precisely to the contrary, they are so substantial that they reach to the bedrock principles upon which our free and democratic society is founded." One week later, the Supreme Court decided for the defendant in *Rosenbloom v. Metromedia.* CBS interpreted this decision to mean that "Red Lion[2] cannot be read as depriving broadcasters of 'the freedom of the press' with respect to what they broadcast in the first instance, or as a ruling entitling the Government to regulate broadcasters in a manner that chills this freedom." By this time also, the big power groups had begun to announce their alignments, with CBS getting the most impressive array of support. And finally, a very well organized lobbying effort was underway on behalf of CBS.

With the suspicion that "Selling" was a poor case and with the weight of endorsement and lobbying for CBS, it was natural that the Subcommittee might have had second thoughts about recommending a contempt citation. Therefore when, after the initial appearance of CBS deputy general counsel Appel, CBS submitted additional material from the production of the documentary, the Subcommittee declared that the network had met all conditions save one of its April 7 subpoena. The only items, according to the Subcommittee that CBS had not provided were the outtakes connected with the production of "Selling." So on May 26, it issued a new subpoena, returnable on June 9, demanding (1) only the filmed or taped sequences including outtakes utilized in whole or in part in the broadcast of "Selling" and (2) the personal appearance of Frank Stanton. This was to serve as a face-saving device. CBS could comply with the new subpoena—since it was limited in scope and therefore supposedly did not involve First Amendment problems—while claiming that it had successfully withstood First Amendment incursions by refusing to comply with the first subpoena. And the Subcommittee could avoid the issue of contempt proceedings (which otherwise seemed inevitable) since it had acquired what it was after—the outtakes.

CBS did not accept this out. Even before seeing the subpoena, Stanton declared his basic position unchanged, and reaffirmed this a month later (April 26) in his four hour, fifteen minute personal appearance where he refused to comply with the second subpoena before the Subcommittee.

The compromise thus refused, there was no longer any chance for rapprochement. Four days after Stanton's testimony, the Subcommittee met an executive session and voted unanimously to refer the matter to its parent Committee on Interstate and Foreign Commerce, along with the recommendation that CBS and Stanton be cited for contempt of Congress. Two days after that, July 1, the full Committee met and voted 25 to 13 to report and refer the matter to the House, recommending that CBS and Stanton be cited for contempt. On July 8, Staggers bid for House

2 In *Red Lion Broadcasting Co., Inc. v. Federal Communications Commission* (1969), the Supreme Court upheld the FCC's "Fairness Doctrine" which requires that broadcasters present discussion of public issues on their stations, and that each side of those issues must be given fair coverage.

support of the contempt citation with a letter to Members and a floor speech. Opposition came from the minority of 13 in the Commerçe Committee that had voted against sending the citation to the house.

On Tuesday, July 13, 1971, Representative Staggers offered a privileged resolution, by direction of the Committee on Interstate and Foreign Commerce, and asked for its immediate consideration. House Resolution 534 would certify the report of the Committee to the United States Attorney for criminal proceedings against CBS and Dr. Stanton for their "contumacious conduct . . . in failing and refusing to produce certain pertinent materials in compliance with a subpoena *duces tecum*. . . ." During the ensuing debate, Hastings Keith, ranking minority member of the Subcommittee on Commerce and Power, declared his intention to offer a motion to recommit the resolution back to the Commerce Committee. Recommittal would in effect kill Staggers' attempt to cite for contempt. Ironically, Keith did this not in opposition to the contempt citation—"Probably the legal position of the committee is sound and CBS should have delivered the outtakes as demanded"—but because he desired to see adequate legislation introduced which would allow the FCC to move in a constitutional way to ensure fairness and honesty in news by the networks. The strategy of recommittal, already approved by House leadership, began to pick up support as the discussion wore on, with members indicating their intention to vote to recommit. Finally the time for debate expired and the speaker accepted Keith's motion to recommit. A voice vote seemed to oppose the motion. Keith demanded a standing vote that resulted in a count of 151 for and 147 opposed. Staggers then demanded a roll call vote, and the count was 226 yeas to 181 nays. The confrontation—and the controversy—was over, and Staggers had lost.

In retrospect, the controversy itself "begged the question." The substantive issues of the documentary dealt with the public relations and promotional activities of the Department of Defense. Few persons challenged CBS' criticisms of these activities. (In fact, in attempting to comply with the FCC's "Fairness Doctrine," the network had to supply opposition to its own documentary. No one from the government had requested broadcast time to reply to "Selling," so CBS itself organized the "Perspective" program on which participants argued pro and con the issues raised by "Selling.") The controversy centered around the *production techniques* employed in "Selling." And it was this peripheral issue—this diversionary tactic—that led to the confrontation.[3]

---

[3] Fred Friendly, veteran of many such controversies from his days with Edward R. Murrow, saw this particular diversionary tactic as one step in a rather classic strategy. In his June 1971 *Harper's* article, "The Unselling of 'The Selling of the Pentagon,'" Friendly constructed a five-step paradigm which detailed the activities of groups who wish to discredit effective documentaries. Step 4 instructed: "Create

The roots of this confrontation originated as long ago as the mid-1940s and perhaps before that. They reflect in part a conflict between the norms of the profession of television news—with specific reference to what makes a "good" newsfilm—and the values of the people—what constitutes "the truth." When "broadcast news" began to mean "television" as well as "radio," the networks faced the task of putting pictures with their words. They used as models for their early efforts the theatrical newsreels produced by divisions of the major Hollywood studios. In fact, some of the original television newsfilm units were the newsreel organizations themselves on contract to the networks. When the networks began expanding their television news operations, they hired former newsreel employees. Naturally these men brought with them the production techniques and values of the newsreels, many of which came in turn from Hollywood. In Hollywood, the emphasis was on anything but reality. Hollywood earned its living by spinning celluloid webs of fantasy, precisely joined to present a slick, polished product. While the newsreel people left behind the fantasy in most cases, they did bring with them to the networks the concept of the slick, polished product and the film editing practices needed to create it. In this way, purely pictorial devices such as avoidance of jump cuts, use of establishing shots, and composite editing found their way into TV newsfilm. They still exist, and TV newsmen accept them as norms of professional behavior, as means to achieving the ends of objective reporting. Finally, to further confuse the issue, the Murrow era of the 1950's established at CBS the tradition of producing documentaries which, at least in some cases, might be more accurately called "advocacy by reporting" or even "editorial."

Given these professional norms, CBS did not consider "The Selling of the Pentagon" as deceptive or unethical; it had done simply what a network was supposed to do in putting together a documentary. The president of CBS News, Richard Salant, wrote that "in accordance with customary journalistic practice, in some cases the editors rearranged material for purposes of the broadcast so that a composite answer was included. Where material from another question was added to a particular answer, it was solely to include points which CBS News felt were relevant to the discussion." To him, such editing techniques, along with "reverse shots," were perfectly acceptable so long as they did not "distort in content or in meaning the *impression* of the questions and answers conveyed to the viewer."

To Staggers and his committee, not having been socialized with the norms of TV newsfilm, these same practices were "questionable manipula-

seeds of doubt over production techniques . . . (A)ttack Hollywood production techniques, 'scissors and paste' editing of interviews which takes them out of context. . . ."

tive techniques [which] allegedly included the *rearrangement of the words of an individual* [Henkin] who was attempting to present a point of view at variance with that espoused by the producers of the program," and the rearrangement of the words of a military officer (MacNeil) *"out of their original order* so as to make him appear to be delivering a statement which in fact he did not deliver." (And to Representative William L. Springer, ranking minority member of the Subcommittee, the Murrow tradition did not square with the definition of "documentary" he found in the dictionary: "(2) of, relating to, or employing documentation . . . FACTUAL, OBJECTIVE" (and objective defined as) "not subjective; hence, detached; impersonal; unprejudiced."

Staggers' rationale for his investigation was based on what he called the fiduciary role of the broadcaster. In the role, the broadcaster is licensed to use a portion of the electromagnetic spectrum, which is public domain, for a three year period of trusteeship. If practices such as those alleged by Henkin and MacNeil were used in the preparation of the TV newsfilm and documentaries, reasoned Staggers, their use would constitute a violation of the trusteeship. This would require corrective legislation. The public, continues this line of reasoning, is not well enough organized nor financed to act for itself in insuring that the broadcaster (here the network) is adequately fullfilling the trust. In this particular case, the Subcommittee claimed to have eschewed any interest in judging the *viewpoint* expressed by "The Selling of the Pentagon;" in the minds of these Congressmen, the First Amendment was not involved in these proceedings. It was simply that evidence indicated the time had come to check on the performance of the broadcaster in his fiduciary role to determine whether new laws were needed, and the Subcommittee was so checking, solely on behalf of the people who could not act for themselves. Said Staggers, "But this position of trust (occupied by the broadcasters), these enforceable public obligations will be rendered illusory if the public cannot act through its elected representatives. Let me make one point clear—we act for the people."

CBS did not share this view of the controversy. The network perceived the situation as follows: (1) it had broadcast a documentary critical of one aspect of the government; (2) the legislative branch of the government was now investigating the documentary, which might or might not result in legislation to correct for what the Congress felt were certain "abuses" in the documentary; (3) this was precisely the kind of situation for which the First Amendment had been written, clearly stating, "Congress shall make no law . . . abridging the freedom of speech, or of the press. . . ;" (4) therefore, Congress had no business doing what it was doing and no right to access to the outtakes.

To be sure, other issues were involved—the equivalency of a TV newsman's film outtakes to a print reporter's notes, applicability of the First Amendment to broadcasters, probability of subpoenas producing a "chilling effect" on TV reportage and newsmen's sources, etc. But these were components and outgrowths of, and supplementary to, the main issue: the right of Congress, representing the people, to investigate what it felt were abuses of a trusteeship versus the right of news broadcasters to protection from government harassment under the First Amendment.

Broadcasting, the radio-TV industry trade magazine, saw the recommitment of the contempt citation as a *First Amendment* victory. Its editorial quoted appropriate statements from the debate to support its conclusion. "Put such legislative sentiments together with the vote to recommit, and the record must be judged to have advanced the cause of broadcast journalism."

Perhaps. Surely such lofty First Amendment sentiments had been the first consideration of *some* Congressmen. On the other hand, the suspicion exists that there might have been more pragmatic reasons for the vote: an effective lobbying campaign, including the subtle pressure of all those media organizations aligned with CBS (which could make a politician pause for thought before voting against their wishes), some not so subtle pressures, (most weekly reports to a Congressman's home district are aired free of charge by the local radio and television stations) and the feeling that, legally, this was not the right time or case to test the limits of legislative inquiry. And the controversy left in its wake two House bills: one called a "truth-in-news broadcasting" bill and another which would embody (and thus codify) some of CBS's new policies for production of TV news and documentary programs.

That this controversy could have arisen at all is a historical paradox. It is, of course, ironic that a government official should seek to "protect" the people from the press, no matter what its form. But what is more ironic is that the people would *support* such a move, much less *allow* it to happen. When the First Amendment was written, press and people were one. "The press" was simply a citizen who owned a printing press. Fresh from the wounds of monarchial repression, the citizens of the new nation were naturally anxious to secure Constitutional protection of one institution—the people, which included the people who printed as well as the people who spoke—against another institution—the government.

As has been pointed out by various commissions, scholars and critics, there are now three institutions where formerly there were two. The press is no longer of the people. In its larger forms, it is big business, and its directors are almost unreachable by the average citizen. Television, the most visible and most popular source of the day's intelligence, is the biggest business in the press and is dominated by three of the largest, most aloof, least reachable, and farthest out-of-touch of all media organizations. This creates a frustrating situation for many people, which helps to bring about the paradox, the philosophical soil from which bloomed the "Selling" controversy. Vice President Spiro T. Agnew had defined and epitomized this frustration in his 1969 Des Moines speech. Now here was Staggers, who was actually trying to do something about what Agnew had called this "little group of men . . . who decide what 40 to 50 million Americans will learn of the day's events" and who force upon these same people their views that "do not—and I repeat, not—represent the views of America." The Government was looking into Agnew's "credibility gap . . . in the studios of the networks of New York," but, as Staggers claimed, "We act for the people."

Viewed in this perspective the outcome of the controversy over "The Selling of the Pentagon" can hardly be said "to have advanced the cause of broadcast journalism." Rather the controversy was the latest manifestation of an increasingly complex realignment of basic institutions in this country. If the press, particularly TV network news, continues its development in perceived isolation from and opposition to both people and government—if the people continue to find themselves aligned with and dependent upon the government for protection from the news media—the possibility of reinterpretation or even rewriting of the First Amendment cannot be discounted.

APPENDIX

Much of the history, particularly the Congressional history of "The Selling of the Pentagon" may be traced in the following government publications: *Subpoenaed Material Re Certain TV News Documentary Programs* (the hearings before the special Subcommittee on Investigations of the House Commerce Committee), Serial 92-16; *Proceedings Against Frank Stanton and Columbia Broadcasting System, Inc.* (the Commerce Committee report), House Report 92-349; and the *Congressional Record,* Volume 117, Issue Numbers 105, 106, and 107 (debate in the full House on July 8, 12, and 13, 1971). All of these reprint in full or in part many source documents involved in the controversy. The weekly issues of *Broadcasting* March 1 through July 19 of 1971, give a blow-by-blow account of the controversy. The *Broadcasting* articles are especially valuable in reporting the various groups that aligned themselves with CBS.

Also, a collection of the more salient documents have been printed in a special issue, "CBS and Congress: The Selling of the Pentagon Papers," *Educational Broadcasting Review* (Winter 1971–72). Available from the National Association of Educational Broadcasters, 1346 Connecticut Avenue, N.W., Washington, D.C. 20036

Many newspapers and popular magazines both reported and took editorial stands on the controversy. Particularly interesting are the editorials and letters that appeared in various issues of the *Washington Post;* the front page editorial of the March 29, 1971, issue of *Barron's;* and the interpretive articles in *Time* (April 19, 1971) and the *New York Times Magazine* (May 16, 1971).

Erik Barnouw provides a concise description of the origins of network television newsfilm in *The Image Empire: A History of Broadcasting in the United States, Volume 3—from 1953* (New York: Oxford University Press, 1970), pp. 40–43. And the Murrow legend is related in Alexander Kendrick's *Prime Time: The Life of Edward R. Murrow* (New York: Avon Books, 1970).

For those who wish to view the documentary, *The Selling of the Pentagon,* it is available for rent from a variety of sources. First check with your state audio-visual bureau which typically is associated with a university (their rates are quite moderate—usually one-half of commercial rental rates).

Two commercial outlets of good reputation renting the film for approximately $25 are:

Pyramid Films
Box 1048
Santa Monica, Ca. 90406

Contemporary/McGraw-Hill Films
330 West 42nd Street
New York, N.Y. 10036

section E Reaction
to
Study Commissions

We conclude this section by reprinting John Tebbel's reaction to the Baker-Ball report.[1] Our purpose, as usual, is multiple.

The recommendations of studies of the press have, as Tebbel notes, been more or less the same since the publication of the Hutchins Commission findings in 1947. The reasons for the redundancy of the various study commissions' findings are difficult to fathom.

Journalistic reform moves slowly. Although journalism certainly has changed since World War II, each improvement or gain has been offset by the increasing population, the shifts in mores, and the growing urban densities. The continued appearance of certain suggestions can be attributed to the fact that some of the suggestions were never tried in the first place. (For example, a national institute to continually study the mass media and their performance, called for in 1947, never came into existence.)

---

[1] This report was prepared for the consideration of the National Commission on the Causes and Prevention of Violence but had little impact except on one or two members. Given its modest price, it is a valuable resource for the student of the news media. Robert K. Baker and Sandra J. Ball, *Mass Media and Violence,* Volumes 9 and 9A, Task Force Report to the National Commission on the Causes and Prevention of Violence (Washington, D.C.: U.S. Government Printing Office, 1968).

Well-meaning and intelligent men have sat on these commissions to investigate and study the press. However (as Tebbel points out), no journalists were ever appointed to any of the commissions. Certainly the next commission should include a number of journalists on its panel. But if experience with press councils is any indication, the principal contribution of the journalists will be to teach laymen how "the press" operates. This would undoubtedly be beneficial (and is one of the things we try to do in this reader). To teach this requires some time, and the commission should not draft a final report until its members learn how a newspaper or newscast is assembled, and the various constraints the media are subjected to. Interaction between the bureaucracy and the various personalities which are a part of it should be investigated. Then, viable field studies should be formulated to determine and attain the improvements that we outsiders insist on from time to time.

If changes in bureaucratic policy and personnel training are implemented, it also means changes in the content and structure of the daily news product. The public must be alerted and reconditioned to accept these changes in order to maintain economic support of the enterprises.

In spite of all the recommendations from the various study commissions, the journalist will always have the last word. With the strength of the institution of the press behind him, a journalist feels free to accept or reject any suggestion put forth by an outside group.

chapter 19 Studying the Mass Media

JOHN TEBBEL

Like blind men examining the elephant, the thirty-three-member study group on the mass media, set up by the National Commission on the Causes and Prevention of Violence, has warily circled the animal and, in the dutiful manner of such committees, has taken testimony from what it characterizes as a wide range of witnesses, done some research of its own, and produced a report that is obviously meant to be constructive and helpful. Unfortunately, to a good many who have spent their lives in the media, it appears both unrealistic and uninformed.

Since the study group was largely made up of lawyers, sociologists, and other non-media people, this result is hardly surprising. One may well imagine the reaction that would follow if the ANPA and the ASNE had formed a study group to examine what the bar and bench have contributed to our national distress, and laid down a series of suggestions by which the legal fraternity and the judiciary might be brought to public

John Tebbel "Studying the Mass Media," from the *Saturday Review*, February 14, 1970. Copyright 1970 Saturday Review, Inc. Reprinted by permission of the author and the publisher.

account. The publishers and editors would be lucky to escape with their lives. Yet such an inquiry, in fact, might be far more fruitful than the study group's work, since the lawyers and judges collectively hold far more power over the nation and its citizens than do the publishers and broadcasters. Indeed, there is ample evidence to suggest that the power of the press in this century, in contrast to the last, has been highly exaggerated. One must always remember that the public holds a power over the media that no other institution faces. People can always switch off the television set or radio, or stop buying the magazine or newspaper. In any single instance, it would not take even a majority of viewers, listeners, or readers to end the life of a medium the public did not want or disapproved of.

Nevertheless, the media are today under perhaps the severest attack from the public since the days of the Revolution and the Civil War, when patriots eliminated the newspapers they did not like by the direct expedient of destroying the printing offices where they were published. While such mob action is far from unknown in the world today, control of the press is achieved by a variety of other means, all legal and all short of simple totalitarian control. The number of countries where the press is free of government controls is shockingly small, and it diminishes every year. There is no country in the world where government does not control television and radio transmission.

Obviously, in the United States we are witnessing a movement toward some kind of press control, put forward in most cases with assertions of the highest motives and with emphatic denials that any control is intended. Yet, when the rhetoric is stripped away, the end result is infringement of the freedom guaranteed by the First Amendment. The study group's recommendations need to be examined carefully by everyone who cares about that amendment, because the suggestions are plausible and because it is far from impossible that shrewdly organized public pressure could bring them about.

The group's report begins with the assertion that few American institutions "are as free from responsible and systematic analysis as the American press," a dubious statement at best, and then notes that the press "has been reluctant to undertake self-analysis." The last is unfortunately true. The press not only is reluctant but fiercely resists self-analysis.

Linking its work to its parent, the National Commission, the study group makes some observations on "the traditional relationship between violence and the press," dating its economic importance "at least since the time of Benjamin Day and the 'penny press.'" This gross distortion of journalism history rests on the erroneous proposition that the press has made its money largely "by openly marshaling the most exaggerated and detailed reports of violence and sex." One could cite a few newspapers in any period that did just that and achieved fame and fortune thereby, but this has never been the burden of the whole press in any period of American history, not even during the famous "jazz journalism" of the Twenties. Furthermore, the number of newspapers that make their sales pitch on a combination of violence and sex has diminished steadily in this century, and the number doing so today (aside from the underground press) could be counted on the fingers of a hand. It may be added that, with only three exceptions, the most influential newspapers since the Civil War have not depended on this formula for their success.

When it comes to making specific recommendations, the study group is strong on fantasy and short on facts. It divides its suggestions between "Action by Government" and "Action by News Media." In the area of government action, the group wants to put the Corporation for Public Broadcasting into competition with the network news organizations by giving the corporation a "comparable" amount of money to broadcast news programs. "Comparable," in this case, means $40- $50-million dollars for the corporation, as opposed to the $150-million or so the networks spent on news last year. If Congress agrees to spend such a sum, which would be little short of miraculous, the group believes that the government can be persuaded to exercise the necessary restraint in accounting for the expenditure of its money by "requiring that all communications between government officials and the corporation relating to news content be a matter of public record, and that all hearings be open to the public." This, if realized, should result in the largest debating society since human parliaments were first convened, and potentially the most troublesome box of mischief since the one Pandora opened.

Besides financing news programs only to relinquish control over them, the report goes on, the government should end single ownership of newspapers and television stations in the same community by requiring that station licenses not be renewed in such instances unless the station or newspaper is sold within three years. The number of newspapers that would certainly go under as a result of these divorces is not discussed, but, as several studies have shown, it would be considerable.

The report comes out strongly for protecting the development of CATV as a common carrier, free from monopoly control, and here the group is on solid ground, as it is when it goes on to recommend that the FCC clear up the present ambiguity surrounding the Fairness Doctrine. It is equally sound in pointing out that the FCC cannot properly pass on nearly 2,500 broadcast license renewal applications every year without developing broad guidelines to insure that the cases that raise serious questions can be separated from the others.

But then the report turns to "Action by News Media," beginning with an elaborate disclaimer that, though the study was funded by the government, its recommendations are entitled "to no special weight," and "should be given no special significance or weight beyond whatever persuasive force they may have." No doubt this will have a *déjà vu* sound to those who have studied the conflict between press and government here and abroad.

The report then unintentionally gets to the heart of the disagreements between press and public and press and government. Journalists, it declares, "should re-examine the degree to which existing news judgments incorporate obsolete standards, including a tendency to report violence because it is sensational, rather than because it is significant." In whose judgment, one may ask, does the press report violence because it is sensational, rather than because it is significant, and whose measuring standards are to be used in determining what is "sensational" and what is "significant"?

The report advocates that interpretative news stories, "which can be written with time for calm reflection and balanced judgment," be run regularly on page 1. As several commentators have already noted, this suggests that the group's members have not been reading the newspapers lately. It also ignores the fact that some of the sharpest criticism from both Right and Left has been directed at these same interpretive news stories. Calm reflection and balanced judgment usually produce the kind of stories people with strong opinions don't want to read, or believe are biased and unfair.

Similarly, in advocating that network television extend its evening news programs to an hour and change to a mixed hard news/news magazine format, the group forgets that every effort the networks have made to employ the news magazine technique has resulted in criticism and severe pressures from several quarters. One recalls how these pressures abruptly ended David Brinkley's "news magazine" show after he lifted the lid only slightly on the incredible and still unexposed scandal of the waste in the federal highway program. Every move, in fact, that the networks make to dig into the nation's real problems—and many people believe these moves are negligible—is met with heavy criticism and pressure from whatever special interests are involved. A medium that is utterly dependent on both the government and its advertisers for existence can hardly fail to respond.

Next the report turns to the idea that the media deny "equivalent access" to the media. It recommends that the media hire and train increased numbers of newsmen from minority groups, which of course they have been doing for some time and as rapidly as is possible considering the short supply, which they are also trying to increase in various ways. The media, says the report, should cover minority group activities regularly, and again one wonders what newspapers the group is reading. One thing presently angering the great Silent Majority is their belief that the media devote altogether too much space and time to minority groups, and consequently "stir them up."

A singular recommendation is that the media provide information to local groups about preparing press releases and so gain access to the press —as though the press release were the only way to get into the paper, or even the best. It would be difficult to prove that local groups who have anything to say cannot get their views into print. The complaint of the groups is that the press does not invariably take up and prosecute their causes, good, bad, or indifferent.

Ghetto "stringers" are suggested, although how this would improve the coverage of ghetto news is not spelled out. Only a fanatic would argue that such news is ignored today by big city dailies; indeed, it is often out of proportion to domestic and world news. As for including members of minority groups in day-to-day coverage of such news as births, deaths, and weddings, this is certainly yesterday's failure in newspapers of any consequence, outside those of the Deep South. True, there is still room for improvement in the North, but progress is more rapid here than in almost any other phase of race relations.

It is also difficult to understand the report's recommendation that "more background and in-depth stories on social issues and particularly those stories dealing with facets of the American scene with which a majority of the audience have little actual experience" be published. Difficult because such stories are appearing in unprecedented abundance every day in the nation's press. Such papers as the Kansas City *Star*, the Louisville *Courier-Journal*, the Los Angeles *Times*, and *The Wall Street Journal* have been particularly outstanding in this respect. There are many others.

But the recommendation made by the group that is likely to cause the most controversy is the proposal to establish a national study center to evaluate press performance. This is no more likely to be welcomed by the media than it was twenty-two years ago when it was first proposed by the Commission on Freedom of the Press, or when it was recommended two years ago by the National Advisory Commission on Civil Disorders. It is, perhaps, significant that the final report of the National Commission on the Causes and Prevention of Violence did not mention the study center idea in its final report.

The study group has some corollary suggestions in this respect that are directed toward what it calls the "need for greater interaction between the news media and the community and for responsible criticism of media performance." These include the creation of grievance machinery by news organizations to hear the complaints of people who think they are treated unfairly; the establishment of local press councils; the inculcation of critical attitudes in students by journalism schools (the study group ought to talk to a few of them); more publications that would provide a forum for public debate on media performance; more criticism of each other by news organizations; midcareer training programs to elevate professional standards; and a series of proposals designed to tell the media how to handle stories of riots and demonstrations.

With a few exceptions, the essence of these proposals is that a professional group, traditionally a Fourth Estate, is to submit itself to examination and scrutiny by nonprofessionals who will, presumably bring public pressure to bear to make the media conform to "balanced," "fair," and "responsive" concepts of the news. To professional media men, this can only seem incredible naïveté on the part of the study group. In the political and social climate of this country (or any country, for that matter), it would be impossible to write and edit a newspaper or a news broadcast that would be considered fair and balanced and responsive by any more than a varying percentage of its readers or viewers, as daily experience proves.

In fact, there is a serious question, which the study group might better have devoted its talents to exploring, whether Americans really want a free press. Several recent polls assessing their attitudes suggest strongly that many are indifferent to the concept of press freedom, others think the press has too much freedom, and still others want the press to conform to such ideas as "printing good news and not always the bad news," or "helping the government, not criticizing it." The solid public support for Vice President Agnew's criticisms of the press and recent proposals from several sources to create governmental or public monitoring agencies, of which the study group's proposals are only the most recent, confirm this impression.

We are shown examples of a press that prints only good news in Vietnam, where the Armed Forces' communications services censor out the bad news in the name of morale, and the Saigon government simply closes up papers that insist that all is not well. Nor is there any bad news in the press of China or Russia, where airplanes never crash, trains never collide, floods and famines and violence are never or seldom reported, only the good news that is not critical of the government but is intended to help it.

Is this the kind of press Americans want? The fact is that, in spite of the conventional denials, we don't really know. What we do know is that this is the kind of press they will get if apathy, hostility, and government encroachment keep on increasing as they have been doing for the past decade.

part four ALTERNATIVES
IN
MASS NEWS

Introduction

Any future change in the news media will require clearly formulated strategies and the mobilization of those of like mind into some coherent pressure group. The power for change or continuance rests with the following clusters of individuals and organizations: (1) the media owners and licensees, (2) viably organized groups of reporters and editors, (3) the government, and (4) the public. Change in the news system is difficult because, like religion, sex, and politics, the news media are and always have been controversial.

Almost all the news media are business enterprises. Although each business requires its owners and executives to have the usual management skills, the news media today also require a touch of (for lack of a better term) show biz. But the core of the value structure is in the business community. The news media owners and executives belong to the same clubs and service organizations as do plumbing executives and missile contractors. They are moderate or conservative, Republican, and insular. At the local level, the TV or radio station manager and newspaper publisher are dependent upon their friends and acquaintances for continued advertising support.

Consider now what occurs in a businessman's mind when you suggest a change that could influence his investment—such as paying his reporters a living wage, or hiring and training a black reporter. He is convinced that sooner or later any change will show up in the accountant's ledger, and usually in red ink. Each and every news media owner and manager wants to serve the public interest, but within reasonable fiscal limits. These men are not superhuman intellectuals and may be as confused as their readers concerning the social changes being reported. It is well to recall this when confronting these individuals with proposals for change.

Most movements or groups discussed here exist outside of journalism and operate like pressure groups. What changes can occur within the journalism fraternity?

In general, reporters are poorly organized both as an occupational group and as "professionals." Often their principal concern is with working conditions, not editorial decisions. Among the younger reporters there is some demand to control story assignments and to begin to cover what seem to be the important social issues of the day, rather than the traditional newsbeat. Two articles are included in this section dealing with reporter's power (or lack of it) and the possibility of their becoming a more coherent professional group.

Although reporters must begin to make elementary moves to control their own fate, the government is inching toward some interesting decisions. In broadcasting, these changes have occurred in the Federal Communication Commission, which is beginning to move toward allowing the public, in the form of political and minority activist groups, to have some input into deciding who shall receive a broadcast license. More important, the Supreme Court recently held in the *Red Lion* decision (discussed in a number of readings) that the First Amendment rights rest with the *citizenry* rather than the licensee. This interpretation of the First Amendment by the court could promise far reaching changes in the news media. The premise is that few citizens can afford a broadcast station. In order to insure a range of opinion and information, it is the broadcaster's obligation to insure the public of varied opinions concerning community needs and goals. Access to the broadcasting media then is a right of the people. The owner can broadcast what pleases him, but he must offer those of differing opinions equal time. (This does not hold true for newscasts.)

If you will recall the introduction in part one, this appears to be the continued seepage of the social responsibility idea into a judicial view of the news media. Needless to say, the media owners are not pleased with this decision. In the following article, you will see how a number of professionals are suggesting that this right of access be extended to *all* media, especially newspapers.

Any social action group has basic levers for applying pressure to media owners. One is to enlist legal and governmental experts to help frame a case within existing legal precedents and procedures. It is necessary to know the subtleties and rituals of judicial and governmental bureaucracies in order to enlist their power to attain one's goals.

To mobilize the government, for good or ill, also requires concerned individuals to mount a public campaign to effect the desired changes. This requires that public opinion be generated and organized to support the proposed goals.

In the introduction to part three, we dealt with controversies, emerging norms, and how campaigns are typically organized. With perhaps one exception, all of the following readings deal with emerging norms. They posit alternate views or requests for change in the system. Their ultimate success rests on the commitment of their proponents to engage in long persuasion campaigns. Sooner or later they must go to the public for support. By this time, it should be clear that there are *many* publics—clusters of committed and informed people who "specialize" in certain problem areas. For example, bureaucrats, professors, students, and a few internationally-minded citizens regularly read and view with close attention the foreign affair news. Others concern themselves with civil rights, state house politics, consumer needs and rights, and so on. It is often from these clusters of concerned individuals that pressure for social change arises. Once the campaign is in motion, these individuals usually recede into the background, and students, lawyers, and the news media take up the cudgel. Proposals for change evolve into policies articulated as new legislation, court challenges, and marches. Any leader, no matter how charismatic, must have his roots or support in the rich soil of his concerned intellectual cadre. This suggests, alas, that any successful social movement (regardless of its political or sociological ideology) ends up creating its own bureaucracy to sustain its existence. The successful social movement then comes full circle in the end; it becomes almost a mirror image of the institution it seeks to influence.

From journalists who seek change in their work and some status for their craft, this entire process will usually elicit a cynical profanity. But perhaps that is not the issue. Rather, it may be up to individual consumers of the news to decide what they need to adequately function as citizens in American society. The public can and does influence the news media with such crass devices as boycotts and bombing. It is possible, however, to demonstrate concern with rational objectives—the key issue, it would seem, is to articulate these needs. We suggest that the best protection of the media owners and editors is time, their insular existence, and the expectation that concerned citizens will tire of the engagement and turn their attention to other issues.

The two facets of the news media that succumb most easily to public pressure are the journalist's ego and the owner's financial health. The newsman and editor are public individuals practicing their occupation before all of us. They receive public criticism daily and have erected some clever protective rationalizations. Most complaints are about the content of the story, and the journalist balances the pros and the cons. Their most vulnerable point is their intellectual and journalistic competence. Positive suggestions to improve these skills would be appreciated by most writers and reporters, rather than concentration of criticism on story content. Outside their family and close friends, most journalists look to one another for praise and criticism. Their primary audience is often each other.

If you want to change a journalist, adopt him somewhat like a college film fan does a director or cinema genre. Read or view him over a long period of time, and isolate his strengths and weaknesses. If he has a specialty, then develop some expertise in the field to supply insights and tips that may escape him. Learn the constraints of the trade and the pressures he must work under. And recall that learning psychologists note that positive reinforcements for a response increases the probability of that response reappearing. Compliment a good performance and suggest a slight change or two. Finally, expect to spend a long time at your task.

Changing the publishers and broadcasters requires more stamina. In most instances they have stable quasi monopolies, and economic pressures are difficult to sustain. Here one needs an orchestrated campaign of letters, telephone calls, and displays of public concern and outrage. Make them aware of your existence and needs. Also, they must be made uncomfortable because of public criticism or economic pressure. Numbers are important, since media depends on advertising to support business. Complaints or praise of a newspaper or station to its advertisers flows quickly back to the organization, since ad salesmen in contact with advertisers complain about anything that threatens commissions. A point often missed is the necessity to praise the news media for taking unpopular stands with which you agree. You can rest assured that those who disagree with the position taken by the news media will be quick to voice their opposition.

This then is the core of news and society for the concerned individual. The public opinion process depends heavily on those individuals who can read with facility, who possess opinions with information—not emotion— and who concern themselves with obtaining the "day's intelligence." A recent book about the British news media was aptly entitled *The Press We Deserve*. Until the public generates and sustains interest in the operation and performance of the news media, it will be business as usual, and we *will* have the press we deserve.

section F Change
by the
Government

In the following article, Alan Reitman and Trudy Hayden of the American Civil Liberties Union, review Jerome Barron's new theory of the First Amendment. This article is excerpted from a longer position paper reprinted in *Educational Broadcasting Review* (December 1968).

In reading the Reitman and Hayden paper, note how some issues presented earlier in this book are connected. The evidence of the growing concentration of mass media ownership presents a possible danger to the free flow of ideas in a democracy. To date, the newspaper industry has little in the way of restriction or regulation. The broadcasting industry has a number of regulations such as the Fairness Doctrine and the equal time for political candidates under section 315 (these have already been reviewed in an earlier section).

In a sense, Reitman and Hayden ask: Does the government have an affirmative obligation to meet the compelling social needs of its citizens? If so, then what steps should be taken to insure access to the news media and what safeguards would be required? It is a complex issue, as the authors note, but it must be confronted. How are minority and unorthodox ideas going to reach the public unless they are allowed access to the channels of communication?

chapter 20 # Should Government Impose the First Amendment on Media?

ALAN REITMAN
and
TRUDY HAYDEN

The First Amendment to the Constitution states that "Congress shall make no law . . . abridging the freedom of speech, or of the press. . . ." Written as a negative commendment, it was the young American Republic's answer to centuries of experience with the English government's suppression of political and religious writings that were not to its liking. The founders were determined that the pamphleteers and publishers and editors of the new nation would be free to speak out uninhibited by the fear that official licensing agents were poised to silence whatever the gov-

Alan Reitman and Trudy Hayden, "Should Government Impose the First Amendment on the Media?" from *Educational Broadcasting Review*, December 1968. Reprinted by permission of the American Civil Liberties Union and the author.

It should be noted that this review paper in no way constitutes an official position by the American Civil Liberties Union, but rather is a background document for the Union's Board and committee studying the access question. The ACLU Board has rejected the idea of a *right* of access as applied to the issue of political advertising. The Board turned down a policy recommendation authorizing the initiation of law suits to challenge publications that refuse to carry paid political advertising. However, the ACLU is making a study of instances of denial of access and will review the issue again in the near future.

ernment of the day might deem "undesirable." Traditionally, the Amendment has been interpreted to prescribe a "hands-off" stance by the government regarding its citizens' freedom of expression. The First Amendment asserts that which the government cannot do: it cannot interfere with the people's protected right to free speech.

By the middle of the twentieth century, however, it has become abundantly clear in almost all aspects of our national life that the simple statement of a constitutional right does not automatically entail the guarantee that all of us as individuals will actually enjoy the exercise of that right. Examining this discrepancy as applied to expression, many people today are asking whether free speech can be an actuality without some further guarantee of access to the key channels of speech. They are pointing out that today's communications industry is gigantic both in financial terms and in the size and scope of its audience, yet its control lies in the hands of a very small group, many of whom look upon the media simply as a profitable business enterprise. They are also beginning to analyze the tremendous influence of the media upon the electoral process itself, and the ways in which the media handle, or avoid, different kinds of socially important but controversial issues. A growing awareness of the complexities of all these relationships has been an important factor in bringing about a re-evaluation of the meaning of the First Amendment. Should the government be restrained from all activity in this area while the private management of the media, a group whose views are colored by economic and other strong interests, may be exercising the very sort of abridgment of expression that is feared on the part of the government?

A second contributing factor in the emergence of generic free expression questions is the rising recognition of government's affirmative obligation to meet the compelling social needs of citizens, as implemented, for example, in the many new anti-poverty programs.

The direct involvement of government in the enforcement of constitutional guarantees of civil rights is a familiar and accepted concept. Government has long been looked upon as the protector of these rights. But lately, with the growing urgency of social problems rooted in racial strife, the government has been forced to assert a more affirmative responsibility actually to promote the realization of equality. It has become evident that laws which simply forbid discrimination are not adequate; it is necessary to act positively in terms of what *shall* be done rather than only negatively in terms of what shall *not* be done. The affirmative theory has taken us beyond the mere redress of wrongs by judicial decision.

Steps toward the development of an affirmative government obligation are also to be seen in the due process area. Because the right to counsel, although supposedly guaranteed to all, means nothing to a man who is

unable to pay for legal services, the government has assumed the burden
of providing counsel for any defendant who cannot provide it for himself. Thus, the government is not merely forbidden to deprive a defendant of counsel, but must in addition take positive steps to see that all
defendants can effectively *exercise* their right to legal representation.

A NEW THEORY OF THE FIRST AMENDMENT

Our society requires agencies of mass communication. They are great concen-
trations of private power. If they are irresponsible, not even the First Amendment will protect their freedom from governmental control. The amendment
will be amended.

. . . Everyone concerned with the freedom of the press and with the future
of democracy should put forth every effort to make the press accountable, for,
if it does not become so of its own motion, the power of government will be
used, as a last resort, to force it to be so.

. . . Under our system the legislature may pass no law abridging the freedom
of the press. But this has never been thought to mean that the general laws
of the country were inapplicable to the press. The first Amendment was intended to guarantee free expression, not to create a privileged industry.

Thus was the problem stated in 1947 in a report by the Commission
on Freedom of the Press, entitled "A Free and Responsible Press." The
Commission, under the chairmanship of Robert M. Hutchins, undertook
to evaluate the functioning of the entire communications industry in
this country as it was twenty years ago. Its recommendations for remedial
action foreshadowed many of the specific suggestions that will be touched
upon in this paper. Although the Commission did not articulate an "affirmative governmental obligation" as a legal concept in so many words, a
perusal of its report leaves no doubt of its belief that if the communications industry persists in its abdication of public responsibility, the government will be forced to enter the field to make freedom of expression
a reality.

In recent years the chief spokesman for a new approach to the interpretation of the First Amendment is Professor Jerome A. Barron, whose
ideas are outlined in a lengthy analysis entitled "Access to the Press—A
New First Amendment Right" (*Harvard Law Review*, vol. 80: 1641).

Professor Barron begins: "There is an anomaly in our constitutional
law. While we protect expression once it has come to the fore, our law is
indifferent to creating opportunities for expression. Our constitutional
theory is in the grip of a romantic conception of free expression, a belief
that the 'marketplace of ideas' is freely accessible."

The basic question which Barron poses is this:

The free expression questions which now come before the courts involve individuals who have managed to speak or write in a manner that captures public attention and provokes legal reprisal. The conventional constitutional issue is whether expression already uttered should be given first amendment shelter or whether it may be subjected to sanction as speech beyond the constitutionally protected pale. To those who can obtain access to the media of mass communications first amendment case law furnishes considerable help. But what of those whose ideas are too unacceptable to secure access to the media? To them the mass communications industry replies: The first amendment guarantees our freedom to do as we choose with our media. Thus the constitutional imperative of free expression becomes a rationale for repressing competing ideas. First amendment theory must be reexamined, for only by responding to the present reality of mass media's repression of ideas can the constitutional guarantee of free speech best serve its original purposes.

According to what Barron calls our "romantic view" of the First Amendment, we tend to assume that as long as government does not intervene, there is a free market for ideas, an assumption which Barron traces to the free speech opinions of Justice Holmes. But although our acceptance of this theory has made us alert to the evils of government censorship, it has left us totally indifferent to some other implications of the "free market theory in the realm of ideas." Our indifference to nongovernmental obstructions to the free exchange of ideas "becomes critical when a comparatively few private hands are in a position to determine not only the content of information but its very availability, when the soap box yields to radio and the political pamphlet to the monopoly newspaper."

Many reasons have been advanced to explain why the modern mass media have come to wield so strong an influence on the content of ideas that reach the marketplace of expression. The first that comes to mind is that the people who control the media may deliberately foreclose from access any idea that is inimical to their interests, or simply to their prejudices. Accentuating this is the decline of newspaper competition both economically and editorially, due in part to the rising costs of production and the rise of competition by other media. The wane of competition and the growth of the monopoly enterprise, which together have created so many one-newspaper towns, naturally increases the power of those papers that remain to suppress opinions or even facts at their discretion.

A second view is the now-famous McLuhan thesis. McLuhan sees the very nature of modern media as being "at war with a point of view orientation." In his analysis the electronic media have replaced the older typographical media and have engaged us not through the content of the ideas expressed but through the very form of the media itself; our involvement is not intellectual but emotional. The electronic media which dominate modern communications are not suited to presenting public issues in a meaningful way, because they mesmerize us to the point of indifference to their content, and to the content of the older media as well.

A third analysis points to the media emphasis upon majoritarian values: the prime importance of reaching the largest possible audience at all times, hence a predisposition to conform to already accepted public taste and opinion. This is blamed not so much upon the profit motive as upon the technology of the various electronic media themselves. Thus, each of two conflicting points of view might receive media attention so long as each is a well-recognized point of view about a controversy that is already in the public eye, but a subject about which a large number of people have not yet demonstrated interest will not be aired at all. In sum, we are given only what might be called "approved dissent." This Barron lays to the odd fact that "the controllers of the media have no ideology. Since in the main they espouse no particular ideas, their antipathy to all ideas has passed unnoticed." It has not always been this way, however; the radio "voices" of the thirties and forties had tremendous impact.

But, says Barron, "retreat from ideology is not bereft of ideological and practical consequences. . . . It is not that the mass communication industry is pushing certain ideas and rejecting others but rather that it is using the free speech and free press guarantees to avoid opinions instead of acting as a sounding board for their expression. What happens of course is that the opinion vacuum is filled with the least controversial and bland ideas. Whatever is stale and accepted in the status quo is readily discussed and thereby reinforced and revitalized."

> The failures of existing media are revealed by the development of new media to convey unorthodox, unpopular and new ideas. Sit-ins and demonstrations testify to the inadequacy of old media as instruments to afford full and effective hearing for all points of view. Demonstrations, it has been well said, are "the free press of the movement to win justice for Negroes. . . ." But, like an inadequate underground press, it is a communications medium by default, a statement of the inability to secure access to the conventional means of reaching and changing public opinion. By the bizarre and unsettling nature of his technique the demonstrator hopes to arrest and divert attention long enough to compel the public to ponder his message. But attention-getting devices so abound in the modern world that new ones soon become tiresome. The dissenter must look for ever more unsettling assaults on the mass mind if he is to have continuing impact. Thus, as critics of protest are eager and in a sense correct to say, the prayer-singing student demonstration is the prelude to Watts. But the difficulty with this criticism is that it wishes to throttle protest rather than to recognize that protest has taken these forms because it has nowhere else to go.

Professor Barron asserts that there "is inequality in the power to communicate ideas just as there is inequality in economic bargaining power. . . . A realistic view of the first amendment requires recognition that a right of expression is somewhat thin if it can be exercised only at the sufferance of the managers of mass communications." Yet changes in the communications industry since the early part of this century have completely destroyed whatever equilibrium in the "marketplace of ideas" might have existed at some earlier time.

Barron criticizes the "romantic view" for its "simplistic egalitarianism. . . . New media of communication are assimilated into first amendment analysis without regard to the enormous differences in impact these media have in comparison with the printed word. Radio and television are to be as free as newspapers and magazines, sound trucks as free as radio and television." Urging a "contextual approach" which takes into account media differences, Barron suggests that "the test of a community's opportunities for free expression rests not so much in an abundance of alternative media but rather in an abundance of opportunities to secure expression in media with the largest impact." Thus, he asks, "if a group seeking to present a particular side of a public issue is unable to get space in the only newspaper in town, is this inability compensated by the availability of the public park or the sound truck?" Barron thinks not. Not only do different media command different audiences, but they serve different functions: "criticism of an individual or a governmental policy over television may reach more people but criticism in print is more durable."

The difficulty under our present constitutional theory is that if the courts or the legislature were to guarantee some right of access to the media for ideas that could not otherwise be effectively presented to the public, this would constitute "state action" violating the First Amendment. Yet today it is not the state but the media themselves which hold the power to abridge freedom of expression. "Indeed," says Barron, "non-governing minorities in control of the means of communication should perhaps be inhibited from restraining free speech (by the denial of access to their media) even more than governing majorities are restrained by the first amendment—minorities do not have the mandate which a legislative majority enjoys in a polity operating under a theory of representative government."

> What is required is an interpretation of the first amendment which focuses on the idea that restraining the hand of government is quite useless in assuring free speech if a restraint on access is effectively secured by private groups. A constitutional prohibition against governmental restrictions on expression is effective only if the Constitution ensures an adequate opportunity for discussion. Since this opportunity exists only in the mass media, the interests of those who control the means of communication must be accommodated with the interests of those who seek a forum in which to express their point of view.

•   •   •

**FOR AND AGAINST THE NEW THEORY OF AN
AFFIRMATIVE OBLIGATION**

Arguments in favor of a right of access. One of the justifications for the
constitutional guarantee of freedom of speech and press is that in a free
society it is imperative that all ideas be heard and considered if citizens
are to exercise their rights and duties in an informed and responsible
manner. It has been argued that the right to hear—otherwise deemed the
right to know—is the other side of the right to speak, and that the right
to speak and the right to know are indispensable concomitants of the
right to vote. Whether or not this posited right to know legally rises to
the level of a constitutional right—and there is disagreement on this
point even among those who support the argument—it is commonly
thought to constitute an integral part of the relationship between the
right of expression and the right to vote. If, therefore, it is true that certain minority viewpoints are effectively blocked from a public hearing
through the mass media, whether by government or by private action,
then citizens are not able to exercise fully their right to speak, their right
to know, and ultimately, their right to vote.

The case for a right to know is bolstered by the strategic impact of
media participation in the electoral process itself. The American two-
party system puts third parties at a tremendous disadvantage. It discourages the formation of new political parties because of the foregone
conclusion that minority groups have meager prospects of winning any
important office. Minority parties are hard-pressed financially—increasingly so as the costs of campaigns soar upwards—and often must fight
even to get a place on the ballot. It is an oft-heard argument that the
function of third parties in American politics is to influence the plat-
forms of the major parties, not to capture office themselves. Given so
strong a two-party bias, it is natural that the pronouncements of third-
party candidates are not as newsworthy as those of the major party candidates, and that the media will ignore them on this basis alone. Yet the
smaller parties do not have the organization or the financial resources to
reach the public directly and depend almost exclusively upon media
coverage to bring their ideas into the arena of public debate. Put the
other way, the public will not ordinarily hear minority party dissent except through the media. It is clear that the soapbox and the flyer have
lost their political importance except on a very limited local basis, and
that the mass media now hold a key position in the national electoral
process. The question then arises whether the media should be allowed
to exercise so vital a public function without being subject to some standards of responsibility to society's right to know.

In the broader context of the functioning of a free society, the need for a "marketplace of ideas" has been emphasized as a means whereby society works out the answers to its most pressing problems. This, of course, is at the basis of both the "romantic theory" of the First Amendment and Barron's "new theory" as one purpose of the constitutional guarantee of free speech. If it is true that certain minority views are not disseminated through the mass media, then society is the weaker for not being able to hear and consider all possible solutions to its problems. Moreover, if society is to function through a system of representative government, it is necessary that the voices of minorities be heard, even if they do not carry the day. Otherwise representative democracy will succumb either to tyranny by the governmental majority or to tyranny by the non-governing minorities who happen to control the machinery of communication.

A third argument in favor of an affirmative right of access to the media is posited on a theory of the relationship between free speech and public order. If minority views cannot be placed before the public by the ordinary means of communication through the mass media, then the proponents of these views are forced, in their desperation to be heard, to turn to more extreme ways of expressing themselves in order to attract public attention. This inevitably leads to expression by action rather than by the more traditional avenues of speech. It also bespeaks a loss of faith in the justice and efficacy of existing institutions: For the people who cannot be heard, the system no longer works.

For all these reasons it is argued that an affirmative obligation on the part of government to assure the right of access to the major media is necessary as a counterweight to the concentrated private power now in control of the mass media. The risk of a strictly limited government involvement in First Amendment territory may be smaller than the risk of having the enormous power of the press in the hands of a privileged minority. The controlling minority is dominated by economic and other privately motivated interests, and is in no effective way accountable to the public. Government is at least ultimately answerable to the public.

Arguments against a right of access. Those who argue against an affirmative government obligation to enforce a right of access to the media do not necessarily deny that a problem of access exists. They do, however, dispute the seriousness of the problem—asking proponents to name important minority positions that do not get publicized in some way by the media—and they dispute the theory of a "right of access" as the proper answer to the problem.

Critics of the affirmative obligation theory believe that the basic definition of freedom of the press is simply the right to print, or not to print —that is, freedom for the publisher. The First Amendment provides that the government will pass no laws abridging this freedom. Any government interference to decide what *will* be printed (leaving aside the pure censorship aspect of what will *not* be printed) abridges the right of the publisher to decide this matter for himself. Freedom of the press is not the same thing as freedom of information—the right to know—and the media are under no obligation to make available all the information in their possession.

Answering the public order argument, critics of the affirmative obligation theory challenge the premise that activism in protest is the result of a stifling of expression. More likely, in their view, activism is the result of a thwarting of objectives. It is one thing to express one's ideas to the public, but it is quite another to see one's objectives adopted as public policy. People resort to "action" protest not because their purely verbal protest has not been heard, but because it has not brought results. This analysis may have particular relevance to the civil rights movement: The arguments have certainly been heard, but have the demands of the protesters been achieved?

The theory of a government-enforced right of access is believed to fail the moment the abstract concept is applied to the actual workings of the media in society. What is a minority opinion? Which minority opinions have a claim to be heard? On what standards will the decision be made? Who will decide? Some answers to such "practical" questions are necessary if the theory is to be carried out, yet any determination on these matters requires a basic value judgment about what is "good for society." Even if some limitation of editorial self-determination might be socially desirable (and there are many who dispute this), not everything that is socially desirable rises to the level of a government-enforceable right.

To objections that questions of practical application ought not be allowed to obscure the goal of access for all, the critics reply that there is no possible application of the principle which does not inherently involve deprivation of liberty, discriminatory judgment, and at bottom, paternalistic government. This is because the goal itself is restrictive, discriminatory, and paternalistic—in every way inimical to the democratic ideal.

On the question of the facts, the critics ask whether an appraisal of today's media must not take note of the vast increase in the entire scope of the media industries and their expansion into many different kinds of publishing and broadcasting activity. Is it valid to say that because a particular viewpoint will not be carried by a mass circulation newspaper or a nation-wide broadcasting network that it will never come before the public at all? Do the circulation statistics of dissenting magazines and "underground" papers uphold the contention that minority views do not manage to get a public hearing?

Finally, it is argued by many who accept the present governmental regulation of editorial self-determination in the broadcast media that the same kind of regulation cannot be applied to print media. It is felt that the distinctions between the two kinds of media would preclude at least the direct regulation of the print media, although some indirect kind of affirmative governmental action might be appropriate. The basic differences in market and advertising problems, distribution systems, limitation and costs of facilities, competition, and historical function are all cited as objections to the transferral of a kind of fairness doctrine from broadcasting to print media.

A final consideration. In weighing the various arguments for and against a theory of affirmative obligation, there is one important factor that must always be borne in mind. Many people are not fully aware of the extent to which the one-newspaper and one-channel community has become the norm in America. The complex interrelationships among supposedly competing media within one community are often overlooked. Only in New York and in a few other huge metropolitan areas is it possible to savor such a broad diversity of printed and aired opinion and information on a full range of important—and unimportant—political, economic, and social topics. Whether this so-called diversity is actually nothing but multiplication and confusion, whether it is more apparent than real, can honestly be argued. Whether the achievement of this high level of diversity is a necessary or even desirable goal in smaller communities can also be debated. But in analyzing the present media situation and in trying to formulate an answer to the problems facing us, it is essential that we deal with the system as most Americans experience it, in rural areas, small towns, suburbs, and even large cities.

The arguments outlined in the preceding paragraphs suggest a number of basic questions which the American Civil Liberties Union must answer in its evaluation of the theory of an affirmative governmental obligation. Among them are the following:

1. Does open access to the media, even if socially desirable, rise to the level of a constitutional right?
2. Does any governmental regulation of expression, even if it is meant to encourage expression, constitute abridgment of expression?
3. Is government intervention in the First Amendment area always too dangerous to be risked because of the possibility of censorship and discrimination?
4. Is it valid to assert that because alternative means of communication are available it is not necessary that the mass circulation media give full coverage to all views?
5. Is it valid to assert that opening the media to make possible a true demo-

cratic discourse will prevent more extreme forms of "communication by action"?

6. Are the media a purely private enterprise or, because of their privileged constitutional position, must they be forced to serve some public purpose?

7. Are there distinctions between the broadcast media and the print media that preclude the application to the print media of government regulations that presently operate in broadcasting?

8. Would it be proper for the government to attempt, whether directly or indirectly, to remedy financial inequalities which prevent some groups from availing themselves of access to the media?

9. Might systematic governmental intervention to enforce a right of access have the unintended effect of sapping the vitality of dissenting groups by removing some of the impetus to fight for public acceptance of their views on their merits alone?

10. How would the functioning of the electoral process be affected, if at all, by government action to assure a right of access to the media?

IMPLEMENTATION OF A RIGHT OF ACCESS

Three general approaches. If it should be decided that the theory of an affirmative governmental obligation to assure a right of access to the mass media has some validity, then we must begin the search for ways in which such an obligation will be implemented.

Barron suggests three basic approaches worthy of trial, all of them referring primarily to print media. The first is judicial. Appeal to the courts would provide a remedy for individuals and groups who feel they have been denied the chance to voice their views on public issues, guaranteeing that they would have a non-discriminatory right of access to a community paper. The focus of this approach would be the letters-to-the-editor columns and the advertising sections (with reference only to non-commercial advertising) as the appropriate province for a judicially enforced right of access.

A statutory solution might be to impose a modest requirement that access to a paper cannot be arbitrarily denied but must be based on some rational and previously determined standard. The law might provide that a publisher could not be held for libel for publishing any statement under the statutory mandate. Constitutionally, such legislation could be passed on either the state or federal level. Barron emphasizes that "a provision preventing government from silencing or dominating opinion [the First Amendment] should not be confused with an absence of governmental power to require that opinion be voiced."

In considering an administrative arrangement similar to the present function of the FCC in broadcasting, Barron warns that the right of access must be closely defined lest the daily press find itself at the mercy of "the collective vanity of the public." But he asserts that the right could be administratively enforced after a careful determination as to whether the material for which access is being sought is in fact suppressed and underrepresented within the context of the total communications picture of a given community.

Some ideas for an affirmative government program. The general solutions proposed by Barron can be translated into a number of specific measures that might be considered as part of an affirmative governmental program to encourage and implement the exercise of freedom of expression. The few outlined here are only illustrative.

1. Creation of a government-subsidized network, paralleling the BBC. Because this would be a completely public enterprise, rather than a private business merely under governmental regulation, it would be possible to assure the expression of many different points of view on all kinds of social and political issues.

2. A variety of government subsidies, both direct and indirect, to private broadcast media owners and producers to finance certain kinds of public service programming that are not now possible or profitable. These might include direct government aid to station owners as recompense for public service programming (similar to the OEO grants under the poverty program and the aid given to small businessmen through the Small Business Administration); special grants to station program directors and other creative personnel who desire to do special public service programming that stations cannot or will not support (paralleling National Defense Education Act research grants); and special tax benefits for marginal stations that produce public service programming, particularly those experimenting with controversial issues. The rationale behind these proposals and other related measures is that if the objective is to increase diversity of expression on the air, then the power of the public purse can be wielded to encourage private action in this direction.

3. Application of sanctions requiring media acceptance of non-commercial controversial advertising and representation of particular points of view. This would mean reversing, in regard to advertising, the Union's previous rejection of government sanctions to enforce a right of access. This proposal would apply to broadcast and print media alike and would encompass the full range of judicial, legislative and administrative devices suggested by Barron. One aspect of such sanctions might be the application of the "equal time" approach now used in broadcasting to newspaper advertising on controversial issues, in particular during political campaigns. (The ACLU's "equal time" approach urges a legal provision that broadcast licensees "offer legally qualified candidates opportunities for the expression of their views during political campaign

periods. The licensee shall both initiate political broadcasts and decide on requests for time within the general definition of meeting the community's needs and with emphasis on fairness and balance." The requirement is to be administered by the citizens' committees discussed earlier.)

4. Government subsidies to start newspapers in communities that are now served by only one paper. This might be seen as a logical extension of the purpose of the proposed Failing Newspaper Act, which is meant to bolster papers in danger of financial collapse in order to avoid the creation of more one-newspaper towns.

5. Direct government participation in areas of controversial expression, particularly in connection with electoral campaigns. This approach is already being tried in some states which distribute free of charge to every registered voter a pamphlet containing statements of position by every qualified candidate for every office. These states are taking upon themselves the responsibility to see that the voters will hear directly the views of every candidate regardless of how the mass media have treated the candidates and issues.

6. Increased use of federal buildings and other facilities for public meetings, open to all on a non-discriminatory basis. An extension of this proposal might entail construction of new facilities at government expense where none now exist.

7. Stimulation of discussion among citizens as a specific and conscious policy of certain government agencies. For example, although the Department of Health, Education and Welfare cannot determine national curriculum standards, it is in a position to encourage discussion of controversial social issues in the schools, perhaps by sponsoring essay contests and debates with federal money as prizes.

8. The establishment of a permanent citizens advisory commission whose sole task it would be to evaluate on a continuing basis the functioning of the mass media. Its work might include self-initiated analysis of newspaper and air coverage of controversial issues, the hearing of complaints on media treatment of controversial issues, and the recommendation of measures that might be used to further the exercise of freedom of expression.

THE PROBLEM OF SAFEGUARDS

No matter how attractive the theoretical justification of an affirmative obligation to further freedom of expression, the entire theory will fall flat if in practice safeguards cannot be found to prevent abuses both by government and by private pressure groups. The spectre of frivolous and arbitrary discrimination and of actual government censorship raised by the opponents of the thesis is not an imaginary one. Every one of the suggestions proposed in the preceding section of this paper involves the application of some standards of access and in many cases the exercise of judgment on matters of substantive content. Since these are all human decisions, what is to prevent merely an intensification of the arbitrary kind of treatment that is given to expression of minority opinion under the existing system?

There is no easy answer to this. One possible solution is the application of the ombudsman principle to establish machinery for evaluating the functioning of the media on a nation-wide scale. This might involve the appointment of an actual "ombudsman of the media," a single man whose integrity and whose stature in the field are so universally recognized that his opinions and recommendations could not comfortably be ignored either by government or by the private media. (A man such as the late Edward R. Murrow comes to mind in this connection.) From a disinterested enthusiasm for the furtherance of all expression this person could plead a specific grievance with the government or with the private media owners on behalf of a petitioner. In conjunction with some kind of citizen advisory commission he could formulate general evaluations and recommendations for approaches to diversity that can be implemented both by government and by the media owners themselves. By virtue of his distance from any interested government agency and from the private media he could command the respect of both and the confidence of the public. Nothing will eliminate the human factor. But it is certainly possible that an ombudsman and a representative citizen body together could oversee the implementation of an affirmative governmental program to further freedom of expression in a fair and progressive manner.

section G   Change by the Media

The following three articles survey a variety of possible changes that can occur in or directly affect the journalist and his work. Diamond reviews the gamut of new directions being explored by a variety of journalists. In general, the journalist is poorly organized. The various unions associated with journalism are usually interested in work conditions, *not* editorial matters. In general, the unions can often inhibit the development of a professional journalist.

It is this topic that is taken up by LeRoy in the second article. The first portion of the article delineates current thinking about "what is professionalism?" This is important since everybody uses the word "professional" with a variety of different meanings. The last portion of the article deals with some suggestions for change in the field of journalism, noting that some avenues have proven, in the past, to be dead ends.

In the third article, Butler reviews the evidence to date dealing with the impact of press councils. The idea of meetings between a representative portion of the public and the local newspaper publishers has met with little enthusiasm from the newspaper owners. However, the reader should be aware of the existence of press councils and of the fact that this may be an appropriate strategy in some communities. For those interested in press councils, *Backtalk*, a new book (as yet unpublished) edited by William Rivers will prove to be a valuable resource.

chapter 21 'Reporter Power' Takes Root

EDWIN DIAMOND

One of the most significant and underreported social experiments of 1969 took place in the small northern California community of Willits. There, forty-three-year-old George Davis, a football coach who describes himself as "a small man with nothing to lose," fielded a football team each Saturday using the principle of participatory democracy; the players themselves voted on who should be in the starting lineup. The team lost its first four games of the season but rallied and ended in a tie for the league championship. This record, of course, might have been as much due to talent as to democracy. Still, the implications of the Davis experiment are clear: in an era marked by the pervasive and passionate questioning of all authority, even the football coach—that traditionally rigid hierarchical figure—is trying to bend with the times.

In American news media most communications caliphates are more like Vince Lombardi than George Davis—they are big men with a lot to

Edwin Diamond, "'Reporter Power' Takes Root," from the *Columbia Journalism Review*, Vol. 9, No. 2 Summer 1970. Reprinted by permission of the author and the publisher.

lose, so to speak—and so the principle of electing editors or announcers has not yet been established. But a sampling of attitudes in a number of city-rooms, magazine offices, and broadcast studios indicates that day may not be far off. In various cities journalists have banded together to impress their professional beliefs and occupational misgivings upon management.

At the Gannett papers in Rochester, N.Y., editorial staff members have begun sitting in with the papers' editorial board on a rotating basis. In Denver, a new Newspaper Guild contract signed in mid-March establishes an ethics committee and a human rights committee that will meet regularly with management. The human rights committee plans to take up the question of minority employment (women as well as blacks) at the *Post;* the three-member ethics committee, which will meet with three representatives of management, wants to discuss such hoary *Post* practices as trade-outs—editorial puffs written about an advertiser to fill out a special section. And in Providence, R. I., a Journalists Committee has held several meetings with management about specific staffing and policy changes on the *Journal* and *Bulletin.* The Committee acted after surveying a sizable portion of the editorial staff, then compiling the survey and mimeographing it for distribution.

Guild contract negotiations are still grimly contested in the news media, as are labor contracts in most business enterprises. But the new benefits that journalists have begun to seek go far beyond the usual guild bargaining points of wages and hours. The new grievances involve, first of all, moral—almost theological—concerns. When the Association of *Tribune* Journalists was formed by reporters at the Minneapolis *Tribune* last February, for example, it carefully stated that the group was not a collective bargaining unit but an agent for bringing "our best thoughts into a dialogue with management." There had been the usual grumbling at the *Trib* about shortages of staff and space, but there was a new element in the talk. As an association member later explained, "There was a feeling on our part of loss of respect. We were being treated like army privates and the editors were officers; we were to do what we were told and like it and no one gave a damn if we thought our orders were sane or insane."

On May 25 the *Tribune's* enlisted men and women moved decisively to assert "rights of participation" in the choice of their junior officers: when two *Trib* assistant city editors announced that they planned to leave the paper, the local Guild unit adopted a resolution stating that "reporters, photographers, and copydesk editors should advise and consent to management's nominations." The next day management met with the Guild and said that while it was not giving up its prerogatives it was willing to take the staff's nominations into account. It is a small step for the *Trib*, but a giant leap for American journalism—which more and more is moving toward the model of *Le Monde* and other European publications described by Jean Schwoebel in these pages.

Similarly, the men and women who produce programs for public television have formed an association concerned not with residuals but with, among other subjects, the social content of programs and the racial hiring practices of their industry. And reporters in several cities have founded journalism reviews [see *Passing Comment*, Spring].

The concerns that have stimulated these various activities are immediately recognizable as the concerns that have dominated much of the news covered by media men and women in recent years. Journalists who have followed the fight of parents to decentralize schools, the demands of students to have a say in the investment policies of the universities, and the blacks' and radical whites' challenge to the established institutions of society, have now begun to think about applying to their own lives principles of community control, participatory democracy, and collective action.

The development of this new consciousness is fairly recent. Ten or fifteen years ago, unions battled to win wage increases and to protest mergers, but the way a publication or station was run—from the color scheme of the newsroom walls to the overall editorial policies—remained the prerogative of the owner. The journalist's attitude was, typically, acquiescent; after all, was it not management's bat and ball—and ball park (although in broadcasting, the air *does* belong to the public and the station owner has only the loan of it)?

With affluence, the new temper of times, and the seller's market for young talent, this attitude has changed. Media executives now know (and graduate school studies show) that the brightest young people, on the whole, are not going into journalism, and that even those who are graduated from journalism schools often choose public relations work over reporting jobs. Even more alarming to an editor or news director with proper regard for talent is the attrition rate of good young newsmen and women after two or three years in the business. Money and bylines alone are no longer sufficient inducements; if executives want to attract and keep good young people, they must be attentive to or at least aware of their opinions. As often as not, a good university-trained reporter who is now in his or her late twenties picketed for civil rights while in high school, spent a freshman summer in Mississippi or Appalachia, and sat in at the Dean's office during senior year—or covered these events for the school paper. Now they are turning reformist toward their own profession.

Recent unrest at the *Wall Street Journal* is a case in point. The *Journal* reached its present eminence in part by hiring good young people right out of college, training them, and giving them the time and the space to develop long, informative reports and tiend stories. Now, says an older hand at the paper, "these younger people are much more activist-minded and more willing to needle management." During the Vietnam Moratorium Day last October, several younger reporters wanted to march on Broad street, a block from Wall, with at least one sign saying *Wall Street Journalist for the Moratorium.* Management's position was that it didn't mind the marching but didn't think the wording of that one sign was proper because it might "raise questions about the *Journal's* objectivity in the reader's mind."

A confrontation on Moratorium Day was avoided—according to one witness, the sign was carried but not held up. But the young activists then dispatched a petition to management asking for a clarification of the *Journal's* "position" on what they could do with their private lives. In response, executives Warren Phillips and Ed Cony issued a memorandum noting that "we must be concerned not only with avoiding bias in our news columns but also with avoiding the appearance of bias." They concluded: "It is the individual's obligation to exercise sufficient judgment to avoid such embarrassment." The younger reporters also have expressed their concern about what the *Journal* does on the editorial page; when the *Journal* ran an editorial that seemed to blame New York City's telephone troubles on allegedly slow-witted welfare mothers hired to operate switchboards, a newsroom caucus told management that reporters didn't want to be associated with a paper that had such mossback views.

The *Journal's* radical "cell" remains largely an *ad hoc* group springing to life when an issue presents itself. At the Minneapolis *Tribune,* however, the new consciousness of younger journalists has manifested itself in a formal organization. Last Fall, by all accounts, the *Tribune* had a morale problem compounded by a high turnover and some admitted paranoia on the part of the staff. A group of reporters began meeting on Sunday mornings—for a while they were known as the Underground Church—to see if anything beside complaining could be done. The Underground Church members repeated the usual litany of cityroom complaints—the need for more phones, better files, more out-of-town exchanges —but they also were concerned with such traditional domains of management as the size of the travel allowance, the company's fiscal and budgetary procedures, and the circulation breakdown by area. More important, the Underground Church challenged the *Tribune's* news judgment, most particularly on those issues that have polarized so much of the country. One young reporter drew up the following indictment:

> The *Trib's* sins tend to be those of omission, rather than commission. We
> sent no one to the Chicago Conspiracy trial despite repeated requests from

staffers who wanted to go. We sent no one to Washington last November with the thousands of Minnesotans who participated in the Vietnam Moratorium. We do have a D. C. bureau which handled Moratorium coverage but we did not, like our rival paper, the *Star*, see fit to send anyone on the buses of demonstrators from our state. . . . The November Moratorium was our right-hand, front-page lead story, with a front-page picture of masses of marchers going along peaceably. The story by Chuck Bailey of our D. C. bureau devoted the first five paragraphs to general comments on the demonstration. The next six paragraphs were on the violence that occurred there. Then followed twelve paragraphs on the speeches, color, etc. We used only the official 250,000 figure for the number of participants and did not mention any higher estimates.

On the second front page only one of the five pictures showed a peaceful scene (Coretta King marching). One was rioters getting tear-gassed, another a draft-card burning, another an American flag being carried upside down, and the fourth a flag-burning which turned out, on close inspection, to be counter-demonstrators burning a Vietcong flag. According to our own figures, one-250th of the people at that demonstration got at least three-fifths of the pictures on the second front page and about one-fourth of the main story. . . .

We do, of course, often do a good job breaking a story. Give us a cyclone or a postal strike or the Governor saying he won't run again, and we're all over it. We get the sidebars and the reactions and the whole thing. But in trying to explain what the hell is happening in this society in any larger way— perspective, context, whatever you want to call it—the *Trib* just ain't there.

The Underground Church soon realized it could go in two possible directions: the reporters could start a publication modeled after the *Chicago Journalism Review* which would regularly monitor the local press' performance on stories like the November Moratorium, or they could try to work within the organization by establishing a "dialogue" with management. The Church chose the former course, and plans for a *Twin Cities Journalism Review* were put on the back burner. Early this year, John Cowles, Jr., president of the Minneapolis Star and Tribune Co. (and also the majority owner of *Harper's* magazine), and Bower Hawthorne, vice president and editor of the *Tribune*, were invited to meet with some of the staff and discuss the paper's direction. Hawthorne, meanwhile, had invited all staff members to his own meeting to discuss the paper—the two invitations apparently crossed in the interoffice mail. The meetings took place—"by this time we were communicating like hell," one reporter recalls wryly—and the dissidents formally organized into the Association of *Tribune* Journalists.

The managing editor, Wallace Allen, drew up an extensive questionnaire which was distributed to some 100 staff members; forty-seven returned their forms. Allen's own summary of the responses reflects the low opinion the workers had for the paper and the management. Five of the nineteen "impressions and conclusions" he drew from the replies are especially noteworthy:

—You want a great deal more information about company direction, through direct and personal communication with management up to the highest level.

—Some of you feel strongly that staff members should play a part in policy-making and decision-making. You do not wish to run the newspaper but you would like to be consulted on what is done and informed in advance of both major and minor decisions.

—You feel that news policy and direction are not being handed down fully or clearly. You have only a vague idea—or no idea—of what we are trying to do and where we are trying to go.

—You feel that our approaches to covering the news and the ways we present it are not up to date. You want to see change and progress in an orderly, responsible but exciting way.

—Many of you feel that the *Tribune* was a progressive and exciting newspaper until about six months or so ago. You indicate that the letdown may have come from confusion in management's mind about news direction when it discovered the silent majority. You feel management switched direction in an attempt to respond to changing social conditions but switched in ways that revealed ignorance of basic issues.

Allen's efforts at communications apparently had a calming effect on the staff, which by and large adopted a "wait and see" attitude. As of late Spring the Association continued to meet every other week or so and was reviving plans for the *Twin Cities Journalism Review*.

The Association of Public Television Producers, another group of journalists who went "above ground" out of a deep concern about their professional lives, has also become engaged in management matters. Men and women on every level in public television are worried about the continued unfettered operation of noncommercial TV in the United States, especially because the new Corporation for Public Broadcasting has to go to Congress each year for funds. The Association came forward during Congressional hearings last year to discuss alternative plans for financing public TV; its spokesman, Alvin Perlmutter, a National Educational Television producer, told the Pastore Committee that he personally favored financing PTV by a tax on the profits of the commercial networks rather than the present arrangement in which public TV is dependent on the goodwill of 535 Congressmen. Perlmutter was rewarded with a lecture from Senator Pastore, advising him not to bite the hand that is feeding him. More recently, the Association publicly protested the decision of some local public TV stations not to show the NET documentary *Who Invited US?*, a highly critical study of U.S. foreign policy. Like the reporters at the Minneapolis *Tribune*, the public TV producers want to see certain stories run—and they are prepared to challenge past assumptions about whether the people who have the bat and ball can make all the rules of the game.

The women's movement at *Newsweek* also has been willing to try its case in public. The conditions that the *Newsweek* women found objectionable—segregation of women into the scut work of research, the lack of writing opportunities (fifty male writers to one woman), and the general atmosphere of exclusion—had for years existed unopposed except by one or two editors. In the last year or two, however, many of the young women had been covering the black revolution and student unrest. As reporters they had listened to the rhetoric of "power to the people"; they had been "used" by militants who staged news conferences and other media events to get across their messages. When the *Newsweek* women decided to press their collective claims they arranged a media event: they timed the release of their complaint to the Equal Employment Opportunity Commission in Washington to coincide with the Monday morning newstand appearance of the *Newsweek* cover story "Women in Revolt." They called a news conference and phoned contacts at other news organizations to insure full coverage. Then they appeared in force, well groomed and intelligent, flanking their lawyer, a young, attractive black woman named Eleanor Holmes Norton. Their widely covered action had the desired effect, galvanizing the top echelon of *Newsweek* into a long series of meetings with the women and winning from management pledges to open the entire editorial hierarchy to women.

The editor may justifiably grumble that the women should have come to his office first, but the women believe it was the public nature of their action that produced results. Their experience replicates that of a Minneapolis *Tribune* reporter who now believes the "only power that we staff members really have in these matters is the power to embarrass management." This power also was demonstrated last March when a group called Media Women flooded into the office of the *Ladies' Home Journal's* editor and publisher, John Mack Carter, to stage the first "liberation" of a mass magazine. The resulting publicity may not have immediately hurt the *Journal's* advertising revenues or circulation, but it certainly affected that evanescent quality known as aura—and it made many readers who heretofore had not paid much attention to the feminist cause conscious of the magazine's assumptions.

For the time being at least, the tactics of "liberation" have been the exception rather than the rule. If there is a pattern in developments around the country, it is the tactic of internally rather than publicly making the case for a larger staff role in policymaking. Thus, some sixty New York *Post* activists (over as well as under thirty) have been meeting with the *Post's* publisher, Mrs. Dorothy Schiff, to force a break from the penurious policies and lackluster journalism of the past. The reporters have asked for more specialist beats, a larger travel budget, more black and Puerto Rican staff, and more coverage of minority groups. At the New York *Times* a loose confederation of reporters and editors have also met to discuss a long list of grievances, some of them water-cooler complaints but others centering on the *Times'* coverage of politics, race, the Chicago Conspiracy trial, and the Black Panthers. Some of the *Times* reporters are chafing under what they consider the harsh yoke of Managing Editor A. M. Rosenthal and his bullpen editors, and one step being considered calls for the selection or election—in the *Le Monde* and Minneapolis models—of a top editor.

And in Philadelphia, the senior editors of the *Bulletin* have been conducting regular Monday afternoon "seminars" with some fifteen of the younger—and more activist-minded—staff reporters. The weekly seminars began last March after managing editor George Packard had heard complaints from staff members that story suggestions and opinions about news coverage were not "trickling upward." A typical meeting allows equal time for a senior editor to explain his particular operation (news desk, photo assignments, etc.) and for reporters to ask questions or otherwise respond. The trickle—some say, torrent—of underclass feelings loosed by the seminars has already resulted in some changes in the way the *Bulletin* handles racial identifications in stories. *Bulletin* editors are also opening up channels so that younger reporters can get story ideas into the paper's new "Enterprise" page, and no one seems more satisfied with these developments than Packard himself.

A number of issues could transform these informal internal discussions into overt action groups. Working reporters have been made visibly nervous by recent efforts to subpoena reporters' notes, raw files, and unused film [PASSING COMMENT, Spring]. The Wall Street *Journal* "cell" and the Association of *Tribune* Journalists, among others, have formally protested to their managements about cooperating in such government fishing expeditions. More signficantly, two groups of journalists, cutting across corporate and media lines, have banded together on the subpoena issue. One group consists of some seventy black men and women journalists who placed an ad to announce their intention to oppose the Government's efforts (the Government's first target in efforts to obtain reporters' notes was a black journalist for the New York *Times,* Earl Caldwell).

The second group, called the Reporter's Committee on Freedom of the Press, consists of both black and white newsmen, and J. Anthony Lukas of the New York *Times* has been one of its early organizers. The Reporter's Committee met early in March at the Georgetown University Law Center in Washington. The discussions—attended by men from the Washington *Star,* the Washington *Post, Time, Newsweek,* the Los Angeles *Times,* NBC, and CBS—reflected some of the feelings of staff men that interests of management and employees may not always be congruent in the matter of subpoenas. Rather than rely on lawyers of their individual companies and corporations—who by and large have been uncertain trumpets in recent months—the Georgetown group wants to explore the legal thickets of the subpoena issue directly with law schools and scholars. Already, the group is cooperating with the Georgetown Law Center on an information center and clearing house, and with Stanford University on a legal study of the whole area of confidential material.

Two other issues could also serve to "radicalize" the working press. One issue is race. Black reporters in the San Francisco area and in New York City have organized their own associations, partly to get together to talk about matters of common interest and occasionally to speak out with a collective voice. The other radicalizing issue is the war in Indochina. Shortly after Mr. Nixon ordered American troops into Cambodia, more than 150 *Newsweek* employees met to debate whether they should bring pressure on their magazine to come out against the war; one form of action considered was an anti-war advertisement in *Newsweek*. At the New York *Daily News* more than 100 editorial employees attempted to place just such an ad in their paper, but were refused space by the paper even though they had collected $1,100 to pay for it. The *Daily News*men promptly took their ad to the New York *Times*, where it was accepted— double embarrassment for the *News'* management.

As of mid-1970, then, media activists had a great deal in their favor, including management's fear of a talent drain and its abhorrence of adverse publicity. Ultimately, too, they can count on the *amour propre* of the ownership: the proprietors have a selfish interest in listening. John Cowles, Jr., for example, told his *Tribune* reporters that it wasn't at all pleasant to hear, in his words, that he was "the captain of the *Titanic*." Perhaps a "dialogue" can achieve a new arrangement of authority that recognizes the best qualities of passion, spontaneity, and social concerns of the younger journalists while preserving the established professional virtues of fair play and balance.

chapter 22   Journalism as a Profession

DAVID J. LeROY

Consider the term professional as it is used by newsmen. When Walter Cronkite states, "I am a professional," what does he mean? If I understand him correctly, he means that he controls his emotions and biases in performing his duties. Stories are selected for their news values and reported in as fair and as objective a manner as possible.

Another cluster of values commonly associated with this usage revolves around the idea of the "old pro." In this instance, the term indicates that a person can perform well under stressful conditions. It is the élan or style under pressure which defines the criterion of judgment.

Is this the meaning commonly associated with professionalism as it is employed by social scientists? The answer, of course, is no. There are any number of occupations that require their practitioners to control their emotions, be fair in their dealings with people, and perform well under stress. If these were the only criteria, how could one differentiate between professional football players, policemen, ambulance attendants, and the traditional professions of law, medicine, and the clergy? All of these individuals perform with élan under stress and gain their principal livelihood from their occupation.

The first task then is to examine the current thinking about professions, professionalism, and professionalization. From these concepts we will extract some criteria applicable to an examination of journalism. Along the way a number of ancillary topics must be dealt with, since they are often employed as rationalizations for not effecting desired changes in journalism.[1]

PROFESSIONALIZATION

This term *professionalization* has been around for years, but recently it has acquired a specific meaning for sociologists who study occupations. It refers to the stages through which an occupation progresses to become a profession. The wording of this definition is rewarding since it frees us of some inhibiting prejudices.

First, the process notion does away with the either/or syndrome in considering a specific occupation as a profession. It substitutes instead the idea of an evolutionary process. Since no occupation evolves in the same way or at the same rate, it can possess, in varying degrees, the elements essential for a profession to emerge. Thus, we ask, how professional is an occupation?

Professions are viewed as *relative*, not absolute, phenomenon. One occupation can be said to be more professional than another by virtue of possessing more professional elements than the other. The value of this new approach is that the psychological attributes of a professional are separated from the structural and organizational properties of the occupation (e.g., licensing, diplomas, and professional organizations). This can explain why some members of an established profession can meet all of the external tests required to enter the profession while lacking the necessary psychological attributes to complete the process. This valuable distinction was often lost in the earlier discussions of the profession.

ORGANIZATIONAL PROCESS

The evolutionary emergence of a profession's structural (or external) events can be summarized as follows. A trade becomes a fulltime occupa-

---

1 The discussion of professionalization presented in the text draws heavily from the work of Richard H. Hall, especially his article, "Professionalization and Bureaucratization," *American Sociological Review*, 33, No. 1 (1966), 92–104.

Besides oversimplifying a complex area of investigation, I have also made the assumption that journalists can be professionalized, whereas many authorities dismiss the field of journalism as capable of professionalization.

tion and organizes itself into an association or organization which at first seeks to reinforce and identify like-minded individuals. Eventually, there emerge competing associations, with one finally gaining dominance and absorbing the others. Standards are generated and formalized into codes of ethics, and efforts are made to drive out the quacks and deviants from the occupation. Approaches are made to universities, and after a time, the essential skills and knowledge of the occupation are offered as a specialized academic major. Finally, the occupation seeks legislation from the appropriate sources to protect and police itself.

Prior to 1950, the procession of events outlined above proceeded at a leisurely pace, allowing one scholar to label it a natural history of professionalization. Today, however, the process is often proceeding simultaneously on all fronts. Efforts to establish an academic major may precede development of a code of ethics. Ancillary and competing occupational associations may still be vying with each other while introducing academic majors in special interest categories (such as that which occurred in separate divisions or departments for broadcasting and journalism). This suggests that any occupation, but especially journalism, is proceeding in a number of directions at once.

At present, most journalism organizations and associations are quite weak and disorganized. Most are organized around a parochial core of occupational attributes. There are associations for owners, editors, broadcasters, Congressional correspondents, Associated Press managing editors, and so on. The organizations have little control over their members. The various codes of ethics are more often statements of principle rather than enforceable standards of practice.

With the exception of scholarly journals published by the two educational associations, Association for Education in Journalism and Association for Professional Broadcasting Education, the periodical literature generated by journalism associations is chatty, trivial, and remedial. At best, like *Quill,* they funnel in ideas for the practitioners to contemplate. The most promising development in terms of publication is the appearance of local press reviews, where standards of practice and concepts or professionalism are discussed without Chamber of Commerce boosterism.

As Wilensky has pointed out, competing organizations retard the professionalization process. Journalism is in dire need of generating a single coherent organization.[2]

PROFESSIONALISM

Before any substantial changes can be affected in the professional associations, there must be some coherence in the psychological orienta-

---

[2] The article is Harold Wilensky, "The Professionalization of Everybody?" *American Journal of Sociology,* 70, No. 2 (1964), 142–46.

tion of the occupation's membership. The following five belief clusters, labeled *professionalism* by sociologists, have been suggested as the necessary attitude structures for any type of professional.

1. The professional uses his professional organization or group as his principal reference group. The goals and aspirations of the professional are not those of a particular employer or one's local status in the community; his allegiance is to the field.
2. The professional has a belief in public service. The professional's purpose is to serve the public good. He is altruistic.
3. The professional possesses a sense of calling about the field. This commitment reinforces and complements the belief in public service. He practices his profession because he feels a deep commitment, and this sustains him through periods of training and times of stress.
4. The professional possesses a feeling of autonomy. The professional makes his decisions and is free to organize his work within certain functional constraints.
5. The professional believes in self-regulation. He controls his own behavior. Given the complexity of his job and the skills required, only his peers have the right and competency to judge his performance.

It can be seen that the five categories are not independent, but complementary. To summarize, the professional is committed to his occupation and practices it because of his altruism or belief in public service. Given the complexity of his various duties, he is the best judge of how the job is to be performed; and when questions of malpractice and ethics are concerned, only his peers have the competency to judge his behavior. He is sustained in his beliefs by the existence of a national or regional fraternity of like-minded individuals formed into a strong association.

Missing from this list is any mention of the older concept of client-professional relationships. This is subsumed under the altruism concept or belief in public service. This is necessary because, in some instances, professions lack an individual human being as a client. Examples would be corporation lawyers, accountants, or clergy engaged in theological speculations. Some observers note that there is a primitive version of the client-professional relationship in the interaction between a reporter and his news source. But this phenomenon is true for only a limited range of journalists whereas others in the occupation have little or no public contact.

Another concept not mentioned here is the grant of public esteem and professional status, because some professions are rarely known to the general public (as in the case of CPA's, certain types of engineers, and the pure research scientists). However, somewhere in the social system the professional is given a grant of autonomy to pursue his goals without bureaucratic interference.

Also omitted was any mention of an isolated and unique body of knowledge assigned as the exclusive property of a given profession. This may have existed at one time for clergymen and lawyers, but it is certainly no longer in existence. Specialized knowledge bases are now the property of the pure research scientist or scholar. It is he who receives the Nobel Prize, not the professional, who develops the application of the knowledge. More and more professional training is emphasizing performance skills, as well as ways to locate, abstract and synthesize information for a task. The internship, an early form of simulation study, is still the major testing ground for the neophyte professional.

For journalism, the knowledge base is varied and poorly systematized, since most of the crucial training occurs in the field and not at the universities. The special skills of the journalist include locating, processing and in some cases evaluating information. The failure to crystallize the activities composing the occupational tasks can be attributed to both the university educator and the owners and editors of the news media (points to which we will return shortly).

Another topic excluded from the discussion of professionalization was the notion of professionals as salaried employees. In our mass society, the individual practitioner is rapidly disappearing and being replaced by clinics, law firms, and consultancies. The assumption by the Hutchins Commission and others—that professionals are usurped by bureaucracies for whom they work—has not been supported by recent research. Ironically, the professionals employed by government and business often turn out in these studies to be more professional than the lone practitioner.[3]

What is clear about professionals and bureaucracies is that the organization must make a number of compromises with its lawyers, doctors and CPAs. The result has often been the "professional department," which is characterized by a loose informal structure. The head is a fellow-professional and he leads by indirection and appeal to professionalism. The crucial facet is the grant of autonomy to the professional department and its members.

Let us be very clear about what is meant by autonomy. Any activity has functional interdependencies. A surgeon, for example, makes a decision to operate, but the act is dependent upon everyone following required procedures and schedules to successfully complete the operation. A similar example is that of lawyers who must follow court procedure and argue their case from precedent and jurisdiction.

Traced to its epistemological roots, autonomy is a relative rather than absolute phenomenon. In most instances, the professional is choosing between alternates for which he bears responsibility, whereas, the bureau-

[3] The research literature is reviewed in an excellent and nontechnical summary in Richard H. Hall, *Occupations and the Social Structure* (Englewood Cliffs, N.J.: Prentice-Hall, Inc., 1969).

cratic worker has standard rules and operations which prescribe how he is to proceed with little or no direct personal responsibility.

Finally, we come to an issue of great emotional impact in journalism, namely licensing. It should be obvious that the only tolerable or acceptable control over entrance and policing of a profession must rest with its members. In America, this power is held by the owners and managers of the various news media. The First Amendment restricts Congress only from passing any inhibiting legislation in regard to speech, religion, and the press. It clearly forbids the government from entering into a licensing role. However, the Supreme Court has held in a number of broadcasting cases that the rights of the First Amendment rest with the public and not with the licensee. The broadcaster should, the court argued in *Red Lion*, conceive of himself as a fiduciary between the public and its government and environment. Some scholars have already noted that many similarities exist between broadcasting licensees and single newspaper towns. The extension of the reasoning in *Red Lion* to newspapers, in terms of casting the newspaper publisher as a fiduciary rather than a businessman, is assumed by some to be a foregone conclusion. The principal issue is to locate an appropriate test case.[4]

Thus, it cannot be assumed that the Constitution or the Supreme Court is going to automatically retard the process of licensing journalism if it were advanced by some parties in the private sector. Besides, there is already a de facto licensing practiced by the publisher, editor, and news director in deciding who shall work in the field. This suggests that the career journalist has "compromised" enough to stay within the organization. The key is that the role is defined and supported by management, not by professional journalists. At present, the journalist is almost powerless in defining the parameters of his craft. Evolving into a profession is one method of enlightened self-defense. Professionalism also contains positive benefits for management and the news public.

WHY PROFESSIONALISM?

The more cynical will note that everyone seems to be seeking or appropriating the title *profession* for their occupation. Although those who do this may have a philistine motive, consider the alternatives. Does one wish to identify himself as a middle-level bureaucratic administrator or refer to oneself as a door-to-door "salesman?" There seems to be a

---

[4] The idea has been introduced by a number of scholars and lawyers. For an introduction to the problem see Lee Loevinger, "Free Speech, Fairness and the Fiduciary Duty in Broadcasting," *Law and Contemporary Problems*, 34, No. 2 (1969), 278–98.

dearth of psychological satisfaction in occupational labels for our bureaucrats. Whatever the reasons for the polarization of labels, bureaucrat or professional, being identified as a professional has its psychological satisfactions for many functionaries in our industrial society.

The reason that society and the employer seek and reward professionalism is that in a complex and difficult to define position with little in the way of structure to audit in terms of performance or, ever-present temptations in terms of money or ethical compromise, a profession is society's "best insurance." Actually, professionalism is a rather old-fashioned ideal of behavior, what Riesman years ago called the inner-directed man—the individual with his own internal moral gyroscope, performing with aplomb a difficult task without a hint of compromise.

When a journalist calls himself a professional, how does one distinguish between those occupational members who have a commitment to professionalism and those who merely seek a rationalization for their daily labor? One way is to evoke the criteria from the area of professional beliefs. The assumption is that in evolving or developing professions, professionalism usually precedes any significant change in the external power of occupational organizations.

RESEARCH ON PROFESSIONALISM

Jack McLeod and his students at the University of Wisconsin began and are pursuing a course of research in the area of professionalism. They have taken an admittedly abstract concept and studied it in the field; this is an important first step.[5]

In summary, McLeod has shown that editorial staffers differ significantly from other employees of the paper. The staffers stressed responsibility and objectivity in reporting in comparison with ancillary personnel (such as accounting and advertising personnel). Further, McLeod studied differences within editorial staffers for implementing professional goals and categorized the resulting groups as either semiprofessional or professional. The semiprofessionals, although not resembling the ancillary personnel, did however differ from the "pros" in stressing internal advancement, job security, and congeniality as important employment variables. The professional group was more apt to stress the implementation of professional goals and was more critical of their paper's performance than the semiprofessionals.

In subsequent studies, mostly in the area of international journalism, McLeod's findings continue to demonstrate cognitive differences be-

[5] Jack McLeod and Searle J. Hawley, Jr., "Professionalization Among Newsmen," *Journalism Quarterly*, 41, No. 3 (1964), 528–39.

tween a professional cadre and other editorial staffers. The evidence suggests that the germative core for professionalism in journalism exists in a wide variety of countries.

In a study of a small, somewhat unrepresentative sample of television journalists, I found a similar core of professionalism to exist. It was found that when a reporter or news director perceives himself as an autonomous individual in his work, a germative factor of professionalism emerges. An interesting corollary finding was that when an individual is denied autonomy in his work, a bureaucracy factor of awesome repressiveness emerges. When an individual has this type of environment, he negatively evaluates the public service components of his profession. At the risk of overgeneralizing from a small battery of research findings, it can be suggested that some crude germative attitudes exist which could form the necessary nucleus for a profession.

(An interesting sidelight is that in some studies (by myself and Beckwith[6]), as market or urban size increases, so does some element that crudely represents professionalism. In addition, this factor emerges for group or chain owned media and not independent organizations. Whether it is the higher salaries or the autonomy of a large organization which accounts for this is not known, but group ownership is at this stage a good predictor of professionalism for journalism and especially for the factor of altruism.)

WHO SHOULD PROFESSIONALIZE?

What roles should be professionalized? There is very little agreement about this among concerned observers of journalism. Most would agree that the back shop is best dealt with as a bureaucracy protected by its union, as are mailers, engineers and truckers. Should everyone in the newsroom be a professional? There are, ironically, a number of forces at work that may decide the issue for us.

Some ancillary personnel are evolving toward a professional model of their occupation without any outside pressure. Whether they attain or wish to attain full professional status is another issue. This seems to be the conclusion that one can draw from Coldwell's study of newspaper photographers.[7] In this study an interesting cluster of attitudes emerged.

[6] David J. LeRoy, "Measuring Professionalism in a Sample of Television Journalists" (Unpublished doctoral dissertation, University of Wisconsin at Madison, 1971); and Gerald C. Beckwith, "An Investigation of Role-Orientation and Reference-Group Identification in Systems of Broadcast Communication" (Unpublished doctoral dissertation, Michigan State University, 1968).

[7] Thomas Coldwell, "Professionalization and Performance Among Newspaper Photographers" (Unpublished master's thesis, University of Wisconsin at Madison, 1970).

An independent panel of judges rated the photojournalism of a sample
of newspapers. The photographers completed McLeod's Professionalism
Scale and Wilcox's ethical judgments for photojournalists. The photographers associated with the excellent papers had significantly higher
professionalism and ethical scores. This convergence of performance and
cognitive valuations resembling professionalism is most encouraging.

The above example suggests that portions of the journalistic enterprise can and probably will continue to evolve in their own manner.
Further, the model of professionalization advanced here does not require that each and every occupation evolve into one type of profession.

Besides this natural evolution, some scholars have postulated that a
few key roles in journalism should or must be professionalized in order
to insure the process for all.

Gerald, in his *The Social Responsibility of the Press,* argues that the
key role to professionalize is the newspaper publisher or owner, since he
controls the assignment of editors and expenditures for reporters and
equipment. Gerald feels that professionalization of other roles will be
insured by the existence of a professionalized owner.

Gillis, in discussing broadcasters, takes the opposite view that professionalism will never emerge because the manager or licensee are
committed to making a profit. This motive is seen as antagonistic to the
professional's commitment to public service or altruism. However, as
has been alluded to earlier, in large multi-station and/or multi-paper
chains, the enterprise is so vast that responsibility must be delegated.
These corporations can afford professionalism. They give a grant of
autonomy to the news director or managing editor. Given autonomy, the
issue is then the editor and his vision of the journalistic endeavor. Editors who constantly talk about the "product," the cost per thousand impressions and increasing circulation are pathetic, not because they lack
vision, but because they are usually such poor managers or businessmen
they would be drummed out of any regular industry. The reason they can
remain is rather simple. The profit margins for both broadcasting and
newspapers are three times the national average for regular industry.
Given the quasi-monopoly status of most of the daily news media, it
takes more than inept management to go bankrupt.[8]

It is one thing to *ask* publishers to develop a professional attitude and
to retain and develop professional reporters. However, there is no way
to *compel* professionalization from the publisher. Since most of the news-

[8] Profit margins are dealt with in a variety of sources. See, for example, "Newspapers Death Held Exaggerated," *Forbes* (October 1, 1969), and Chapter 4 in Ben
Bagdikian, *The Information Machines* (New York: Harper & Row, Publishers,
1970).

paper industry is already a quasi monopoly, the assertion that a paper cannot afford professionalism appears moot. Editors who employ the show business razzle-dazzle to justify shoddy and sensational coverage of community affairs are no longer justifiable.

But can editors be required to become professional? At present this is an impossibility, but given the quasi-monopoly status of newspapers and the right test case, *Red Lion* could be extended to certain types of newspapers. The Court has held that the key element is the marketplace of ideas, which must be preserved, not the melodrama of the *Big Story* or *Front Page.* This new role requires the editor to function as a fiduciary. Some industry sources feel that the fiduciary role will reduce newspapers and broadcast journalism to nothing more than community bulletin boards. However, this is somewhat extreme since there is nothing in the fiduciary role which reduces the journalist into being a mere pipeline between the news source and the public. However, this type of professional role is more appropriate for the editors than reporters.

A fiduciary role for journalism would require a double-faceted orientation for the editor. (W. E. Moore in his book *Professions: Roles and Rules,* unfortunately employs the term "two-faced" for this role, which is, to say the least, a deplorable choice of words.) The editor here would not only serve in his regular capacity of overseeing the paper or news program, but would also insure that all news is sought and published. His obligation for professional behavior is to insure that the public has a marketplace of ideas. Since many editors already attempt this, the crystallization of this role is not that difficult to imagine. The principal difficulty will be in obtaining recognition from the owner in a quasi-monopoly market.

There is another ownership system represented by communities or markets where there exists free enterprise competition between separate news media owners. The evidence that competing dailies results in journalistic excellence (i.e., professionalism) is less than compelling.

Looking at the top ten American dailies, it is not competition or the lack of it that is the distinguishing characteristic, but rather the people responsible for the enterprise. The conclusion seems to be that competition depends upon the "quality" of the opposition—it may lead to excellence or sensationalism. A second point, somewhat disquieting to the open competition proponents, is the existence of superb papers without a trace of competition. This suggests that we have come full circle. Excellence in journalism is dependent upon the men involved and the commitment to excellence by the owners. In the concluding section, a number of suggestions will be advanced which seek to place journalism on the road to professionalism.

BEYOND THE CORRIDOR OF MIRRORS

There are times in discussing journalism and its current problems that one feels like Alexander and the Gordian knot. The impulse is to lift the sword and come down with one swift move upon the complexities which confront the field. My assumption is that there is a saving remnant, a cadre of concerned men and women both in the occupation and aspiring to it, who can, by dint of application, close the locks and back up the waters to save what is valuable in the present system, while eliciting the required changes in the system.

The key to professionalism is of course, autonomy—a psychological freedom within a flexible number of functional boundaries required to produce the newscasts, newspapers, or magazines. If change is to come, it must evolve from within the occupation. The courts may or may not help, while the general public continues in its blissful ignorance of the complexities of the journalistic task.

Let us dispense with some counterarguments or diversions that are offered as possible sources of change to hasten the day of professionalism and to make present immediate action unnecessary.

The first of these I call the new millennium argument. Journalists are told that when the new cable systems are in operation, or when the home facsimile newspapers arrive, there will be this vast cornucopia of news and the news system will finally be able to accommodate one and all. Those who advance this argument are no doubt well meaning, but they have failed to absorb the lessons of history.

Since the introduction of film in the 1890s, each new technological device is introduced with essentially the same arguments. *This* new media (be it film, radio, television, weekly news magazines) will automatically generate a genuine marketplace of ideas, culture, and intelligent comment. The new media always promises to be the real democratic "town meeting of the country." But none of the new media has fostered cultural pluralism, much less professional behavior on the part of the journalists.[9]

Further, each new media is controlled and often developed by the owners of the existing mass media. To be profitable, the managers of the system must control either the input or the distribution of the product. Economic viability is based upon the cost of production and distribution

[9] For a summary of the literature see Robert E. Davis, "Response to Innovation: A Study of Popular Arguments About New Mass Media" (Unpublished doctoral dissertation, University of Iowa, 1965). Davis reviews approximately 65 years of periodicals and books dealing with arguments of both the proponents and the critics of film, radio, and television. New proponents should develop some new arguments, since they have been saying essentially the same thing since the days of the nickelodeon.

being less than the income derived from either advertisers or purchasers. The new medium thus falls victim to the same financial constraints as its predecessors. Minority opinion, be it ethnic or intellectual, must either return its investment or be carried as a public service supported by what is popular and profitable.

It seems naive to assume that in the next decade, minority or intellectual news media will suddenly be able to pay its own way. Wilensky has shown that increased university education results in such unaccountable facts as engineering doctorates resembling the unemployed black in media habits. Mass higher education has not resulted in cultural or intellectual pluralism. The evidence suggests that there is no large untapped news audience awaiting the millennium. In the final analysis, given the distribution and financial systems required for mass media entertainment systems, the millennium will once again be postponed.

If the future cannot be depended upon to generate the spawning grounds for professionalism, neither can the universities. At present, journalism educators are pleasant sorts of failures in this capacity. Since the training process is still in the hands of the editors and publishers, the educators lack control of the intellectual core of the occupation.

The reasons for this academic failure are varied. To oversimplify, most curriculums embody archaic notions of monkey see, monkey do. The traditional production curriculum is a shoddy reproduction of journalism's bureaucratic structure. Courses are set up to mirror editing rooms and the student "plays editor." Essentially, this type of curriculum has sought to reflect the field and not lead it. Today many journalism departments are in a battle to survive within the university, which is critically evaluating the presence of these expensive vocational schools.

In graduate education, the "green eyeshade" practitioners are locked in combat with the "chi-square" researcher. This latter type of doctorate no longer looks to journalism for his role models, but rather to sociology and psychology. In many schools the journalism and broadcasting departments are being absorbed into the new colleges of behavioral science.

The thrust of the "new" curriculums will be in the area of task analysis, behavioral objectives and simulation systems. This new curriculum provides rigorous analysis of the journalistic task in terms of information processing skills, ability to understand statistics, economics, and politics. It is one thing to "get the story;" understanding what it means and its social ramifications for the citizenry is the critical need. We can only hope that journalism departments survive long enough to test the veracity of these new programs.[10]

[10] For an example of the newer ideas see Philip M. Burgess and Paul S. Underwood, "New Approaches to Educating the International Journalist," *Journalism Quarterly,* 47, No. 3 (1970), 519–29.

Apparently then, we can expect little influence in the near future from new media systems or the universities in fostering the emergence of a professional journalist. Earlier I had suggested that the best role for the editor is that of a fiduciary; but what about the reporter? Why are so many of them intellectually inept?

BUREAUCRACIES' TOLL

One of the crucial problems today is assembly-line journalism. Its justification is bureaucratic, its origins are nineteenth-century mass production methods, and its *raison d'etre* is the romanticism of a deadline-a-minute news objectivity and a melodramatic cynicism toward life.

The reporter has absorbed the brunt of this type of journalism. He is no more than a blue-collar worker. Initially the journalist was an essayist, not a short story writer. The intellectual nuances were not plot, angle, tension, and narrative gimmicks, but critical insight through investigation. The goal was epistemology, not entertainment. At its heart, journalism is a human being thinking, evaluating, and reaching conclusions about events, government, and man's inhumanity to man.

Is it little wonder that generations of American news "consumers" have grown up with little awareness of this process? The typical reporter's personality has been filtered out of the writing task so that the result is a news story which resembles a dried sponge.

To rethink the journalistic enterprise is going to be traumatic. The basic arguments against the change are not intellectual but rather, economic. The whole idea of daily news, wire services and electronic headlines resists change, but (as in the case of the automobile's internal combustian engine) the time has come to weigh alternatives.

A numbing recitation of the thousands of newspapers and radio stations, and the few hundred magazines and television stations is often given as proof of diversity in American journalism. But most of these outlets merely repeat wire service copy. Consider that 75 percent of the American public use their newspaper and their television sets as their principal source of news. This is the mass news system. Weekly news magazines and a few monthlies are definitely minority sources of news. If there is to be a marketplace of ideas for the American public it must occur in the daily newspaper and evening newscast. Everyone from Walter Cronkite to Spiro Agnew knows that television and even the newspapers do not furnish enough daily intelligence for the citizen. But to insist that it is the reader's duty to read more and diverse sources of information is sophistic. To argue that one news media's inadequacies are counterbalanced by another's in terms of scope of coverage, depth of report, and intelligence, is naive when most of their news is torn from the same wire teletype service.

The key issue is to reinstitute the reporter as intelligence seeker rather than as "fact grabber." The exact role need not be an issue; as Bill Rivers and Howard K. Smith agree, the more diversity, the better. The reporter as a professional represents a human intelligence at work. The profound antiintellectualism of the American press flows from its assembly line bureaucracy, considering the "news product" as if it were an automobile. The act of assembly has become the focus of attention. The melodrama of deadlines insures the banality of the product. Free enterprise news media competition (if it can be said to exist today) has had little impact upon the quality, scope and rigor of the newsman's thought. The manner in which the reporter must function on the assembly line is an almost classic example of work alienation.[11]

Who then is the villain in retarding the development of professionalism in journalism? Probably the editors who hold to stereotypes of circulation as an excuse for the mediocre papers or newscasts. The editor who says, "I don't care what the impact of this story is, or what the public thinks about it, because in my news judgment, they should know about it," is often the same man who talks circulation, track records and the scoop. These individuals are profoundly out of touch with reality. Audience research reveals they share little in common with their news audience.

Some of the hostility about the press is due to the "bad" news syndrome, the mirror theory of journalism and the inane idiot savantism of fact recitation without coherence or shaping intelligence. The hard news-objectivity syndrome, like popcorn, is filling but not very nourishing. The editors have presumed to know what is news; and, like some kind old aunt, they insist upon giving us our daily dose of cod liver oil. But when asked to justify editorial practices, the intellectual bankruptcy of much American journalism becomes obscured as the editors scurry to First Amendment protection.

Journalism is a public act open to public scrutiny. Professionalism is the public's defense against malpractice. We must trust the journalist. But the journalist must accept responsibility for his actions. Reintroducing the reporter as an intelligent, reasoning and responsible figure in journalism is essential to the survival of the democratic process.

---

[11] While a number of papers exist comparing roles, reporters might enjoy reading a former reporter's notes on her transition from a reporter to a sociologist. Ruth Harriet Jacobs, "The Journalistic and Sociological Enterprises as Ideal Types," *The American Sociologist*, 5, No. 5 (1970), 348–50.

chapter 23   Press Councils:
A
Brief Review

NANCY BUTLER

The argument has been advanced that if the press is to be responsible
and free, then as Blankenburg has noted, "ways are needed to strengthen
the responsibility without constricting the freedom."[1] One suggested
means of achieving this goal is through the establishment of community
press councils. The actual form of the press council varies from country
to country and from region to region. The crux of the idea of a council
is to assemble a group of people, usually some journalists and laymen,
who meet to evaluate the performance of the press in a given community
or in some cases the entire nation. There are a variety of ground rules that
restrict the discussion and render some comfort to the media publishers
and editors.

Nancy Butler, "Press Councils: A Brief Review." Published here for the first time
by permission of the author.
[1] William B. Blankenburg, "Community Press Councils," Unpublished Ph.D. Dissertation (Stanford University, 1968), p. 1.

FOREIGN PRESS COUNCILS

Before discussing a number of American experiments with press councils it will be beneficial to review briefly the variety of press councils that exist overseas. Sweden has the oldest council which dates back to 1916. Switzerland has the second-oldest council which was established in 1938. These organizations were established by the press of each country.

There are councils, however, which were not adopted freely by the press. Councils in West Germany, India and South Africa were instituted by the governments for a variety of reasons. West German publishers acted upon plans from the Interior Ministry. The Indian council was established directly by the federal parliament. The South African press was confronted with the threat of government statutes and reacted by establishing its own council.

Councils in Italy and the Netherlands concentrate on professional journalistic standards, whereas West German and Danish councils confine their activities to publishers. There are councils in Turkey and South Korea, but little is known about them except that there are lay members on the boards as well as professional newsmen.

Perhaps the best known council is found in Great Britain. In 1946, two members of the House of Commons, who were journalists, introduced a measure to appoint a Royal Commission to inquire into the finance, control, management, and ownership of the press. The bill passed and the Royal Warrants were issued in 1947. Seventeen members were appointed to the Royal Commission on the Press. The commission limited its inquiry to the management, ownership and free expression of opinion.

The commission recommended that the Press establish its own council. Known as the General Council of the Press, its primary concerns were: "(1) the recruitment and training of journalists, and (2) the maintenance of professional standards."[2] The British press disapproved of the first recommendation, and a series of debates ensued. Eventually, the General Council adopted eight revised objectives suggested by the Royal Commission:

1. Preserve the established freedom of the British Press.
2. Maintain the character of the Press in accordance with highest professional and commercial standards.
3. Keep under review any developments likely to restrict the supply of information of public interest.

[2] Paul B. Snider, "The British Press Council: A Study of its Role and Performance, 1953–1965," Unpublished Ph.D. Dissertation (The University of Iowa, 1968), p. 7.

Also see Norman E. Issaacs, "Why We Lack a National Press Council," *Columbia Journalism Review* (Fall), 1970, pp. 16–26. His comments are valuable in suggesting ways in which the British press council idea could be adopted to the American situation.

4. Promote methods of recruitment, education, and training of journalists.
5. Promote proper functional relations among all sections of the profession.
6. Promote technical and other research.
7. Study developments of the Press which may tend toward greater monopoly.
8. Publish periodic reports reviewing its own work and reviewing from time to time various developments in the press and factors affecting them.[3]

The General Council of the Press lasted for ten years. In 1961, Parliament established a second Royal Commission which recommended the establishment of a new council with lay members and a new constitution. In 1964, the House approved the new council under the simpler title of The Press Council. Five nonjournalists, representatives of the public, were added to the Council. The provisions dealing with recruitment, education and training of journalists, the promotion of functional relations among all sections of the press, and the promotion of technical and other research were deleted from the new constitution. The present council has become an arbiter of the ethical conduct of the British Press.

AMERICAN EXPERIENCE

Perhaps the first mention of press councils was made by the Hutchins Commission who examined the state of the press in the mid-1940s. In their report, among other things, they called for something akin to a press council. This, and the other recommendations of the commission, were greeted by the press with howls of indignation. The very notion that the commission, much less the public, should be allowed to sit in judgment of the press' performance was considered a ridiculous if not seditious act.

In the intervening years little transpired in the way of press councils. More by osmosis, rather than by concious critical evaluation, many of the original notions advanced by the commission have seeped into the executive suites and city rooms of American newspapers. Today it is possible to hear a publisher discuss the responsibilities of the press employing paraphrases of some of the commission's initial recommendations. However the difficulty remained, how does the concerned citizen and university scholar offer advice and comment upon a newspaper's performance in reporting community affairs?

In the 1960s, the rise of a number of social activist groups, especially among the racial minorities, brought to light some of the glaring shortcomings of the press in reporting the ghetto and other daily affairs of the poor and oppressed minorities. Press performance in reporting assassinations, civil disorders and political dissents against the war in Vietnam

[3] Ibid., pp. 20–21.

reinforced the notion that improvement was in order. To criticize newspapers is a sticky issue since the First Amendment guarantees the protection of freedom of the press. Telling the press what to do by law is forbidden, while the more informal practices of complaint by letters to the editor or the locker room chat with publisher at the local country club seem at best haphazard.

The notion of a press council seems to some concerned newspapermen and academic critics to be a viable alternative that retains the First Amendment rights of the press but allows the publisher to enter into dialogue with a broader range of community leaders and citizens.

However, experience has shown the ground rules for American press councils have to be altered, since there is nothing to require a publisher to attend council meetings. Thus, to bring into being and sustain its existence the organizers of a community press council are required to engage in persuasion, not coercion. Secondly, the topics under discussion will have only an advisory tone since there is no way to require a publisher to follow the advice offered. If anything, the whole idea represents more informal chat rather than a "council." In counter distinction to the English council, the American versions can do no more than comment and react to the performance of a given newspaper.

THE MELLETT FUND

In 1967, the Mellett Fund for a Free and Responsible Press made funds available through universities for the establishment of press councils in four small cities: Bend, Oregon; Redwood City, California; and Sparta and Cairo, Illinois. Ground rules were established by the Fund for the sponsorship of community press councils.

1. The local council would have no power to force change upon the newspaper.
2. The council would not be organized by the paper but must have cooperation of the publisher involved. The council members and publisher would meet as equals.
3. The design, implementation, and reporting of the council experience would be in the hands of a university researcher.
4. The major objective of the enterprise was to be "a detailed analysis of the experience by the researcher, the results to be given the widest practical dissemination."[4]

The council in Cairo was termed a failure because of the refusal of

[4] Blankenburg, Community Press Councils," p. 26.

white citizens to sit with black members of the community. The Sparta and Bend councils are still in operation because the publishers are pleased with the results of the meetings with members of the community.

Two councils, Redwood City and Bend, were formed by William L. Rivers and William B. Blankenburg. The councils were comprised of a cross-section of citizens in both communities. Of the experience Blankenburg says,

> In each council, the publisher braced himself for cudgels and lances, but none was wielded. Apparently we had told the members so much about press responsibility that they resolved to be terribly responsible themselves—even to the point of reticence. What they could—and did—do extensively was to ask for information about journalism. The first, and easily overlooked, chore of a press council is to educate itself in the mechanics and traditions of journalism.[5]

Blankenburg goes on to say that the mere presence of a press council can have significant effect on journalists. "A hidden value in press councils is their ability to require busy journalists to reflect on their work."[6] Attitudes toward the press held by members of the council underwent significant changes, as did those of citizens in the community who were aware of the council's existence.

Both publishers allowed the councils to "roam freely across newspaper performance."[7] Neither publisher considered the councils as infringements to press freedom.

The give and take between council members and publishers afforded avenues of communication to both groups that were previously closed. Because of the representativeness of the community at large by council members, the publishers were able to gain knowledge about the community that was not known before. Similarly, the workings of the press became known to members of the council. Because of the successes in Sparta, Redwood City and Bend, the Mellett Fund expanded to two major cities, St. Louis, Missouri and Seattle, Washington.

The St. Louis experiment was less than successful, primarily because only one newspaper participated. However, the experiment in Seattle, though not termed a success by the council organizer, did make progress in the areas of race relations and minority reporting.

Established in early 1968 by Lawrence Schneider, the council was comprised of newspaper and electronic media decision makers and members of the black community representing the entire spectrum of

---

[5] William B. Blankenburg, "Local Press Councils: An Informal Accounting," *Columbia Journalism Review*, 8 (Spring 1969), 14.

[6] Ibid., p. 16.

[7] Ibid., p. 17.

viewpoints. Six commercial media of Seattle supported the council after the Mellett grant ended. Meetings were held from June 1968 to December 1969. The council met without publicity in order to allow free flow of discussion.

> . . . the council sought (1) to inform the media members of the concerns of the black community so that the media would be better able to communicate those concerns, and (2) to provide a clear, strong, continuing channel through which a powerless minority could readily communicate with the decision makers of the mass media.[8]

The Seattle Communication Council became a useful channel of communication and was effective in bringing about changes in media coverages of minority groups. However, as Schneider points out,

> Black dissatisfaction with the society of which the media are a long-established, relatively comfortable institution is so considerable that much more than communications councils will be necessary if that dissatisfaction is ever to disappear.[9]

NEW DIRECTIONS

An interesting phenomenon to be observed closely is the development of the newspaper ombudsman established by a few papers. Here an editor is assigned to deal with public complaints about the paper's performance and to publish a column or reply to a variety of concerns.

One example is Mel Marth's the *People's Voice* column published a few times a week in the *St. Petersburg Times*. Besides the typical corrections about names and omissions, many of Marth's columns are in reality short little education pieces for the public. In one he will discuss how the newshole is decided (by the editorial staff not the advertising staff of this paper), why a newspaper publishes "bad" news, what occurs in editorial conferences, and so on.

Certainly an honest and conscious ombudsman can defuse some public anger and increase good will, but here the issue is not so much reaction as public education. The issue remains to open up the lines of communication between the minorities and their local news media. Letters to the editor and telephone calls are the biased product of indignant readers or those with special causes. A press council could serve this function since an important facet of it could be to generate a systematic and regular

---

[8] Lawrence Schneider, "A Media-Black Council: Seattle's 19-Month Experiment," *Journalism Quarterly*, 47 (Autumn 1970), 440.
[9] Ibid., p. 449.

input of comment and evaluation. A case could be made for a visible press council which could receive the citizens' complaints. The discussion and the conclusions reached need not be public, but at least the citizen could be assured a hearing on important and substantive issues. Certainly the few experiments reviewed here demonstrate that the publishers have little to fear in the way of confrontation. If anything, the acceptance of a press council by a publisher may be taken as a sign of maturity and the acceptance of public responsibility that follows from owning and publishing a newspaper in America today. With the demise of competing papers, only three percent of 1,589 cities with dailies have competing managements, there is little in the way of a media self-correction for poor press performance. The snide and flip answer, "if you don't like it, don't buy it" is spurious since in a *majority* of American cities there is only one newspaper. Newspapers continue to be the source of local information which people require that is not supplied by television and radio journalism.

The possibility, no doubt tangential and remote, is that the government could move to establish something similar to a press council, such as the English system, or enact something similar to the suggestions offered by Barron in his new theory of the First Amendment.

The issue could also be solved by a more active and concerned public who set up and direct their own press councils. Sooner or later the publisher could be enticed to sit in. But if the Mellett studies are any indication, public apathy and ignorance of the press are the principal barriers to spontaneous enactment. Meanwhile the credibility of the press continues downward as indicated by a recent Gallup poll where only 37 percent of the American public feel newspapers deal fairly with political and social issues. Press councils may be *one* way to break the vicious cycle of apathy, ignorance and distrust that so many of the American people seem to feel for the American press.

section H Change by the People: New Media

The following three selections deal with essentially people-oriented changes in the news media; the underground press, public pressure on the broadcasting establishment, and the role of the public in cable television.

The reemergence of an "underground" press in the last few years is seen by many as a valuable sign of democracy's viability. It should be clear that the appearance of both politically right and left weeklies suggests the shortcomings of the mass news establishment in serving the needs of political and ethnic minority groups. Also, a weekly newspaper, regardless of its politics, can only exist alongside a viable daily newspaper. What is unique about the underground and right-wing papers is that they are often muckraking papers interested in digging up a story on some skeleton in the establishment's closet. Some of these papers cover the news that the mass media avoids or that the daily newspaper overlooks. And in some areas, the weekly newspaper gives one a sense of community whereas the daily newspaper is market-oriented (recall Bagdikian's essay). The question remains, can the weekly press evolve into a fifth estate to offset the numbing prattle of the middle of the road press? You can judge for yourself by reading a few issues of your local weekly.

271

The second selection (by Prowett) offers part of a manual for citizen action in broadcasting, published by one of the most active church groups working to change the operations of American broadcasting. It is unlike the other two selections in this final section because it is written as a series of advising instructions rather than as a description. Note that the major steps include concerted group action (individuals have little effect acting alone), being informed (knowing the status quo and reasons for it is essential to suggesting or advocating change), and steady escalation (trying to settle differences "through channels" before going to court, for example). Much of the basic information in Marsha O'Bannon Prowett's article is applicable to other media as well, for while the government role in print media is nowhere near as important, the need for group-informed escalated action exists here as well.

Prognosticators tell us that another communications "revolution" is just around the corner. For mass news, one possible innovation is the spread of cable television to the large urban centers of America. The essence of cable TV is that a large antenna receives both local television stations and those in distant cities. An operator, for a monthly fee, hooks your television set to this master antenna. Besides delivering clear and crisp signals, cable television gives you access to more than three network signals.

As the industry matured, federal regulatory agencies have sought to control cable growth to retard the decay of the over-the-air broadcaster. The issue is no longer whether the cable industry will be controlled by the Federal Communication Commission, but how and with what benefits for the citizen. It is now clear that each and every system will be required to maintain a certain number of access channels for use by the public. In its crudest version, the channel is nothing more than an electronic soap box. Almost anyone can arrange for free time and appear at the studio to deliver a sermon, harangue, or lecture on whatever they wish. But, with a little equipment and some expertise, small productions concerned with consistency journalism will also now be possible.

Certainly, the development of cable television promises to change the electronic landscape. For mass news, the access channels will not be a serious threat, but like the underground press, these new access channels promise to diversify the marketplace of ideas. The type of programming that is evolving is largely dependent upon those who wish to become involved with cable at this stage. In the following articles, the authors speak of two types of programming. One is street media—the use of light portable one-half inch videotape equipment—used to collect news in its rawest form. The second type of programming is somewhat disdainful of the first method, opting, instead, for a more "professional" programming. This type of cable programming will tend to resemble in technique and treatment much of the programming now on over-the-air stations.

We would argue that cable television is essentially a "new" medium that requires rethinking of the old mass audience syndrome. Given a variety of popular programming, the 20 channels of a cable system leaves plenty of room for exploration and innovation. These programs, at least in the area of news, need not appeal to mass audiences, but those of a specialized interest. In a sense, cable can demassify the audience. For those of a rigid frame of mind, these changes portend great upheavals in the marketing and distribution of mass production industries. But with forethought and diligent planning, cable television can help reconstitute the community that has been lost in the marketing philosophy now pervading newspapers and over-the-air broadcasting.

For those of you with a cable company in your own community, we can only reinforce the authors of the following article in their point about "experiencing" cable television. Make arrangements to visit your local outlet or one nearby. If possible, ask to examine and use the portable videotape equipment. Phenomenologically, cable and videotape are similar to the seventeenth-century pamphlet. With modest skills (no more than that required to operate an 8mm motion picture camera or take a Polaroid snapshot) each individual can begin to construct his own polemic.

However, it is still too early to predict the shape of cable television. It is a unique opportunity for people to express their feelings in the shape of a new medium.

The last selection which follows is taken from chapters eight, nine, and eleven of *On the Cable: Report of the Sloan Commission on Cable Communications* (McGraw-Hill, 1971), and detail the news and public affairs potential of the nations future cable systems. For those desiring further information write to the following agencies:

National Cable Television Association, Inc.
918 16th St., N.W.
Washington, D.C. 20006

Sloan Commission on Cable Communications
Sloan Foundation
630 Fifth Ave.
New York, New York 10020

Urban Research Group
1730 M Street, N.W. (Suite 405)
Washington, D.C. 20036

chapter 24 # Emergence
of the
Fifth Estate:
The
Underground Press

WILLIAM FUDGE
and
JOHN W. ENGLISH

The underground press, or counterestablishment press, represents the ideal of freedom of dissent, and is a voice of those alienated from the American mainstream. As a vehicle of dissent, the underground press was employed in principle during pre-Revolutionary times by a young, long-haired radical named Benjamin Franklin. He was followed by other anti-establishment writers—Samuel Adams with the Patriot Press, pamphleteer Thomas Paine, while Matthew Lyon was organizing radicals in New England.

A phenomenon of the past five years, the underground press of today is not different than its predecessors in passing acerbic commentary on the system—social, political, and economic. It blends together the Bohemian/ Beatnik cult of the fifties with the affluent—flower child—hippie cult of the sixties. The idealistic, cynical, and antiestablishment cries of Norman Mailer, Jack Kerouac, Allan Ginsburg, Paul Goodman, Aldous Huxley, Lenny Bruce, and others in the fifties and early sixties were articulated

William Fudge and John W. English, "Emergence of the Fifth Estate: The Underground Press." Published here for the first time by permission of the authors.

through essays, prose, and readings or lectures to those of like mind. Without a media that reached larger numbers with increased regularity, many of the *messages* of these figures remained in the same cults.

However, in the sixties, young and old radicals fused together in a kaleidoscope of social movements beginning with civil rights and progressing through the bloody decade which saw assassinations, riots, free speech movements, and the ultimate hysteria, Vietnam. Little wonder that a decade which began with a virginal dream of peace and justice for all men should end with the ultimate bummer, an undeclared war which left the nation schizophrenic. The children of middle class white America began to drop out, not (like the silent generation of the fifties) to the suburbs and grey flannel suits of the Organization Man, but to Haight Ashbury and the communes. The Hippie phenomenon, a creature of the straight press, came unglued with Mafia drugs and Vietnam.

The early underground papers dealt with rock music, psychedelic art, and the San Francisco mystique. The radical and politically oriented university types continued to run their college dailies. They carped and hassled but they were still in the system. They were guerrillas but still took finals and hitchhiked through Europe in the summer. Somewhere around 1967 *Ramparts* revealed that the CIA was everywhere, even supporting the various student publications arm of the National Student Association. The movement to end the war came and went, people were killed, bombed, and beaten. Richard Nixon became President of the United States of America. During this time the underground press came into existence. The papers were soon into the politics routine, for grass and against hard stuff, and antiestablishment. Many became concerned with and developed a sense of community. They took positions, muckraked the establishment and reported the hassles confronting the street people, long hair, the new politics, draft resistance, and rebellion.

The haunting technology that helped created the counterculture has been a boon to the production of the underground papers. Photo offset printing which is a fast and relatively inexpensive process has allowed even shoestring papers to get started and proliferate. Typewriters with interchangeable type faces and right hand margin justifiers as well as pasteup type have made the job of type setting and page makeup simple and fast. An estimated 4,000 copies of an eight-page paper can be printed for about one hundred dollars.

Today, about 350 recognized underground papers are published worldwide, and 500 or so unofficial high school papers, which vary in format from professionally printed publications to mimeographed single sheets, circulate among the teen set.

This underground press represents, for the first time in several years, another newspaper voice in many cities. It doesn't claim to be in competition with the major dailies, but is in the business of feeding peoples' heads with a counterpoint to the reported day's intelligence.

A few recent accomplishments that this underground press can lay some claim to might include: they provide an outlet for diverse opinion or dissent; they helped launch the peace movement which has grown to worldwide proportions; they dropped out and put down irrelevant education and touched off a new period of academic change or reforms; they berated a federal government that drafted 18-year-olds but denied them the vote, thus, encouraging courrent national legislation; they mobilized others to sponsor an Earth Day to focus attention on environmental abuse and urge action in restoring natural balance; they lashed out at the dehumanizing aspects of technology and bureaucracy and bigness and preached the worth of an individual, love, art, and playfulness; and they have taken up the traditional press' role of fighting for the underdog, even for such fringe groups as the Gay Liberation and the Hare Krishna cults. In short, these underground papers provide readers with articles that the established press either doesn't find or won't print. In upholding their self-assigned role as the "people's press," many underground papers tirelessly pursue the views of their constituency.

Journalistically, the writing style of the underground press has both strengths and weaknesses. A freewheeling nature often provides a channel for creative, albeit weird, writers and poets. More conservative media would stifle much of this creativity. Most of the writers specialize in subjective journalism, often personal witness reporting, full of biased perception and introspection. Yet, many reports are especially candid or frank, if sometimes lurid. On the other side, many articles are frequently superficial, factually inaccurate, illogical, and incomprehensible to those unfamiliar with the pop idiom or contemporary mode of expression. Too often, the communication gap is based more on educational levels than age or class differences.

Profanity is the most sensationalized part of the underpress content and probably the least important to its readers. The language of the streets, as field linguists will tell you, has always been rough; its reality has been ignored in the conventional media. Profanity is rarely used to shock others; it is just that obscenity and profanities have been devalued. They tend to be noticed and irritating only to the more conservative.

Intellectually, the underground press stresses the global thinker and publishes frequent interviews or articles on gurus such as Buckminster Fuller, Marshall McLuhan, Herbert Marcuse, and Robert Theobold. In fact, while some sociologists say that today's young have no heroes, the underground press is filled with cult figures: Bobby Seale and Angela Davis, John Lennon and Mick Jagger, Peter Fonda, Nicholas Johnson, Charles Reich, Tom Wolfe, Ken Kesey, and so on.

All alternate media, including the press, currently seem to be going through a period of testing commitment. Lack of money for salaries and editorial operating expenses, long a critical problem, have become severe. Most papers can afford to pay only a few staff members meager salaries and are often unable to do significant muckraking or investigative reporting within its circulation region because of chronically empty cashboxes. This limitation often makes them carry national news when the editors would prefer more local and regional material.

Founded in 1966, the Underground Press Syndicate is a cooperative federation of about 200 papers, published worldwide, held together by trust. Members exchange papers and news. In addition, UPS coordinates national advertising, promotes national distribution of papers, and generally supports the underground press by holding conferences to discuss and help resolve common problems. UPS is administered by the Free Ranger Tribe which also publishes an internal newspaper for the underground press, *Intertribal Clear Head*. Tribal headquarters function as a storehouse and clearinghouse of information about the underground press.

The Liberation News Service, with more than 800 subscribers produces packets containing news stories, essays, poetry, comics, and visual materials. While most of the LNS subscribers publish the materials received in the packets, many subscribers use the materials for their own self-edification, to get a better understanding of the counterculture.

The underground press and the business establishment find peaceful coexistence in advertising. Many underground editors acknowledge that America's affluence allows them to exist. Most underground papers carry advertising, and while some of it is saucy, risque, and sometimes considered pornographic, much of the advertising is centered on new products and services such as water beds, freaky boutiques, crafts, and organic foods. Record, tapes, and music companies spend more money on advertising in the underground press than other advertisers. These advertisers have looked to the underground press readers as an innovative market, leading, far ahead, the others in the use of new products and services.

Advertisers also see the underground press as an efficient medium in costs. Generally, the page rates are low, and in addition to the total combined primary circulation of about five million nationwide, the advertisers also enjoy a pass-along circulation approximately four to five times that of the actual circulation, reaching 20 million readers weekly.

Generally, all underground papers have standards of advertising acceptability. Underground Press Syndicate reports typical products and issues that are usually incompatible with editorial viewpoints: "products and advertising related to, or produced by companies involved in the production of military equipment and services; products which are potentially harmful to individuals or the environment, such as cigarettes, alcohol, insecticides, etc.; advertising which dehumanizes or depersonalizes people, such as ads which utilize women in male-defined roles to sell products. These ads would be defined as 'sexist' and would be totally unacceptable."[1]

Some underground papers report that they will accept advertisements for abortion services, while others state that they will not, but rather, will run the abortion service information in special sections of their papers free of charge.

Several distinct offshoots of the "conventional" underground press have emerged in recent years so that specific information could be carried to special interest groups—women, servicemen, college and high school students, blacks, and religious groups.

Collectives of women, irked with the chauvinistic views of most media men, have initiated a spate of newspapers espousing the views of liberation: abortion, equal opportunity and pay, day care centers for children, etc. *Everywoman, Aphra,* and *The Rat,* among others, have built national circulations among feminists.

A whole new segment of the underground press has sprung up agitating the military establishment from within. In addition to strong antiwar sentiments carried in these papers, the editors fight to resolve the differences between military demands on individuals as compared with civilian ways of life. The military editors are subjected to more severe hassles than their civilian counterparts because of considerably stricter ground rules of operation on military bases. The editor of the *Last Harass* was dishonorably discharged only a few days before his hitch was up despite a perfect record as a soldier. Others have received stiff sentences resulting from hassles due to their editorial positions. The absolute number of military underground papers is not known, but there are 57 such papers listed in W. D. Lutz's *Underground Press Directory.*

From *About Face* at Ft. Pendleton to *Head On* at Camp Lejeune, *A Four Year Bummer* at Chanute Air Force Base to *Fatigue Press* at Killeen, Texas, the military underground papers are found on most military bases in the country, as well as papers such as *Bond, Task Force,* and *Ally* which are also internationally distributed.

The Berkeley *Barb,* Madison's *Kaleidoscope* and Austin's *The Rag* are among the many underground papers serving the communities of major universities. These papers—whose muckraking often focuses on the university power structure and sensitive issues—has provided the college press with competition for readers' attention. The challenge has given collegians additional sources of news and opinion of wider diversity. In

[1] Thomas K. Forcade, *Free Ranger CO-OP Directory* (New York: Free Ranger, 1971), p. 4.

general, the underground press' activities have sparked lackadaisical college editors to provide much more thorough campus coverage.

These papers are usually unofficial organs; however, the administrators generally feel that policies banning these papers from campuses would prove the suppression the papers' editorials have spoken against.

During the last decade an increasing number of high school students have become disenchanted with their school systems, family life, and society in general. The necessity of a vehicle for the high schooler's voice has resulted in several hundred papers emerging and carrying fare that deals with serious community issues, antiwar movements, and crucial school problems.

The High School Independent Press Service, HIPS, offers weekly packets of news and illustrated features to supplement materials carried in the high school press. Generally recognized as being the most outstanding of the high school underground papers is the *New York High School Free Press.*

Another spinoff from the underground press has been a few papers devoted to black student affairs and black militancy. *Uhuru* and *Black Panther* at Oakland, *Black Politics* at Berkeley, and *Black Mask* at New York, are among black-oriented underground papers established to bring the black community together.

An indication of the success of the underground press in reaching young opinion leaders is seen in attempts to imitate their formats by church groups to get Christian messages through to the young. One such publication is *Student Action,* extolling in freewheeling underground style the philosophies of the Campus Crusade for Christ organization.

How does one summarize this polyglot of newspapers, tearsheets and rip-offs? These newspapers supply a voice to minority opinion be it young, political, organic, or otherwise. The alternate media are the expression more often of a group of people which float alongside the American mainstream. But, as media, they represent what the founding fathers envisioned in writing the constitution, that the press reflect the marketplace of ideas and debate. With the rise of media market philosophy, cost per thousand impressions, and corporate journalism, the underground press reflects values that were once essential to the republic, individualism, liberty, and the pursuit of happiness. In a sense, the papers reflect the lost innocence of the white middle-class children. However, print—underground or otherwise—in many ways is not a good reflection of the racial minorities, whose culture (for a variety of reasons) is still oral and locked into music and street rapping. Still to be developed is an alternate radio and video underground, although there are signs of its struggling into existence.

Finally, the nice thing about the underground press is that anybody can do it. Anyone with 100 dollars and a typewriter can start a newspaper. And ironically, the first people asking for a mail subscription are often the *New York Times* and *CBS News*. Gives one ideas, doesn't it?

INFORMATION ON UNDERGROUND MEDIA

A list of papers appears from time to time; see William D. Lutz, Underground Press Directory, 5th edition, Box 13603, University Station, Reno, Nevada 89507, and Underground Press Syndicate run by Free Ranger Tribe, P.O. Box 26, Village Station, New York, N.Y. 10014. This latter group provides a free pamphlet, *How to Publish Your Very Own Underground Newspaper*. The other principal source of news is Liberation News Service, 160 Claremont Avenue, New York, N.Y. 10027. For high schools write: Amerikan Press Syndicate, P.O. Box 5175, Beverly Hills, Calif. 90210; FPS, 3210 Grace Street N.W., Washington, D.C.; and High School Free Press, 604 East 11th Street, New York, N.Y. 10009.

Many underground papers are available on microfilm from Bell and Howell Microphoto Division Drawer E, Wooster, Ohio 44691. The Free Ranger Tribe will provide you with the name of the closest library having a set of the Bell and Howell series.

A small but growing cadre of underground television people has emerged. They use a variety of portable videotape recorders and circulate tapes. They have been especially active in attempts to gain access to various channels on the growing cable companies (CATV). For information write, Raindance, 8 East 12th Street, New York, N.Y. 10003. This group issues a quarterly, *Radical Software* and a handbook *Guerrilla Television*, New York: Holt, Rinehart & Winston, 1971. A valuable source of organizations, addresses, and related materials is *The Organizer's Manual*, New York: Bantam Books, 1971. The group has established an office, O.M. Collective, 211 Bay State Road, Boston, Mass. 02215. And finally, the *Alternative Press Index*, Radical Research Center, Carleton College, Northfield, Minn. 55057 issues a quarterly index of articles and publications of interest to underground media people.

chapter 25 # Effective Public Action: Television and Radio

MARSHA O'BANNON PROWITT

As a first step ask yourself the following questions about the nature of broadcasting by stations in your community:*

1. Does the station make a serious effort to consult with representatives of community groups about the kind of programming it is providing and how it might improve its service?
2. Does the station present a balanced program schedule, offering programs in each of the fourteen areas enumerated by the FCC as representing local needs?
3. Does the station program include discussion of controversial issues that are important to the community? Does this programming give opposing points of view the opportunity to be heard or does it give voice to only one point of view? Are members of minority groups included in discussions

Marsha O'Bannon Prowitt, "Effective Public Action: Television and Radio," from *A Guide to Citizen Action in Radio and Television.* Reprinted by permission of the author. (The complete manual is available from: Office of Communication, United Church of Christ, 289 Park Avenue South, New York, New York 10010.)

* Jennings, Dr. Ralph M., "How to Protect Citizen Rights in Television and Radio," Office of Communication, United Church of Christ. 1969.

of community issues? Are news and documentary programs biased toward one viewpoint or a limited number of viewpoints?

4. Do announcers or guests of the station attack individuals or groups? Does the station feature "call-in" programs on which anonymous callers are allowed to make attacks on individuals or organizations? If such attacks are made, does the station offer those attacked an immediate opportunity to reply?

5. How much time does the station devote to public service broadcasting for non-profit organizations within the community? Are these programs aired during hours when people are likely to be viewing or listening or are they on the air at a time when people are in bed, at meals, or in church? Are the programs aimed at a variety of audiences, or are they directed at a particular segment of the community?

6. Are the interests, tastes, needs, and desires of minority groups, such as Blacks and Chicanos, adequately served? For example, do Blacks receive treatment equal to that accorded to whites? Do they appear regularly on the station on all types of programs at all times of day? Are racial issues and the affairs of the Black community dealt with fairly and objectively? Do Black leaders have regular access to the station to present their views? Are the lives and problems of Blacks portrayed to the whole community with depth and meaning?

If the answers to any of these questions indicate that a station is not living up to its responsibilities to the public, you may want to pursue the matter further. Remember, there is strength in numbers. Seek out other individuals and interest other organizations in your community that share your concern. Join with them in deciding what practices in broadcasting you find objectionable and how radio and television service can be improved.

After you have decided upon your objectives, you have two alternative courses to consider: 1) non-legal action: complaints and negotiation or 2) legal action. The first alternative relies largely on the power of persuasion, the second upon the power of legal enforcement by the FCC and the courts. If you try to mobilize the forces of persuasion and fail to achieve your reforms and objectives, you can then consider the kind of legal leverage available to you. Many groups have used both persuasion and legal action in their campaigns with considerable success: it often has been the case that the ability to take legal action at the FCC if necessary has been the prerequisite to successful non-legal negotiation with a station or network. Therefore, you should inform yourself of all alternative courses of action at your disposal.

Let us first explore the three most commonly and successfully used non-legal means of citizen action: complaints or suggestions; organized community letter/PR campaigns; and organized negotiation with stations.

NON-LEGAL ACTION

Complaints

Any person or community group, at any time, may file a complaint either with his local broadcaster or directly with the FCC. This is often a very effective device when there are specific standards to be enforced. For example, fairness, personal attack, equal time and equal employment are all covered by specific rules which stations are obligated to follow. When you prepare a complaint be sure that you

1. *State the facts.* Give your name, station call letters, and your specific complaint or suggestion.
2. *Cite a standard.* Relate your grievance or proposal whenever possible to one of the standards set forth in Part II of this Guide "FCC Standards for Programming and Performance." This establishes a recognized basis for your complaint.
3. *Ask for a specific remedy.* For example, ask for a new kind of program, levy of a fine, an opportunity to reply to a personal attack or one side of a controversial issue.

If you do not get a satisfactory response from the station, send the complaint to the FCC and enclose copies of your correspondence with the station.

If you send your complaint to the FCC, the Commission usually asks the station for a response to your complaint (often enclosing your letter). In extremely rare instances, the Commission might investigate the complaint by sending its own staff into the community where the station broadcasts. The FCC has the power to levy a fine or issue an order demanding that the station take action to remedy your complaint. If you are not satisfied with the explanation or action of the FCC, you may wish to consider initiating one of the other alternative actions discussed here.

Three kinds of complaints require specific procedures and information. These complaints involve compliance with the Fairness Doctrine, the personal attack rules and the requirement of equal time for political candidates.

Fairness Complaints. If you wish to make reply or have offered by the station other viewpoints to a one-sided presentation of a controversial issue the station (or network) broadcast, you should send your letter first to the broadcaster, and then to the FCC if you do not get a satisfactory response from the broadcaster. A fairness complaint by the public has traditionally been one of the most commonly used citizen rights. It is a means by which citizens can gain access to the media for expression of their views on issues of importance dealt with on the station.

Include in your letter to the FCC the following specific information: (1) the particular station or network; (2) the specific issue of a controversial nature of public importance which was broadcast; (3) the date and time when it was broadcast; (4) the basis for your claim that the issue was controversial; (5) the basis for your claim that the station or network was not offering contrasting views on the issue in its overall programming; (6) that the station has not afforded or does not plan to afford an opportunity for the presentation of contrasting views.

Personal Attack. If you believe that you or your group has been personally attacked during presentation of a controversial issue, and if you are not offered an opportunity to respond, you should complain to the station (or network) involved. If you are not satisfied with the response, you should then complain to the Commission. . . .

Your complaint should contain the following specific information: (1) station (and network) involved; (2) words or statements broadcast; (3) the date and time the broadcast was heard; (4) the basis for your view that the words broadcast constitute an attack upon the honesty, character, integrity or like personal qualities of yourself or your group; (5) the basis for your view that the personal attack was broadcast during the presentation of views on a controversial issue of public importance. If you are writing the FCC with your complaint, include reference to any dealings you have had with the station on this matter.

Equal Time Requests. If you are a legally qualified candidate for public office, you should obtain from the FCC the booklet containing interpretive ruling under the equal time requirements and follow the complaint procedures set forth there in detail.

PR, Letter and Education Campaigns

While individual complaints directed at the station and the FCC are often successful in remedying a situation where a specific rule or standard has been violated, citizens frequently have much more broad concerns with media performance and find that existing standards are vague and not easily remedied by the single shot complaint route. For example, citizen concern with the infrequent and poor quality of children's programs or of public affairs or dramatic presentations are bases for community concern. In such cases, an efficiently organized community campaign combining letter complaints, discussions with broadcasters, demonstrations, talks with community groups and press coverage may be used to highlight the issue and bring pressure upon the broadcaster.

Networks and stations frequently comment that they receive very few constructive suggestions and criticisms from the public. But for your suggestion to be effective, it is usually necessary to have a considerable number of suggestions or complaints about a subject before a network or station will consider the pressure to be sufficient for them even to recognize the need, let alone respond to it.

The work of a parents group concerned with children's television, called Action for Children's Television (ACT), brings into focus the effectiveness of a combination of efforts. ACT has used a variety of tactics to give voice to the concerns of those people interested in the use of TV as a creative force for the development of the child and society. ACT has met with the FCC and with local broadcasters, network representatives and government officials; commissioned studies to document the way TV treats children; educated other groups throughout the country through newsletters, conferences and speeches; monitored children's programs and organized support groups in many communities. Its achievements include persuading the FCC to consider the area of children's TV programming for the first time; new network programs for children; designation by the networks of an individual with particular responsibility for developing children's programs; and heightened awareness by national and local educational organizations of the importance of television in the life of children. ACT has also initiated a number of newspaper and magazine articles about the subject.

Questions about the usefulness of boycotts against objectionable station programs are frequently raised. One piece of information should put into perspective the questionable nature of this tactic: stations have the advantage of being able to measure the effectiveness of any boycott through the information they receive from their rating services—information that you cannot get.

Community Negotiation with Stations

It is possible for well organized and representative community groups to negotiate with radio and television stations and obtain significant improvement in service. Based on past experience, this kind of action must be supported by a substantial number of people and organizations in the community, it must root proposed reforms substantially in the law, it must be supported by careful research and observation of the media, and it must have the assistance of attorneys briefed in communications law. The key to a successful negotiation effort between community groups and station management is the ability and readiness to take legal action against the station—usually in the form of a Petition to Deny its license renewal—if efforts to reach a satisfactory local settlement fail.

While this type of effort requires extraordinary organization, research and work for a period of 3 to 5 months and sustained interest thereafter, groups in a number of cities, including Atlanta, Chicago, Rochester and Nashville, have won significant reforms in station performance in their cities and believe the benefits well worth the effort. Such reforms have included new training programs, scholarships and employment for minority persons, regularly-scheduled consultations with community groups to discuss policies and programming, increased news coverage of Black community events; public service spot campaigns about community problems; institution of procedures to screen advertising for demeaning reference to ethnic and racial groups, development of programming of special interest to the Black community, additional children's programs, public affairs, and consumer information programs and announcements.

Agreements vary from community to community as they reflect circumstances and needs in each city. Predominantly-Black and, recently, Chicano groups who have documented discrimination in employment and programming have been most vigorous and effective in using this negotiation route to improved broadcast services.

How does a community organize such a negotiation effort? What have been the elements of the successful endeavors? Six steps have been essential to every successful effort.

1. Organizing a Citizen Group
2. Briefing Members on Rights in Broadcasting
3. Enlisting Legal Support
4. Research and Observation
5. Determining Goals for Improvement
6. Negotiation with Stations

Step 1: Organize a Citizen Group. Most communities have formed a loose, ad hoc coalition of individuals and community organizations, broadly representative of the community, who share a common concern to improve television and radio service. The coalition structure enables diverse individuals and organizations to focus on the specific objective of negotiating reforms with selected broadcast stations. The citizen group in Nashville included more than 40 large and small community organizations in addition to well-known community leaders.

Once organized, the group should elect a chairman authorized to sign documents and act on its behalf. The extent of this authority should be specific. Statements made on behalf of the group should be agreed to by its membership. Individual members should agree not to make statements to the press or have unilateral contacts with representatives of radio or television stations or with the FCC.

Your group will need the use of a temporary office once research activities and negotiations are underway. Try to locate an office, with a telephone, typewriter and mimeograph machine and office supplies. You will need volunteers to make calls and type letters and documents. It is also important to select a coordinator of research and appointments. Community organizations who may be members of your group are often generous in loaning facilities and personnel for this purpose.

Step 2: Briefing Membership. Members of the citizen group should be fully conversant with citizen rights and responsibilities—and broadcaster obligations—under the American system of broadcasting.

Step 3: Enlisting Legal Support. Legal assistance is absolutely essential to a successful negotiation with broadcasters. Cooperating attorneys are necessary partners in your community effort: they must do much of the work and bear much of the responsibility. Cooperating attorneys render assistance in four ways: aiding the research effort, advising you on points of the law as you frame proposed reforms and later as you negotiate in meetings at the station, preparing whatever legal documents may be required, and bearing the burden of any subsequent litigation.

Try to enlist the support, on a voluntary basis, of public-spirited attorneys in your community. Contact the local chapter of one or more of the legal groups which have aided citizen groups in broadcasting in the recent past, such as the NAACP Legal Defense and Educational Fund, the ACLU (American Civil Liberties Union), local Legal Aid Attorneys, or the Lawyer's Committee for Civil Rights Under Law. Investigate what assistance the Young Lawyer's Section of the local bar or a neighboring law school may volunteer. Estimate you will need one lawyer for each station you negotiate with. Try to get one of the interested attorneys to coordinate the volunteer legal assistance to your group.

Few local attorneys specialize in communication law. Most will need special briefing materials. Three good aids are the FCC's new booklet, *The Public in Broadcasting: A Procedure Manual,* the *Primer on Citizens Access to the Federal Communications Commission* available from the Citizens Communications Center, and the *Lawyer's Sourcebook for Citizen Action in Radio and TV* available from the United Church of Christ.

Inquire of one or more of the national groups if they can aid your effort by providing experienced communication attorneys to brief local attorneys on relevant communication law. Consultation with one of these groups may provide the "know how" with which to avoid undue vexation and pitfalls which only experience with broadcasters and the FCC can provide.

Step 4: Research and Observation. Initially your group will need to assemble basic information about radio and television stations in your community; the number of radio and TV stations, their call letters, channel, network affiliation (if any), ownership, senior management, license renewal dates and recent profit figures overall for both radio and TV.

The group should become familiar with the actual program service offered by the television and radio stations in the community. A plan for systematic listening and viewing should be developed. It may be useful to tape record radio programs and the sound portion of television programs. Various monitoring systems have been designed to incorporate necessary data gathering and viewing procedures. You may wish to seek the help of one of the organizations offering such guidance. The Office of Communication, United Church of Christ has developed forms for TV and radio observation and monitoring.

A careful examination of the employment reports and license renewal applications of the stations should be made. You will find very useful in this task the *Guide to Understanding Broadcast License Application* offered to community groups by the Office of Communication, United Church of Christ. Compare your findings from these two station reports with the information developed from your systematic listening and viewing of stations.

Based upon the information gathered, tentative conclusions should be reached about the strengths and weaknesses of local broadcast stations. Has each station lived up to the promises made in its license application? Has each station properly ascertained the needs and interests of the entire community? Do the programs offered truly respond to the needs of the community as identified on the license renewal application? Is fair employment opportunity reflected in the station's employment figures or only in policy statements?

Step 5: Determining Goals for Improvement. It will be necessary to define goals for improvement of television and radio service in the community. Assuming your citizen group has agreed to act upon the information it has gathered, it must now decide upon the moves it will make. Do not overlook the opportunity to commend stations whose performance you have found truly outstanding.

It is also likely that you will have found stations defective in their performance and that the citizen group will want to seek improvement in the service of one or more stations in the community. At this point, the group may wish to limit further consideration to a few stations of particular interest because of serious deficiencies in service.

The specific recommendations of the citizen group should be set down in writing and the substance and language of each proposed reform discussed by the members of the group and its assisting attorneys. These recommendations can usefully be incorporated in a single document for discussion with the management of a given station.

Step 6: Negotiation with Station Management. Once you have set out your recommendations and identified what station or stations you will seek to talk with, a citizen group should designate a team of representatives to meet with station management. If more than one station is the target of your concern and there is limited time, you may need to set up separate negotiating teams of three or four persons each. Each negotiating team should be assisted by one attorney. The members of a station negotiating team should be thoroughly familiar with facts about station performance and should have reviewed and evaluated the license renewal application and equal employment report for that station. Do not attempt to meet with broadcasters until you have full command of the facts and proposals you wish to discuss. Be sure your appointment is set up with a representative of the station, usually the president or general manager, who has the authority to act upon your suggestions.

In your negotiation, keep in mind that beginning Fall, 1971, all network-affiliated local stations will have available to them an extra half hour of prime time each evening, usually 7:30–8:30 p.m., for locally originated programming. This time slot has previously been used for national network programs but was returned to local stations by a recent FCC decision with the hope that local stations would use this time for programs responsive to needs and interests of its local community.

Allow at least four to six weeks for your negotiations with a station. To do so, plan your first meeting with station management at least two to three months prior to the expiration of the station license—keeping in mind that the deadline for submission of Petitions to Deny to the FCC is 30 days prior to the license expiration date. It is possible that one meeting may be enough. Usually a number of long conferences are necessary before you can reach a mutually satisfactory agreement.

It is wise to get any pledges of changes in program or employment policy in writing and to have such document submitted by the station to the FCC as an amendment to its license renewal application. In this way the station will be legally bound to abide by the changes to which it has agreed.

Unfortunately, it is also possible that your recommendations will be wholly rejected. If this happens, the group can consider a formal complaint or petition to the FCC. If your consultations with the station are underway during the period just prior to station license renewal, it is wise to have your assisting attorneys preparing a possible Petition to Deny at the same time you are in negotiation with the station in the event that your negotiations break down. Frequently community-broadcaster negotiations fail very near the cut-off date for formal citizen petitions, i.e., one month prior to license renewal. Unless your group has prepared petitions, you will have passed the filing date.

It is possible to petition the FCC for waiver of the filing date (FCC rule 1580) and a 15 or 30 day extension of time to complete your negotiations. But the station or stations you are negotiating with must join with you in requesting the waiver.

LEGAL ACTION

If your suggestions and complaints have gone unheeded, if citizen group negotiations with stations have failed to bring about desired reforms, then you may want to consider filing an objection or Petition to Deny the station renewal of license. The explanation of these legal procedures will seem complex, but do not be discouraged. Community groups throughout the nation, aided by attorneys, have been successful in using them. Experienced national organizations can also offer you guidance in these undertakings.

The Petition to Deny is the most severe action a citizen group can take against a broadcast station. Such petitions are costly and extremely time consuming to both the petitioner and the broadcaster. It should be considered the last resort when other means of achieving necessary change in local broadcast service have failed. A citizen group will need to have expert legal assistance prior to filing a petition.

The most severe penalty the FCC can impose is denial of the applicants license—but levy of other penalties, such as fines and short-term renewals, is also appropriate. In the past renewals have been denied broadcast stations on public interest grounds including overcommercialization, serious and repeated violations of the Fairness Doctrine, fraud, and consistent racial discrimination in programming.

Citizen groups have used a Petition to Deny license renewal where broadcasters willfully and consistently flout the public interest. Two examples of citizen action demonstrate the effectiveness of this device. In these cases, no compromise agreement proved feasible.

In 1964, the Office of Communication, United Church of Christ, joined by two Black civil rights leaders in the Jackson, Mississippi community, filed a Petition to Deny license renewal of station WLBT-TV on the grounds that the station discriminated against the interests of the black community which represented 45 per cent of its viewers. After years of legal action before the FCC and in the courts, the U.S. Court of Appeals in 1969 revoked the license of the station. A precedent won for all of us in this long fight is the right of the public to be heard and to have our views made part of the official record in license renewal proceedings.

Stations which consistently broadcast extremist propaganda—political, religious and anti-Black and ethnic group—seriously concern citizens in many communities. In Media, Pennsylvania, 19 local civic and religious organizations charged in a Petition to Deny that WXUR-AM-FM carried predominantly right-wing political programming, systematically vilified ethnic and racial minorities and refused to air other viewpoints in violation of the Fairness Doctrine and contrary to the community's interest. They requested and were granted a public hearing in their hometown. After all the evidence was heard, the FCC revoked the licenses of the station owner.

A Petition to Deny begins with an explanation of why you are a "party of interest." A broadly-based citizen group should have no difficulty establishing that it qualifies under this definition. The petition next sets out the "allegations of fact"—the issues in the case. If, for example, one of your charges is that the station discriminates against minority people in its employment, you should support this allegation with specific information which might include statistics on the low employment of minority people in each category of station responsibility as compared with population of minority groups in the city or of minority people who have applied for employment; signed statements (affidavits) of minority persons who have been denied employment, citing specific violations of the equal employment rules and other relevant material.

Attach to the Petition to Deny as exhibits, signed and notarized statements of persons who have personal knowledge of the charges you have made against a station and any relevant monitoring analysis or special research studies you have conducted. Hearsay, rumor, opinion, or broad generalizations are not acceptable. The more thoroughly documented your allegations, the better chance you will have that the FCC will seriously consider your petition and that penalties or corrective action will result.

A Petition to Deny must be filed no later than the first day of the last full month of the license period and a copy served on the applicant. After you have filed your petition, the broadcaster is allowed 10 days in which to file an "Opposition to the Petition to Deny." The petitioning citizen group is then allowed 5 days in which to file a "Reply to the Opposition." The reply to the opposition allows the petitioner an opportunity to further support his original allegations, as well as to counter whatever allegations the station offers to defend itself.

If the FCC decides that your petition raises substantial public interest

questions about a broadcaster, it will set the application for hearing on
the issues you have raised. If you wish the hearing to be held in your
community you should make that request in your petition.

In several instances the submission of a well-researched and documented Petition to Deny has moved the affected station to reconsider
reforms or changes heretofore considered unacceptable. Agreement has
often been reached after a petition has been filed. In several cases the
written agreement was forwarded to the FCC as an amendment to the
license renewal application and the citizen group withdrew its petition.

Much greater detail on the requirements of a Petition to Deny and the
subsequent hearing are included in a new booklet available from the
FCC, *The Public in Broadcasting: A Procedure Manual.* You should read
the sections relevant to the action you contemplate and follow the steps
and requirements set out there.

Informal Objections. Another means of seeking FCC remedy to the objections a citizen group may have to a broadcaster's performance is an
"Informal Objection." Informal objections are not subject to the cut-off
dates which apply to Petitions to Deny and may be filed at any time until
the renewal of a station's license. Filings must be signed by the objector
but there are no formal standards for content. However, as a practical
matter, it is a good idea to follow the standards for a Petition to Deny
and include a factual analysis of the station's application, together with
concrete information supporting the charges. Include as many facts and
figures as possible.

You may wish to consider filing an informal objection if the deadline
for a Petition to Deny is fast approaching or past or if your citizen group
feels that a Petition is unwarranted or if it is unable to assume the bur-
dens of a formal legal action. This is also a useful mechanism for individuals wishing to have their objections to a broadcast renewal considered.

If the Commission concludes that a substantial and material question
of fact has been presented or if it is for any reason unable to find that a
grant of the application would serve the public interest, it will order a
hearing. Otherwise it will grant renewal of the license.

Participation in Other Application Proceedings

Aside from license renewal, there are other times when citizen groups
can enter legal objections to a Commission action affecting a station.
Whenever the FCC has before it an application to grant, modify or approve the sale of a broadcast station, it must make a specific determination that the public interest will be served. Therefore, public interest
questions raised by citizen groups at these times have a great impact

because substantial objections must be considered before the Commission can approve an action as in the "public interest."

When such applications are pending, individuals and citizen's groups may enter their objections in the same ways as they can in license renewal proceedings: by complaint, by Petition to Deny the application or by an informal Objection. Basically the same ground rules as to form, content and filing deadlines apply in these situations as well.

At these times you may raise any public interest question relating to the application or the applicant. If, for example, the applicant is seeking to construct a new antenna tower, you might argue that the application should be denied because the station has engaged in discriminatory hiring practices. In other words, the issues raised need not relate directly to the construction of the tower. You may also support the application.

Frequently the very nature of the proposed change in facilities or ownership directly affects the public interest. For example, when the sale or transfer of a station is proposed, the buyer may wish to change the music or programming format of the station—or his ownership of other media properties may raise serious questions as to whether concentration of control of media would result to the detriment of the public. In these cases, negotiation may not hold the answers to citizen group objections and legal avenues of redress should be considered. You may gain important perspectives from the efforts and successes of other citizen groups who have participated in FCC proceedings involving the transfer or sale of stations.

A recent, most dramatic, $1,000,000 commitment to minority programs and employment demonstrates the leverage citizen groups can bring to bear in transfer proceedings. In November 1970, the Citizens Communications Center filed with the FCC a petition opposing the $110 million sale of radio and television stations in three cities to Capital Cities Broadcasting Corporation. Citizens asserted that Capital Cities had ignored important public interest considerations in the transaction. Encouraged by Citizens, Capital Cities management conducted an extraordinary series of consultations with minority group leaders in the three cities affected—Philadelphia, New Haven and Fresno. After weeks of round-the-clock negotiations, Capital Cities pledged $1,000,000 over a three-year period to programming aimed at reflecting the views and aspirations of Black and Spanish-surnamed Americans. Innovative features in the agreement included community advisory groups to assist in planning programming and minority recruitment, designation of prime time hours devoted to documentaries dealing with controversial issues, goals for minority employment and a self-renewing mechanism whereby portions of revenues from sale of programs will be added to the $1 million fund. As a result of the agreement, the Petition to Deny was withdrawn and the transaction incorporating the agreement has been approved by the FCC.

Another example of effective citizen action occurred in Atlanta, Georgia. The proposed sale of the only classical music station to a buyer who indicated he would change the music format to "middle of the road" spurred the formation of a citizen group of classical music lovers—the Citizen's Committee to Preserve the Voice of the Arts in Atlanta on WGKA-AM/FM. The Citizen's Committee petitioned the FCC for a hearing alleging that the musical interests of a substantial group in the Atlanta community would not be served by the sale. While the FCC denied their request, upon appeal, the U.S. Court of Appeals ordered the FCC to hold the hearing. The Court said that all substantial groups within a community have a right to service from the broadcast stations in their city:

"... (I)t is surely in the public interest . . . for all major aspects of contemporary culture to be accommodated by the commonly-owned public resources whenever that is technically and legally possible."

The Court went on to observe that the 16% of the residents of Atlanta who appear to prefer classical music are:

"not an insignificant portion of the people who make up Atlanta; and their minority position does not exclude them from consideration in such matters as the allocation of radio channels for the greatest good for the greatest number."

In the hearing, the citizen group will try to demonstrate that the needs, tastes and interests of the substantial group of classical music lovers in the Atlanta area, which they represent, will not be served adequately if the one station broadcasting classical music changes its format.

chapter 26 # News
and
Opinion
on the Cable

SLOAN COMMISSION
ON CABLE COMMUNICATIONS

One threat of cable television is that it may reduce the diversity of network hard news programming and affect seriously the availability of network documentaries. One promise of cable television is that it is capable of replacing network diversity and amplitude with a diversity and amplitude all its own that will produce an even richer system of television news.

• • •

Should the time come when the fractionization of audience brought about by cable television begins to affect network revenues, news and news-related programming will be the first to suffer. The costs of entertainment programming are elastic, for talent costs rise and fall with revenues, and talent costs are the largest component of entertainment costs. (A network program which moves from prime-time to daytime, or from network presentation to syndication, is produced at smaller expense even though the talent may be the same.) The fundamental costs of news programming, however, are the logistical costs and the basic labor costs; they can be reduced only by reducing coverage.

One can assuredly conceive of economies. Should only one correspondent and one crew, serving all three networks, be dispatched by charter plane to Peru when an earthquake strikes, each network would reduce its costs for that story by perhaps half. At the extreme, all but the most vital coverage could be pooled, and the networks differentiated (as for the most part newspapers are differentiated) by the manner in which the news program is made up and by the elements which are added in the studio. Such economies, through this decade at least, might enable the network to continue to provide national and international news at much their present level, if in somewhat different form. (They might also, of course, bring about anti-trust requirements concerning access.)

There are, however, no comparable economies for documentaries. At present their cost is diminished at the network level because they employ staff and equipment which must be on hand for coverage of hard news, and are not otherwise fully utilized. Pooling arrangements for hard news would make the documentary, unit by unit, more expensive in a period when the revenues it might attract—even now inadequate—are diminishing.

The promise of cable television lies once again in its capacity to serve, for a fee, the special audience that is particularly interested in access to news and documentaries, or the special audience that would be willing to pay for the convenience of news service provided more or less upon demand. If there can be defined a special audience in either of these senses akin to the cultural audience defined in a previous chapter, one can perform simple arithmetic upon the economics of pay television news.

On the assumption that each of the three network news services operates at a level of $50 million a year, and that each serves, over the course of the year, one-third the viewing audience or 20 million households, it is clear that each network must derive $2.50 per household in revenue for a break-even operation. These revenues come in the form of commercial fees, of which approximately half are derived from the five minutes of commercial announcements transmitted each weekday evening on the early-evening news broadcast.

Against these figures, we may now consider two distinct configurations of cable network news services, each of them charging a fee of $1 per month per household, of which 50 cents would be revenues to the operator of the service. One configuration would be an extended prime-time news service—from perhaps 6 p.m. to midnight—which would contain news, documentary and public affairs programming at the national and regional level. Its costs would be higher than that of a conventional network news operation—perhaps $75 million a year. It would therefore require approximately 12 million households, or half the expected minimum penetration of cable television at the end of the decade. The second configuration might be a twenty-four-hour news channel, similar to existing twenty-four-hour news radio stations, over which there would be considerable repetition of national and international news, time allotments for local and regional news, and a budget of special features. Again setting costs at $75 million a year, a penetration of half the minimum cable households would be necessary. In both cases, however, the degree of penetration could be reduced if commercial announcements were added to the mix. Revenues for such advertising, set at $2.50 per household in conformity with present network expectations (and the figure is indeed substantially higher, since revenues from local advertisements at each end of the news program are not taken into account), would reduce the break-even point below 10 million homes.

In neither case, of course, is it to be assumed that a channel dedicated to news, at a fee, would have a constant audience of 10 million homes, or even any sizable part of such an audience. Like any special channel, it would be avilable when it was desired. A news-hungry family might make use of a news channel each evening; another family might be content to view the channel upon ôccasion, or when a particularly interesting documentary was being presented. The ratings game in cases of this sort, unlike the ratings game to which television usually appeals, deals with cumulative audience over a period of a month, rather than audience per program minute.

• • •

Each of these distinct configurations would provide, in its own way, a service far superior to the present network service; one because it would be richer in documentary programming, the other because it would be permanently available. The demand for news, moreover, is sufficient to give some reason for a belief that competing cable news services would come into being, and that during the decade, at least, the viewer would be able to choose from among two or three network news services and perhaps several cable news services. For a modest price to the viewer, in short, cable promises a greater diversity in international, national and regional news and news-related programming: a wider variety of topics considered worth covering; a wider range of views concerning what is being transmitted.

We admit that this statement of the promise of cable television in the area of hard news and documentaries may be over-optimistic. Yet the penetration we hypothesize, and the cost to the subscriber, are in each case far smaller than comparable figures for the daily press. The numbers we have put forth here we concede are large, but they do not appear to us to be outrageous.

Local news does not respond so readily to the promise of cable. The major costs in producing local news at anything near the level of technical and editorial proficiency with which the networks have made the viewer familiar are not substantially lower than ordinary network costs, and must be recovered on a far smaller economic base. The problems that afflict the local broadcasting television station, if it wishes to produce an acceptable local news program and local documentaries, are to be found in almost equal measure for the local aggregate of cable installations.

The most that can confidently be asserted is that the cable entrepreneur, whether operating on channels he himself controls or, more probably, by means of leased pay television channels, will enjoy a substantially larger cash-flow from news operations than the conventional television station enjoys, and may be able to provide a somewhat more acceptable local news service. The question is, as it should be, fundamentally one of how much residents of a large metropolitan area are willing to pay for the provision of a metropolitan news service. The answer to that question will come as individuals and groups of individuals assert themselves to discover it. What cable television provides, in this instance, is nothing more than the channel capacity to make room for the entrepreneur.

● ● ●

There is a particular flexibility on cable television with respect to what might be called "raw news" or "unedited news." The ordinary news service is a process by which professional newsmen make editorial judgments on the news that passes before them, on behalf of those who wish access to the news, selecting from all the events of a given time period those which it chooses to present and imposing structure on each story and on the presentation of the news as a whole. But there is also possible an unstructured presentation of news, in which it is assumed, for example, that the proceedings of the City Council are of importance, and those proceedings are transmitted in full; it remains up to the viewer to impose structure on the whole.

● ● ●

Cable television, by freeing television from the limitations of radiated electro-magnetic waves, creates for television as a whole a situation more nearly analogous to that of the press. As we have speculated above, the copiousness of cable television makes it possible to conceive of far broader access to its channels by competing entrepreneurs and hence opens up the possibilities of a far broader expression of opinion. The existence of public access channels, and the recommendations this Commission will make concerning their general availability and the principles governing their use, will make possible the expression of an extraordinary range of opinion, in practice as well as in principle. Yet the question remains whether these capabilities that cable television provides will in fact result in "free and open encounter" by means of television. And the power of television is such that it can certainly be argued that television must be treated, in this respect, as an entity: a pamphlet is not entirely a useful response to a television broadcast or cablecast.

• • •

The Commission did not seek to make recommendations regarding the applicability of the fairness doctrine to radiated television. So far as cable television is concerned, the Commission concluded that no such doctrine should be applied to the operations of public access channels, where it will recommend that accessibility be ensured and where accordingly the conditions of "free and open encounter" will be fully met. Channels which merely rebroadcast radiated signals will obviously continue to be covered by the FCC fairness doctrine applicable to those signals.

On channels devoted to cable-originated programming, whether free or subscriber-supported, the majority of the Commission has chosen to await the lessons of experience. A system broken up into many intermediate-sized audiences might require no fairness doctrine at all, upon the assumption that diversity of choice or program would bring about diversity of flow of opinion, and that in any case the accessibility of public channels reduces the need for regulatory intervention. A system in which a small number of channels commanded the great mass of the audience might create the fears of monopoly of opinion to which the FCC has reacted with respect to conventional television.

Questions of ownership and control of cable installations are also relevant to questions of fairness. If the mass of individual cable installations, throughout the country, were to be owned or controlled by a few large corporate enterprises, as networks are today controlled, the spectre of monopoly of opinion would arise in quite a different form. Still another form of monopoly would arise if, within a given geographic area, many communications media, including television and cable television, fell into the same hands. The Commission believes, however, that its recommendations on ownership and control over cable television preclude the likelihood of such outcomes.

• • •

The broadcast television system is not designed to reach the ward or the precinct, or even the municipality; the signal emitted covers an area measured in thousands of square miles, and the cost of buying time on the system is scaled to that kind of audience. A candidate for municipal office in a Connecticut suburb would be obliged, if he wished to campaign by television, to employ a system with a potential audience of some 20 million viewers; to reach the few thousand viewers he seeks to reach, he must pay for reaching all 20 million. At the municipal level, this can rarely be attractive. Even at the state level, it may be inordinately expensive, as when a candidate for Governor of New Jersey is obliged to buy time on New York City stations to reach a large part of his constituency.

• • •

Cable television, by its physical configuration, eliminates some of the disabilities of broadcast television. With channel space to spare, time even on a state-wide basis need not be expensive; the purchaser is not necessarily in competition with the mass advertiser. But what is more important, the cable system is so organized that a political message may be directed to a potential audience more or less identical with the constituency of the candidate: to the ward or the suburb or the state. Each person the message can reach is a person who will be casting a ballot of significance to the candidate who buys time and pays the cost of producing the message. The problem of spill-over becomes insignificant; the costs associated with spill-over vanish.

All this comes into existence without diminishing the power of the present system. The cable television installation will continue to carry channels of mass entertainment, and most of the audience, at any time, will be tuned to one or another of those channels. The candidate who wishes to pay the going price for a spot announcement or a time-slot on those channels can continue to do so, and reap the demonstrated benefits of his choice. What cable television provides is not a substitute for the current mode of political promotion, but a supplement. It can perform all that conventional television performs—and something more.

• • •

The most straightforward approach would be the institution, on a cable system or a set of such systems, of a political channel operating on a regular basis and both producing its own political programs and allotting time to the local, regional and national political parties. Such a channel might be organized and managed by a non-partisan local institution created for the purpose, along the lines of the League of Women Voters. Its viewing audience would rise and fall with the political temperature of the community it served: high during the general election, higher still if a local recall election was exercising the community, attractive most of the time only to the politically sensitive.

• • •

Beyond this simple system it is possible to conceive of the institution of explicitly partisan channels. Since the early days of the Republic, when all newspapers were party- or factionally-run and oriented, the United States has never had an explicit party press. Costs of running such a channel, even on cable television, appear at first glance to be high: if it is estimated that delivery costs via cable come to approximately one cent a day, and a party committee wishes to reach 1 million households during the two-month period before a general election, delivery costs alone would come to $600,000, or approximately 20 cents a voter. The sum is not large, but large enough to make it necessary to reduce most other campaign expenditures. On the other hand, such a channel would be an extremely valuable fund raising instrument, and might well pay its own way.

The question of fund-raising, in fact, arises in its own right even in the absence of party channels. The merchandising capability of an addressed cable system with its capacity for a digital return signal makes it possible to address appeals directly into the home, and either to receive pledges in the system itself or to mount follow-up campaigns that might be extremely efficient. The same announcer who sells kitchen appliances on broadcast television might be available to say "We need funds and need them badly: push the button once for every dollar you want to contribute." Impulse giving may prove to be as profitable to the party as impulse buying to the merchant. "Political parties," to quote our consultants, "may find themselves more dependent on charismatic pitchmen than on a few rich men."

Still another possibility for the campaigner lies in the possibility . . . that the mass audience portion of the cable system may come to provide an all-news channel comparable to those that now exist on radio. Exposure on such a channel, particularly for the local politician, will provide opportunities not now available on broadcast television. It can be a powerful instrument in making himself known to a wide public in a fashion that no other news medium can provide.

All of these are modes in which the campaigner and his party can direct their message and their appeals to the general public. The degree to which they reach the public will depend in large measure upon their skills in presenting themselves and their causes. In a certain sense, they will be competing with relatively scarce means against the mass entertainment that is available on the popular channels, and their audiences will not, at any given moment, be large ones although their cumulative audiences—which essentially is what the advertiser strives for—may be immense.

But there is another kind of audience which is far more dependable, and in some ways even more important to the campaigner. That is the audience, small in total, which is composed of the political enthusiast, the party faithful. It is those people who fund campaigns, promote the candidate of their choice, solicit face-to-face the support of the less dedicated, get out the vote on election day. In a political campaign, much of the effort of the candidate is directed to mobilizing those forces, and maintaining their initial enthusiasm over the long pull.

Closed circuit television, in which the candidate addresses several large gatherings in separated locations, is now in frequent use for that endeavor. Cable television is ideally designed for the purpose. It can reach the campaign worker in his home. There is no problem of attracting that audience; it is eager to participate, anxious to receive the word. Cable television cannot take the place of the candidate's handshake, and a few kind words about the family, but it can be an efficient and an economic supplement.

•   •   •

So far this Report has considered only the contributions cable television might make to the management of political campaigns. The use of the medium in exposing the political process itself, particularly on the local level, is at least as significant. It requires little explanation.

With channel space available, the problem of permitting the community to participate vicariously in the political process itself vanishes. The public hearing which is so fundamental a part of local and state politics can become, in another sense, a public hearing indeed, in which the general public can at least be present, if only passively. City council proceedings can be watched by those who are interested in seeing their government in action. The school board can be forced to debate its several positions in full view of those who will be affected by its decision.

Audiences for such activities will at all times be small except perhaps times of municipal crisis. But the importance of such an audience is not measured by its size. Those who listen tend to be the activists within the community, who themselves take a deep interest in the political process and its outcomes, and who possess a deep personal commitment to the process. They are the enthusiasts, whose principal purpose is to make their own enthusiasms contagious. We have seen, in recent years, a handful of environmentalists profoundly affect the national view of the environment. In a small city or a suburb, a similar handful who are interested in their schools, and who have via cable television regular access to information about the management of their schools, can infect the entire community with pride or with concern, and can bring about profound change.

The effects of all this on the entire practice of politics might conceivably be far more far-reaching than the single items in this catalogue suggest. As stated in the paper prepared for the Commission by Ithiel de Sola Pool and Herbert Alexander:

> If the local cable system serves to delimit neighborhoods, to give a sense of community to a section of a city or to a suburb now mainly dependent on the central city media, then politics could become more decentralized, with less attention to the national and state, and more to the local.

So far as conventional television is concerned, the FCC and Congress have wrestled at intervals with what is known as the "equal time rule." In principle, this provides that time allowed any single political party or its candidates must be made equally available to all political parties and their candidates (except on hard-news programs); in practice, it has led stations to refuse air-time to any party or candidate, except on a commercial basis, for fear of invasion of air-time by every political party, however small, in existence within the state in question.

The Commission believes that if leased channels and public access channels are effectively available and employed the necessity for "equal time" will be removed, and that whatever its status with respect to conventional television, "equal time" need not be regulated with respect to cable television.

The existence of an informed and an engaged public is prerequisite to the healthy maintenance of a political democracy. Cable television, on the face of it, has much to contribute. Unlike conventional television, it does not necessarily call for the investment of huge sums, and it can be made effective down to the local level.

It cannot, of itself, create a politically aware citizenry, for no one can be forced to twist the dial to the channel carrying political information or political news. But cable television can serve, as perhaps no medium before it has been able, those who wish to be part of the political process, and skillfully used it might very well be able to augment their number. Like so much that has been put forward in this Report, its effectiveness will depend upon the skills of those who take it in hand. Politics, whatever opprobrium may sometimes be attached to the word, is important. The cable can literally bring that fact home, and in doing so help the entire political process function efficiently and effectively in the public interest.

THE COMMUNITY VOICE

One large family of possibilities remains to be considered. These are the uses of cable television as a medium for the direct engagement of people with people; as an institution within which the separate voices of the community may be heard.

• • •

Two or more community channels, open to the members of the community for whatever their purposes, might go a long way toward relieving the pressures that arise where communication is in short supply. They will not solve the problems of the inner city, but they may at least contribute toward making some of those problems more amenable to solution.

Nor are the benefits of the public access channel limited to the inner city. It is no doubt true that the problems of the inner city are more deep-rooted and more pervasive, and that the inner city peculiarly lacks orderly means by which to articulate them. But one would be hard put to find any community—the bedroom suburb, the middle-class urban neighborhood, the low-rental area where the newly married are most likely to set up housekeeping—that does not have its internal communications problems, or an urge for cohesiveness that is not met by existing media.

• • •

The problems involved in the provision and operation of public access channels are admittedly enormous. The relationship between a television system and the citizen is a complicated one, and must be resolved by institutional arrangements of some kind or another. This in itself is reason for encouraging control, by preferential franchising rules, if necessary, within the community of a cable system serving that community, particularly in areas which are conscious of profound differences between themselves and neighboring communities. Such control might be lodged in a non-profit organization, or a profit-making corporate activity; in either case, there would certainly be a larger chance that it would be in tune with the community and reflect the community's desires.

The problems of access are still more formidable. Even cable television cannot cope with everyone shouting at once; there must be allotment of time, and a procedure for sharing out the most favorable times. There are problems with those who wish to voice highly unpopular opinions, and far sharper problems when the opinion can be interpreted as incitement to riot, or sedition, or defamation of character.

Public access channels, in short, are not likely to operate smoothly.

But if they can help contribute in any significant way to the solution of the general problems within their communities, the problems they themselves create will be more than tolerable. The Commission recommends, therefore, that public access channels be made an essential element in cable franchises that may be awarded in a large metropolitan area; we believe further that consideration should be given to their inclusion in any other area for which a franchise is sought.

Rate regulation for the public access channels may also become, in time, a matter at issue. It is clear that the phrase "public access" is in practice meaningless if that access must be purchased at rates beyond the means of the general public within the community in question. As long as cable systems maintain excess capacity—and such a condition will certainly obtain over the next few years—economic considerations alone will keep public access prices at their lowest level short of direct subsidization. While the cable operator can only benefit, on balance, from additional diversity of programming, self-interest will keep rates at a minimum. It is true that upon occasions non-economic interests might lead an operator to use his rate structure, for reasons of his own, to restrict access; this is a matter upon which the franchising authority should certainly retain the power to exercise oversight.

As demand begins to challenge capacity, one might expect to see a general rise in channel rates, in which the public access channels would inevitably be caught up; if public access rates remain low, as they must if the channels are to serve their purpose, at some point they will appear to constitute a highly uneconomic use of channel space. That is not merely a problem of the public access channels, however (although it might affect those channels first)—rather, it is a problem of the orderly growth of the cable system, and the degree to which that growth should be governed by regulation.

• • •

The provision of channels, even at highly favorable rates, will not be sufficient to bring public access television into use. Without a promotional force within the community, capable of providing technical assistance to groups who wish to use the channels, they will not flourish.

A study of public access in New York City, where such channels are mandated by franchise agreement, indicates the difficult tasks that must be confronted by any promotional agency dealing with public access channels. They include the monitoring of cable management of access, representation of the public in the formulation of rates and regulations, educating community groups in the manner in which they can use access to further their purposes, assuring the existence of low-cost production facilities, and furnishing seed money and training for actual production.

Where such a promotional force is absent, the public access channels are most likely to lie fallow.

The nature of that promotional force is likely to vary with communities. In those instances in which the cable installation itself is community-owned and community-controlled, the operating entity itself will hasten to provide the promotional efforts which may be required: that, presumably, is one of the reasons for community control. In the short term, while excess capacity is a burden on the installation, the self-interest of the private operator may lead him, for a time at least, down the same road. In other instances, purposeful intervention by appropriate governmental agencies—the Human Resources Administration in New York City, for example—may be necessary. Where high levels of community involvement already exist, the process may be self-starting.

An important role might and should be played by Public Television. Stations within the Public Television system possess technical knowledge and production facilities; the better stations are already in close touch with neighborhoods within their signal area. In Boston, WGBH has made its facilities available to community groups that wish to broadcast over Channel 44, its UHF community-oriented outlet. In New York City, WNET has cooperated with groups wishing to use the city's public access channel, making available space, production personnel, and production skills.

In recommending, as we have, a new orientation of Public Television toward the provision of local news and an involvement in community needs, this Commission may be charged with moving beyond its own terms of reference. We feel we are justified in that the combination of the skills and the devotion of Public Television with the capacities of cable television is such that there can be created out of those components local services that have heretofore been far beyond the reach of the television system. We are made more confident in this view by a communication from John W. Macy, Jr., president of the Corporation for Public Broadcasting, in which he proposes very much this role for the Public Television system.

● ● ●

Thus there must be flexibility in the allotment of time by whoever it may be that makes that allotment. Scheduling must recognize the diverse categories of users, each with special time needs. Applicants should not be obliged to queue up for each hour they wish to reserve; if groups are to be encouraged to plan for the use of public channels and to set aside funds for the purpose, some regularity of scheduling must be assured. Certain periods might be reserved for brief items at reduced rates: the equivalent of the classified advertisement. In the light of the varying nature of the demands that may be made on the channels, to assert merely that allotment will be non-discriminatory, or on a first-come-first-served basis, is in practice to say nothing at all. There will be decisions that must be made, and consequently someone charged with making them.

Because the utilization of the public channels will begin slowly, the Commission believes that there will be time to experiment with a variety of approaches to the solution of the problem of the "traffic director," within a variety of installations. It could be the cable owner himself, although most will shun this role; if cable ownership is sufficiently diverse, this in itself will be an experiment. Our own preferences lead in other directions: we would prefer some such instrument as a public-access commission with representation from civic and cultural groups, or existing civic institutions within a community which assume this task as an additional responsibility.

• • •

Opening a camera lens and a microphone to anyone who may come by involves risks. Any actions designed to minimize or obviate the risks can be interpreted as censorship, whether they take the form of cutting the live communication off the air, refusing to transmit the tape or film or denying future access. This defines the dilemma with which television must live, and it is particularly acute—or at least particularly feared—with respect to public access channels.

Three of these risks are historically bound up with the regulation of radiated television. The risk that opinions will be stated without a corresponding expression of counter-opinion is covered by the fairness doctrine. The risk that there will be a biased presentation of partisan political issues of candidacies is covered by the equal time rule. The risk that a person will be subjected to personal attack, without the opportunity to defend himself, is governed by the right-to-reply rules.

It is the Commission view that the first two of these doctrines are not relevant to cable television, at least at the present time, and further that they are not likely at any time to be relevant to the public access channels. The manner in which the public access channels are established, the manner in which the Commission hopes to see them governed, and recommendations that the Commission will make in this Report to assure their copiousness, provide equal access for counter-opinion and for the expression of competitive political views.

Right-to-reply rules, or some variation upon them, may be required. It seems unreasonable that a person who has been subjected to a personal attack which he did not invite, and over which he had no control, should be obliged to pay for the privilege of defending himself. In some instances he may possess, of course, recourse to the laws of libel, but although they may reward him for injury he has suffered they do not repair the injury. It should be recognized, however, that the invocation of right-to-reply rules implies the right of the cable operator, or his agent, to protect himself by cutting off, or by refusing to air, the original attack. In other words, there will be a kind of censorship at the source, which will at times be exercised by the engineer in control of the transmission. There are many instrumentalities by which the actions of the engineer, or any other censor, may be assayed after the fact, and it is not likely to be surpassingly difficult to see that they will, in general, be exercised prudently; it is true also that personal attacks are easily identified and rarely misidentified, so that the task of justifiable censorship is not unduly arduous.*

Beyond those three special risks are the general risks of criminal libel, incitement to riot, obscenity, sedition and the like. Any one of those offenses may be committed before an open camera, or recorded on tape or film. It is in these areas that there is little disposition to trust the judgment of the individual acting as censor: one man's obscenity may be another man's blunt expression; one man's incitement to riot another man's assertion of a political point of view. Our own society prefers that these issues be left to the judgment of judge and jury, and that offenders be punished *ex post facto* when it has been determined that a crime has indeed been committed.

In conventional television, it has been presumed that the operator of the television station is in the first instance responsible for the commission of any of those crimes over his station; he is thus automatically endowed with the right to censor, in his own protection, and he is likely to make full exercise of that right. It is clear that such a presumption is unwarranted with respect to public access channels (and to other leased channels) and inimical to the most useful operation of those channels.

The Commission therefore recommends that the appropriate legislative bodies modify existing laws to remove the liability of the cable operator in these respects so far as channels outside his direct control are concerned. The burden of meeting the requirements of the civil and the criminal laws will thereupon fall entirely upon those who brought the burden upon themselves.

In extreme cases, the operator or his agent will no doubt terminate a transmission or simply refuse to transmit a recorded telecast; certainly no cable operator will allow what might be called "hard-core obscenity"— of which the definition now appears to alter from year to year—to pass over his system. If a community or an individual should take the view

---

* One member of the Commission, Mrs. Wald, dissents from this general position. Mrs. Wald holds that a cable operator or his agent should not be allowed to interfere with statements because he fears that those statements might provoke invocation of the right-to-reply rules.

that the privilege is being abused, it appears to this Commission that there is a variety of remedies to which the community or the individual may have recourse. In practice, it is not an outcome that is likely to be frequent. The repeated transmission of material that the community in general finds offensive does not in fact appear to be a significant threat. The experience of Channel 44 in Boston is instructive: it stipulates rules that participants in its public access experiments must abide by, and has found that this procedure keeps offensive material at an extremely low level.

On the whole, the Commission is not as disturbed as some in the face of all these risks. It appears to the Commission that they represent situations that will not often occur, and that can be readily managed on those rare instances when they do occur, as they are managed with respect to other media of communication. The greater risk, we believe, would be to impose regulations that would stultify the public access channels.

• • •

part five SELECTED
TITLES FOR
FURTHER
READING

The following pages offer titles of books (and of a few periodicals) with brief annotations on each, which should be a useful guide to further and more in-depth reading of subjects raised in this book. Listings followed by an asterisk indicate that the work was available in paperback at the time we went to press.

The various media self-regulatory codes have not been included in this volume both for lack of space and the fact that they are found easily elsewhere. Some sources for these codes are listed here and cited more fully below:

AMERICAN BAR ASSOCIATION, *Canon 35* (one of the legal canons, this concerns media in courtrooms): Green, pp. 324–325; or Kittross-Harwood, p. 193.

AMERICAN SOCIETY OF NEWSPAPER EDITORS, *Canons of Journalism:* Kirschner, pp. 21–33.

NATIONAL ASSOCIATION OF BROADCASTERS, *Radio Code* (news portion): Dary, pp. 186–187.

NATIONAL ASSOCIATION OF BROADCASTERS, *Television Code* (news portion): Fang, pp. 220–229; or Green, pp. 320–323.

RADIO-TELEVISION NEWS DIRECTORS ASSOCIATION, *Code of Broadcast News Ethics:* Dary, pp. 183–185; or Kittross-Harwood, pp. 194–196.

This list concentrates on books dealing with journalistic topics, and does not include many of the excellent texts and readers on general aspects of mass communications. Only publications known as of early 1972 have been included, and currently available titles are stressed.

GENERAL BIBLIOGRAPHY

ADLER, RUTH (ed.), *The Working Press: Special to the New York Times.* New York: Putnam's, 1966. A readable collection of nearly 60 behind-the-scenes tales of "how I got that story."*

——, *A Day in the Life of the New York Times.* Philadelphia: Lippincott, 1971. Just that—from the initial reports to appearance on the street, all the departments of the paper are covered in a novel-like treatment.

AGEE, WARREN K. (ed.), *Mass Media in a Free Society.* Lawrence: The University Press of Kansas, 1969. A collection of six papers, the first four dealing with media news.*

* Means paperback available.
This bibliography was compiled by Christopher H. Sterling.

AMERICAN SOCIETY OF NEWSPAPER EDITORS, *Problems of Journalism*. New York: ASNE, 1923 to date (annual). Transcripts of annual ASNE convention which concentrate on one or two major reporting/news issues per year.

ARLEN, MICHAEL J., *The Living-Room War*. New York: Viking, 1969. A collection of the author's TV criticism from *The New Yorker*, dealing heavily in news issues.*

ARONSON, JAMES, *The Press and the Cold War*. Indianapolis: Bobbs-Merrill, 1970. Traces the role of print news media since the end of World War II in reporting world tensions, suggesting that press has failed to alert public to policy errors.

————, *Packaging the News: A Critical Survey of Press, Radio, TV*. New York: Little New World Paperbacks, 1971. A short current essay stressing establishment ties of news media.*

BAGDIKIAN, BEN H., *The Information Machines: Their Impact on Men and the Media*. New York: Harper & Row, 1971. An important Rand Corporation study on the current organization of news reporting and technological changes which will effect it.*

BAKER, ROBERT K., and SANDRA J. BALL, *Violence and the Media: A Staff Report to the National Commission on the Causes and Prevention of Violence*. Washington, D.C.: Government Printing Office, 1969. Lengthy report on all aspects of the subject.*

BARRETT, MARVIN (ed.), *The Alfred I. duPont–Columbia University Survey of Broadcast Journalism*. New York: Grosset & Dunlap, 1969 to date (annual). An invaluable source covering selected topics in detail for each fiscal year.*

BLUEM, A. WILLIAM, *Documentary in American Television: Form, Function, Method*. New York: Hastings House, 1965. A unique work analyzing past and present problems and prospects for the documentary journalism format.

BOORSTIN, DANIEL J., *The Image: A Guide to Pseudo-Events in America*. New York: Atheneum, 1962. The standard book on created news (or public relations) and how the media are involved.*

CASTY, ALAN (ed.), *Mass Media and Mass Man*. New York: Holt, Rinehart & Winston, 1968. Second part covers "Mass Media and Information" with case studies.*

CHESTER, EDWARD W., *Radio, Television and American Politics*. New York: Sheed & Ward, 1969. Best history to date of political campaign use of broadcasting.*

CHITTICK, WILLIAM O., *The State Department, Press, and Pressure Groups*. New York: John Wiley/Interscience, 1970. Good examples of media's effect on policy and vice versa.

COHEN, BERNARD C., *The Press and Foreign Policy*. Princeton, N.J.: Princeton University Press, 1963. The pioneer exploration of journalistic effect on policy.*

Columbia Journalism Review (1962–70, quarterly; 1971 to date, bimonthly).

COMMISSION ON FREEDOM OF THE PRESS, *A Free and Responsible Press*. Chicago: University of Chicago Press, 1947. The basic findings of the Hutchins Commission which are still valuable (and still in print) today.

DALY, CHARLES U. (ed.), *The Media and the Cities*. Chicago: University of Chicago Press, 1968. Eight papers on problems of urban news (including riots).*

DARY, DAVID, *Radio News Handbook*. Blue Ridge Summit, Pa.: Tab Books, 1970. A brief and useful how-to-do-it guide for smaller stations.

————, *TV News Handbook*. Blue Ridge Summit, Pa.: Tab Books, 1971. Similar but more detailed coverage for TV operations.

DEXTER, LEWIS A. and DAVID MANNING WHITE (eds.), *People, Society, and Mass Communications*. New York: Free Press, 1964. One of the best readers in the field, this volume has many news-related selections.

DUNN, DELMER D., *Public Officials and the Press*. Reading, Mass.: Addison-Wesley, 1969. Concise discussion of reporters, officials, and the resulting chemistry which makes much of today's news.*

EDWARDS, VERNE E., JR., *Journalism in a Free Society*. Dubuque, Iowa: Wm. C. Brown Company, Publishers, 1970. A basic introductory text emphasizing print media.

EFRON, EDITH, *The News Twisters*. Los Angeles, Nash, 1971. A word-count content analysis of TV network reporting of the 1968 campaign which suggests a strong liberal news bias.

EMERY, EDWIN, *The Press and America: An Interpretive History of the Mass Media*, 3rd ed. Englewood Cliffs, N.J.: Prentice-Hall, 1972. One of the best of the standard print journalism history texts.

FANG, IRVING E., *Television News: Writing, Filming, Editing, Broadcasting*. New York: Hastings House, 1968. Production text with good behind-the-scenes information.*

FIELDING, RAYMOND, *The American Newsreel: 1911-1967*. Norman: University of Oklahoma Press, 1972. Complete illustrated review of once important means of news communication—and the reasons for its decline.

FREEDOM OF INFORMATION CENTER, *Digest* (bimonthly 1958 to date), and *Reports* (two per month, 1958 to date), Columbia, Missouri: School of Journalism. Excellent short reviews of current problems of news access.

FRIENDLY, FRED W., *Due to Circumstances Beyond Our Control . . .* New York: Random House, 1967. The background and problems of CBS TV news in the 1960s.*

FULBRIGHT, J. WILLIAM, *The Pentagon Propaganda Machine*. New York: Liveright, 1970. Collection of speeches critical of military propaganda, much of it using media.*

GILLMOR, DONALD M., *Free Press and Fair Trial*. Washington, D.C.: Public Affairs Press, 1966. Complete discussion analyzing both sides of controversy.

————, and JEROME BARRON, *Mass Communication Law: Cases and Comment*. St. Paul, Minn.: West Publishing Co., 1969, with 1971 supplement. One of the standard texts, with much news-related law.

GLESSING, ROBERT J., *The Underground Press in America*. Bloomington: Indiana University Press, 1970. Best short treatment of trends and content in the counterculture media.*

GREEN, MAURY, *Television News: Anatomy and Process*. Belmont, Calif.: Wadsworth, 1969. Standard text analyses techniques, concepts and functions of news in society.

GREENBERG, BRADLEY S. and EDWIN B. PARKER (eds.), *The Kennedy Assassination and the American Public: Social Communication in Crisis*. Stanford, Calif.:

Stanford University Press, 1965. A grim but fascinating collection on dissemination of crisis news with and without media.

HOCKING, WILLIAM ERNEST, *Freedom of the Press: A Framework of Principle.* Chicago: University of Chicago Press, 1947. The basic theoretical report from the (Hutchins) Commission on Freedom of the Press.

HOHENBERG, JOHN, *The News Media: A Journalist Looks at His Profession.* New York: Holt, Rinehart & Winston, 1968. Discussion of major problems of mass news.

————, *Free Press, Free People: The Best Cause.* New York: Columbia University Press, 1971. History of the freedom of the press concept, focusing on post-1945 events.

HULTENG, HOHN L. and ROY PAUL NELSON, *The Fourth Estate: An Informal Appraisal of the News and Opinion Media.* New York: Harper & Row, 1971. A well written introduction to modern American news media and their varied roles.*

JOHNSON, NICHOLAS, *How To Talk Back to Your Television Set.* Boston: Little, Brown, 1970. FCC Commissioner's polemic on ills of broadcasting and what public can do about them.*

Journalism Quarterly (1926 to date).

Journal of Broadcasting (quarterly, 1956 to date).

KEELEY, JOSEPH, *The Left Leaning Antenna: Political Bias in Television.* New Rochelle, N.Y.: Arlington House, 1971. A right-wing view of liberal bias in TV.

KENDRICK, ALEXANDER, *Prime Time: The Life of Edward R. Murrow.* Boston: Little, Brown, 1969. Very readable biography of broadcasting's foremost commentator illustrating rise of radio then TV news.*

KIRSCHNER, ALLEN and LINDA KIRSCHNER (eds.), *Journalism: Readings in the Mass Media.* New York: Odyssey, 1971. Heavily devoted to print media, but good collection of current viewpoints.*

KITTROSS, JOHN M. and KENNETH HARWOOD (eds.), *Free and Fair: Courtroom Access and The Fairness Doctrine.* Philadelphia: Journal of Broadcasting Publications (Temple University), 1970. Collection of relevant articles from the *Journal.**

KRIEGHBAUM, HILLIER, *Pressures on the Press.* New York: Thomas Y. Crowell, 1972. Excellent current review of news media problems due to both internal and external pressures, concentrating on stories in the 1968–71 period.

LANG, KURT and GLADYS ENGEL LANG, *Politics and Television.* Chicago: Quadrangle, 1968. Collection of studies on effect of TV on political process.*

LOFTEN, JOHN, *Justice and the Press.* Boston: Beacon Press, 1966. Analysis of most major points of view in the controversy.*

LYLE, JACK, *The News in Megalopolis.* San Francisco: Chandler, 1967. Valuable study of all news media in Los Angeles area.

———— (ed.), *The Black American and the Press.* Los Angeles: Ward Ritchie Press, 1968. Major remarks of symposium held at UCLA in 1967.*

McCOY, RALPH, *Freedom of the Press: An Annotated Bibliography.* Carbondale: Southern Illinois University Press, 1968. Massive annotated listing of articles over past three centuries, concentrating on past 70 years.

MacDougall, Curtis D., *The Press and Its Problems*. Dubuque, Iowa: Wm. C. Brown, 1964. Good review of print journalism issues.

McGinnis, Joe, *The Selling of the President 1968*. New York: Trident Press, 1968. The already classic account of public relations methods in Nixon's 1968 campaign.*

MacNeil, Robert, *The People Machine: The Influences of Television on American Politics*. New York: Harper & Row, 1968. Broad discussion of TV news problems, campaign uses of TV, and questions of access.

Marbut, F. B., *News From The Capital: The Story of Washington Reporting*. Carbondale: Southern Illinois University Press, 1971. A history from Jefferson to Nixon which provides a good view of the development of political reporting generally.

Markel, Lester, *What You Don't Know Can Hurt You: A Study of Public Opinion and Public Education*. Washington: Public Affairs Press, 1972. Former *New York Times* editor on the role of news media in creating informed public.

Mendelsohn, Harold and Irving Crespi, *Polls, Television, and the New Politics*. Scranton, Pa.: Chandler, 1970. Political effects of polls and TV.*

Merrill, John C. and Ralph L. Lowenstein, *Media, Messages and Men: New Perspectives in Communication*. New York: McKay, 1971. Another recent and broadbased introduction with a news bias, this volume has a good annotated bibliography as well.*

Mickelson, Sig, *The Electric Mirror: Politics in an Age of Television*. New York: Dodd, Mead, 1972. Former president of CBS News discusses both campaign and noncampaign uses of video in episodic fashion.

Midura, Edmund M. (ed.), *Why Aren't We Getting Through?* Washington: Acropolis Books, 1971. Ten papers on the urban communications crisis.*

Minor, Dale, *The Information War*. New York: Hawthorn, 1970. Government vs. media in gathering of the true story for the public.*

Murray, George, *The Press and the Public: The Story of the British Press Council*. Carbondale: Southern Illinois University Press, 1972. Former chairman of the council tells story of its first two decades which is useful for those arguing U.S. needs for similiar body.

Nimmo, Dan, *Newsgathering in Washington*. New York: Aldine-Atherton, 1964. Detailed account of the people and institutions involved.

———, *The Political Persuaders: The Techniques of Modern Election Campaigns*. Englewood Cliffs, N.J.: Prentice-Hall, 1970. Excellent discussion of all campaign methods with a long section on media uses.*

Oberdorfer, Don, *Tet!* Garden City, N.Y.: Doubleday, 1971. Detailed analysis of the 1968 turning point of the Vietnam war with much information on media reporting and its effects on the home front opinion process.

Price, Warren C. and Calder M. Pickett, *An Annotated Journalism Bibliography: 1958–1968*. Minneapolis: University of Minnesota Press, 1970.

Rivers, William L., *The Opinion Makers: The Washington Press Corps*. Boston: Beacon Press, 1965. Fascinating description of the men—compare to Nimmo (1964).*

———, *The Adversaries: Politics and the Press*. Boston: Beacon Press, 1970. Where print newsmen do better than their broadcast counterparts.*

———— and WILBUR SCHRAMM, *Responsibility in Mass Communication*, rev. ed. New York: Harper & Row, 1969. Mainly devoted to mores of mass news media.

RUBIN, BERNARD, *Political Television*. Belmont, Calif.: Wadsworth, 1967. History of television's political use from 1960 through 1964 elections.*

RUCKER, BRYCE W., *The First Freedom*. Carbondale: University of Southern Illinois Press, 1968. Economic and legal analysis of news media problems.*

SCHILLER, HERBERT I., *Mass Communications and the American Empire*. New York: Augustus M. Kelley, 1969. Role of news media in supporting American economic empire building abroad.*

SKORNIA, HARRY J., *Television and the News: A Critical Appraisal*. Palo Alto, Calif.: Pacific Books, 1968. A good detailed analysis of TV's shortcomings, not all of which the author attributes to the medium itself.

SMALL, WILLIAM, *To Kill a Messenger: Television News and the Real World*. New York: Hastings House, 1970. Insider's (CBS) view of network TV coverage problems and prospects.

SWALLOW, NORMAN, *Factual Television*. New York: Hastings House, 1966. An Englishman's point of view.

TALESE, GAY, *The Kingdom and the Power*. New York: World, 1969. Behind-the-scenes story of the *New York Times* in recent years.*

TUNSTALL, JEREMY, *Journalists At Work: Specialist Correspondents, Their News Organizations, News Sources, and Competitive Colleagues*. London: Constable, 1971. Concentrating on British practice, this is an excellent in-depth examination of print journalism operations.

TYRRELL, ROBERT, *The Work of the Television Journalist*. New York: Hastings House, 1972. British-oriented manual on all aspects of TV news preparation and production, concentrating on key roles.

UNGAR, SANFORD J., *The Papers and The Papers*. New York: Dutton, 1972. Journalistic review of the entire Pentagon Papers legal and political battle concentrating on first few weeks of the confrontation.

WHALE, JOHN, *The Half-Shut Eye: Television and Politics in Britain and America*. New York: St. Martin's, 1969. British point of view on question of effects.

WOOD, WILLIAM A., *Electronic Journalism*. New York: Columbia University Press, 1967. Analysis of national and local reporting as major source of public information.*

WYCKOFF, GENE, *The Image Candidates: American Politics in the Age of Television*. New York: Macmillan, 1968. One man's experience in "packaging" candidates.

Index

North Vietnam, 150, 151
Norton, Eleanor Holmes, 247
NVA (North Vietnamese Army), 151

Oakland, California, 279
Oberdorfer, Don, 317
Objections, informal, in license renewal
   applications, 292
Objectivity in mass news, 132
   black coverage and, 186–88, 282
   factors encouraging, 8
   limitations of, 124, 136–39, 168, 244, 263
   press associations and, 8, 62, 66
   professionalism and, 250
   status quo reinforcement and, 191–92
   television and, 129, 133–34, 207
Obscenity, 110, 308
Ocean Press service, 65
Office managers, 51–52
Offset printing, 51, 275
"Off the record" briefings, 73, 148
Ohio State University, 170, 180
Old pro, 250–51
Ombudsmen on newspapers, 239, 269
O.M. Collective, 280
Oregon *Daily Emerald* (periodical), 111
Organization, professional, 251–53
Organization Man, 275
Organizer's Manual, 280
Oswald, Lee Harvey, 112
Ottinger, Richard, 198
Outside sources, 66, 71–72
Out-takes and subpoenas, 195, 202–4, 207–8
Overcommercialization, 290
Ownership of news media, 221–25, 243,
   288
   monopoly of:
      cable television and, 299
      examples of, 140, 245
      markets and, 29
      in one area, 29, 235, 245, 255
      profitability and, 258–59
      statistics on, 21–23, 27, 270
      steps to reform, 215, 229, 233
Oxford, Mississippi, 106–7

Packard, George, 248
Pagoda battle, 152–55, 157–58
Paine, Thomas, 274
Paletz, David, 191–92
Palmer, L. F., Jr., 184–85, 187–88
Paris, newspapers in, 24, 243, 248
Parker, Edwin B., 315
Parliament, 265–66
Participatory democracy, 241, 243
Pass-along circulation, 277
Pasteup type, 275
Pastore, John, 246
Pastore Committee, 246
Patriot Press, 274
Paulu, Burton, 87
Peace movement, 244–45, 275–76
Pegler, Westbrook, 110

Penny press, 214
Pentagon, The Selling of the, 166, 169,
   200–210
Pentagon Papers, 88, 113–22
People's Voice (column), 269
Perjury, 105
Perkins, Jack, 151, 156
Perlmutter, Alvin, 246
Personal attacks in mass news media,
   282–84, 307–8
   See also Libel laws
Personal life and libel, 107
"Perspectives: Selling of the Pentagon,"
   202, 205
Petition to deny broadcasters license re-
   newal, 285, 289–94
Philadelphia *Bulletin* (periodical), 248
Philadelphia community action in broad-
   casting, 293
Phillips, Warren, 244
Photoengraving, 53
Photographers, 53, 65, 257–58
Photographs in advertising, 110
Photo-offset printing, 51, 275
Photo services of press associations, 65,
   151–53
Pickett, Calder M., 317
Pirating, 110–11
Pluralism, 9, 131
Police Force of South Vietnam, National,
   151, 154, 158
Political crimes and subpoenas, 194
Political parties, conventions of, 91*n*, 143,
   172
Politics, third parties in, 232
Polls:
   Gallup, 171, 270
   Harris, 171, 173
   Roper, 4, 131
Pop sociology, 135
Population increase since World War II,
   211
Postal regulations, 110
Prefab editorials, 3
Presidency, 141–42
President's Advisory Commission on Cam-
   pus Unrest, 171, 178
Press:
   foreign, 17–19
      See also specific countries
   freedom of:
      ambiguity of, 88, 121–22
      controversy and, 83–84
      Fairness Doctrine and, 89–102, 194,
         204
      First Amendment and, 7–11, 24, 71,
         233
      marketplace of ideas and, 7–10, 228–
         33
      Pentagon Papers and, 116–22
      press councils and, 264–70
      right to fair trial and, 72–73, 87–88,
         111–12, 193
      violence and, 129–30, 164